T0113849

Virtue-Based CHRISTIANITY

*Transitioning from
Milk to Solid Food*

DAVE RYTER

WESTBOW
PRESS®
A DIVISION OF THOMAS NELSON
& ZONDERVAN

Copyright © 2022 David Ryter.

All rights reserved. No part of this book may be used or reproduced by any means, graphic, electronic, or mechanical, including photocopying, recording, taping or by any information storage retrieval system without the written permission of the author except in the case of brief quotations embodied in critical articles and reviews.

This book is a work of non-fiction. Unless otherwise noted, the author and the publisher make no explicit guarantees as to the accuracy of the information contained in this book and in some cases, names of people and places have been altered to protect their privacy.

WestBow Press books may be ordered through booksellers or by contacting:

WestBow Press
A Division of Thomas Nelson & Zondervan
1663 Liberty Drive
Bloomington, IN 47403
www.westbowpress.com
844-714-3454

Because of the dynamic nature of the Internet, any web addresses or links contained in this book may have changed since publication and may no longer be valid. The views expressed in this work are solely those of the author and do not necessarily reflect the views of the publisher, and the publisher hereby disclaims any responsibility for them.

Any people depicted in stock imagery provided by Getty Images are models, and such images are being used for illustrative purposes only. Certain stock imagery © Getty Images.

Scripture quotations taken from The Holy Bible, New International Version® NIV® Copyright © 1973 1978 1984 2011 by Biblica, Inc. TM. Used by permission. All rights reserved worldwide.

Scripture taken from the New King James Version® Copyright © 1982 by Thomas Nelson. Used by permission. All rights reserved.

ISBN: 978-1-6642-6502-8 (sc)
ISBN: 978-1-6642-6504-2 (hc)
ISBN: 978-1-6642-6503-5 (e)

Library of Congress Control Number: 2022907839

Print information available on the last page.

WestBow Press rev. date: 06/08/2022

For Tami, Emily, Alexandra, and Rachel.

You are my living stone monument.

Contents

Preface

I love deep Bible study that accomplishes two distinct tasks. First, I need Bible stories to make sense to me. Whether by adding appropriate context and/or humanizing the abbreviated manner by which the scriptures record the human experience, I need to connect with these stories in order to feel that I am appropriately applying the spiritual lesson that God has set before me at the time of that particular reading. Second, I need to connect with deep spiritual truths, for it is here that I find the greatest spiritual motivation. I need to see how the scriptures tie together and, in doing so, be routinely reassured that the concepts held within are neither complicated nor reserved for the learned—rather, they all tie into the common theme that God seeks a relationship with other beings, created in His image, who voluntarily choose a relationship with Him.

With reference to this free will, the only way to accomplish this task was to give those beings the ultimate and uninhibited freedom to choose to foster a relationship with Him or to choose to reject a relationship with Him. Had the downside for rejecting Him been fierce and immediate, then He would have forced our hands and, thus, free will wouldn't truly exist. Rather, God allows those who He knows will ultimately reject Him to live among those who have or will ultimately seek Him. As a result, those who will never seek God are allowed to experience much of the good associated with having a relationship with Him while they live this life. God is patient with all of His people, not wanting any of them to perish, yet He will not intervene in any way that would force our decision one way or another. He will run after us, woo us, love us, bless us, and walk alongside us, but He will not do anything that would interfere in our freedom to choose a relationship with Him, for doing so would undercut the very reason for our existence. We will explore this concept further in the last chapter of this book. For now, it is sufficient to understand that we are gifted life for a set period of time, during which we can choose a relationship with our Creator.

This book began as a personal endeavor to teach the beauty of biblical virtue to my children, something I was ill prepared to do. Second Peter 1 quickly became the theme scripture on which these lessons were built. These teachings were later turned into monthly lessons and provided to a group of parents whom my wife and I were mentoring. The goal was for parents to take each lesson (all of which are now contained in this book as chapters) and integrate them into daily or weekly devotionals that they would focus on with their families over the course of that month.

With that background, understand that these chapters can be lengthy, as they were originally intended (with the exception of chapter 1) as small-group lessons that would provide a month's worth of study material. I thought long and hard about including family devotionals associated with each virtue but came to the conclusion that doing so would lead families down the road of what I believe they should glean from each chapter, rather than allowing God's Spirit to minister to readers, based on their current life circumstances and spiritual maturity. I would prefer that each of us receive from each chapter different aspects of spiritual concepts, depending on a culmination of our own life experiences and our current life situations. My prayer is that those who take the time to personalize the material contained within these chapters and work diligently to incorporate the principles into their lives will develop or refine a perspective of God through the lens of His magnificent virtue. Similarly, parents who take the time to personalize these lessons and instruct their children with humility and passion should find them incredibly useful in helping young people develop a similar perspective.

Irrespective of how this material became a book, it remains the culmination of my own personal journey in pursuing a virtue-based Christianity, rather than one driven by fear of consequence and failure. I pray that God will open your eyes to these deeper concepts, intended to help you to fall more in love with Him and refine you to become one with Him. This book is not intended to be the A to Z of Christianity or an exegesis of the salvation process. Nonetheless, I am fully confident that biblical concepts contained herein have the power to transform the Christian experience into one that not only results in discovering life to the fullest for individual readers but that simultaneously and collectively creates "a shining city on a hill" for a lost world that is fumbling around in the darkness with very few physical examples of the invisible God who is pursuing them.

Chapter 1

THE FATHER, THE SON, AND THE HOLY SPIRIT

IN FIRST-CENTURY ISRAEL, WHEN A MOTHER AND FATHER GAVE birth to a boy, they would soon begin the search for a potential mate. Although in our modern American culture, parents leave finding a mate to the child, it is not really that difficult to understand this mindset. As the father of three daughters, I am acutely aware of young men who are being raised by good parents who share similar moral and spiritual standards. My wife and I have each had our own experiences with dating, courtship, and marriage, and we also have a more mature grasp on young love, infatuation, attraction, the discovery of one's self, and frankly, a more accurate view of who our daughters really are, rather than how they might currently see themselves. If you have been married for more than a decade or two and now look back on who you were when you first married, you can certainly relate by being dumbfounded by how little you actually knew about yourself and your spouse at the time.

Now, before you put this book on the shelf, assuming it is an unabashed promotion of arranged marriage, let me assure you that is not the case. I am simply highlighting the fact that, given the opportunity, most parents would be thrilled to help their children navigate the process of finding spouses who are a good fit, will remain faithful, and who share a morality and spirituality that reflects their family values. Although modern Western parents have this shared interest with first-century Jewish families, we differ in that those first-century parents acted on that impulse and went in search of a potential mate for their children. Sometimes, this search yielded a quick result, and sometimes, the search took many years. When the parents of a son found a like-minded family whom they thought would raise a good potential spouse for their son, they would introduce themselves and attempt to reach agreement to reserve the children for each other. If an agreement could be reached, the son's parents would then return home, and each family would go about the business of raising their respective children.

Now, first-century Jewish families lived primarily in family compounds. Those of you who have seen images of archaeological digs have likely seen the remnants of foundations to family homes built in a single line of adjacent rooms, similar to the layout of a single-story motel. As the family grew, a new room would be added to accommodate the new couple and their future children.

This is a side note, but the first stone laid when constructing the initial home was the called the cornerstone. This was the squarest stone or brick and was placed at the corner of the foundation, hence the name. All other walls in the home would be squared off the cornerstone, allowing the home to be straight, sturdy, and able to withstand the harsh elements of nature. Having the initial room as close to square as possible was especially important, for the entire extended family could have their homes built off a single cornerstone. Not only should we understand the reference to Jesus as the cornerstone of His church but also the importance of spiritually accurate parents in the long-term stability and spiritual integrity of their children and their children's children.

I will mention one other side note, the point of which will become evident later in this chapter. Every Sabbath, the family would cease all chores and participate together in a day of rest. A common practice was to gather the entire family for a time of worship, during which the women would lead the family in song, and the men would perform the teaching, largely through storytelling. The most common form of teaching consisted of the family patriarch recounting stories of how God had intervened to bless the family through both hardships and times of abundance. These stories not only defined God for the family but also created a deep sense of family identity, with God as the family cornerstone.

These Sabbath gatherings remind me of the father-son backpacking trips I took each year of my childhood into the Sierra Nevada mountains. Because most meals needed to be prepared for the entire group at one time, all of the men and their boys would gather to eat together, and the conversation almost always consisted of stories told by the fathers. I remember not only tremendous laughter but great relational bonding and a deep sense of security that resulted from these times. With this reference point in my own history, it is not hard to imagine that these Sabbath gatherings produced similar learning environments and emotional experiences.

The importance of these two side notes will soon become evident, but for now, let's return to our initial discussion. When the potential couple reached marrying age, the groom's entire family would assist the men in preparing to journey to the bride's village or family compound so that the two could meet. Depending on how far away the families lived, it is possible that this would be the first meeting of the future couple. This journey was also tradition and must have been a special rite of passage, as the groom traveled with all the men in his family to meet his potential bride. This trek would have created an opportunity for the older men to pass along their wisdom to this young groom and also a time for him to ask questions of the married men in his family as he prepared to care for a family of his own.

If, after spending time together, the young man and woman agreed to marry, then the fathers would meet to negotiate the *bride price*. This is another concept that can cause consternation in our Western minds. But let us stick to the facts. Absent significant wealth, first-century parents did not have any form of retirement. In fact, their retirement was their children. Children were responsible for taking care of their parents until their death, a practice that remains common throughout the world today. Those of us who live in the United States are actually in the minority with our retirement plans, Social Security, and first-world health care coverage for assisted living, nursing homes, and hospice care. But if the parents' retirement rested solely on their children, and their daughter left to live with her new husband's family, then she would be lost to her parents as a caretaker and source of provisions. The purpose of a bride price was to make sure that the bride's parents were taken care of when they could no longer work, despite the loss of their daughter. This was not human trafficking or slavery but rather a beautiful gesture between the parents of the bride and groom to make sure the bride's parents could live out the rest of their lives with security and dignity, despite the loss of their child. Now, we know from the story of Jacob, Leah, and Rachel that this practice was abused, but for the purposes of our discussion here, let's focus on the original intent of these practices, rather than their misuse.

Once a bride price was agreed upon, the couple was considered betrothed. The bridegroom and his family then left the bride with her family and returned to their property in order to build an add-on to the family home. This is a bit like our modern-day engagement period, except that the couple was from this point legally married even though they had not yet consummated the marriage. Ponder for a moment the anticipation of the groom as he worked diligently with his family to build the future home for his new bride. Imagine also the eagerness of the bride as she awaited the return of her bridegroom so they could begin their life together. It is easy to visualize the groom's entire family, including even nieces and nephews, helping to construct this new home with much care, personalization, thoughtfulness, and craftsmanship so that the new bride would feel embraced and welcomed once she arrived.

If the bride and groom did, in fact, live far apart, the bride would not likely have any way to easily determine when the bridegroom would return for her. This understanding may help place in context Jesus's words when He said what is recorded in John 14:2–3: "My

Father's house has many rooms … I am going to prepare a place for you," and in Matthew 25:13: "Therefore, keep watch because you do not know the day or the hour." Every Jew of the time would have understood exactly what Jesus meant with these metaphors. All of the rich history described thus far had emotional connections for the Jews, just as attending a friend's wedding has an emotional connection for those of us who are already married.

When the new home addition was complete, the bridegroom and his family would travel to the bride's home for the wedding ceremony. Imagine, if you will, a group of a few dozen people, ranging from grandparents to newborns and from uncles and aunts to siblings, nieces, and nephews, traveling in a caravan with enough provisions to both make the journey and hold the wedding, as well as the associated wedding parties and banquets. Imagine the excitement, the conversations that took place along the road, the father-son and mother-son talks, the storytelling, the bonding, and the anticipation that built as each mile passed.

In Western culture, weddings can be highly expensive and very stressful. But contrast that with this first-century family affair. Mom and Dad have suggested a potential spouse, based on the moral and spiritual belief system of the bride's family. The meeting of the potential bride and groom went well, and they chose to marry. The men of the groom's family have traveled to and from the bride's family compound to facilitate this meeting and determine a bride price. The groom's entire family has worked together to build an add-on for the new couple. And now, the groom's family has traveled together to the home of the bride's family for the wedding, wedding banquet, and a great celebration.

With this imagery in mind, I would request that you pause and allow yourself a few moments to contemplate how this atmosphere would darken as the groom's family arrives at the bride's home and finds that while they were away, preparing a home for her, she became pregnant by another man.

Can you imagine the groom's crushing disappointment, the endless deflation in the pit of his stomach? The feelings of betrayal followed by anger? The humiliation? What about the desire of the groom's parents to protect their son? The head-spinning disorientation, followed by the embarrassment the groom would feel, even though this turn of events was in no way his doing? The shame the parents would feel for having selected this girl for their son and promoted her as his future spouse? Would they storm off? Would they demand the woman's life, as directed in Leviticus 20:10? What about the relationships that already had been built with the bride's family? Were those relationships now severed? How could the groom's mother and father look the other parents in the face, and what would they say when they did?

What about the bride's family and the horror of seeing the groom's family face-to-face? The disgrace to their family name? The confusion between a parent's deep love for the daughter and the deep disappointment in her behavior, which didn't seem to be in line with who they knew her to be. For this wasn't simply a woman becoming pregnant out of wedlock but a woman who became pregnant while betraying the groom, to whom she had committed herself. Would the groom's family demand the daughter's life? Did the bride's family still have the ability to repay the bride price? Imagine trying to make sense of what was happening in real time, determine how to respond to it and how to dampen the anger—even hate—from the groom's family.

Although we don't know all of the specific details regarding location, distance, number of relatives, etc., we do know that it was a situation like this in which Joseph, son of Jacob, found himself when he and his family arrived for his wedding to Mary.

THE JOURNEY

If you are like me, you have heard the romanticized Nativity-scene Christmas story for so long that it can be difficult to wrap your head around the fact that this happened to real people—moreover, to a young man and woman who were likely still teenagers.

The Bible, which contains some of history's greatest understatements, only makes a few statements regarding Joseph. It begins in the first chapter of Matthew by stating that he was faithful to the law. Some translations use "being a righteous man." The most accurate translation seems to be "Joseph, being righteous." We also are told that he was not willing to expose Mary to public disgrace. And we are told that he had made up his mind (the actual Greek translation is that "he purposed") "to divorce her quietly," or sever their betrothal. These statements alone are incredible. What honorable character Joseph possessed! Despite crushing disappointment and humiliation and *before he was visited by the angel in a dream*, he chose to remain faithful to God's law and decided to place an unfaithful woman's reputation ahead of his own. He knew that he had to go back home and explain to his neighbors and friends why he was without his new bride. There was no escaping the humiliation and disappointment, but in this moment of extreme emotion and deep discouragement, he was a righteous man (which means that he acted not as he felt but on what was best for strengthening relationships with those around him), and from that core belief system sprang his commitment to protect Mary from any further consequences of her decision to be unfaithful to him.

The Bible doesn't say how Joseph's family reacted, but it is not a stretch to consider the possibility that they were not in agreement with Joseph's desire to protect Mary's reputation at the expense of his own. We can infer from the scriptures that Joseph at least stayed the night at his bride's family compound. For it was during that night that Joseph had a strange dream in which he envisioned an angel informing him that Mary's unborn child did not have an earthly father, instructing him to take Mary home as his wife, and to name the baby Yeshua, which means "Yahweh is salvation."

Now, may I ask that we pause here to have a gut-level discussion about our own hearts? Have you ever been in the middle of a traumatic emotional experience and then had one or more weird dreams about it? In fact, science now tells us that strange and intense dreams are a common way for the brain to process traumatic or highly charged emotional experiences. How many of us would have awoken from Joseph's dream and simply brushed it off as an intensely strange dream in which our brains were trying to process yesterday's events? There is little doubt that is how I would have responded. In contrast, how many of us would have awoken from that dream and concluded that it was not simply a strange dream but an actual angel of God, telling us what to do? And if we were so sensitive to the Holy Spirit as to come to that conclusion, how many of us would have had the courage to then act on it?

I can tell you with confidence that I would not have concluded my dream was God's actual voice, and even if I had concluded that it was God speaking to me, I cannot be confident that I would have obeyed. There are times in the scriptures where God speaks to certain people physically and while they are awake, but there are other times where it is recorded that God comes to people in a dream. Joseph's experience is the latter, and this is an important distinction to make, for God coming to you in a dream is much easier to rationalize away than a commanding voice from a bush that spontaneously combusts before your eyes.

With nothing more than a strange dream during the night, which followed the most emotionally charged day of Joseph's life, he concludes that this was not just a dream but an actual angel. In response to that very personal decision, Joseph then chooses to take a pregnant woman as his wife and tell his family that he is doing so. How do you think his family reacted to that news? How would you have reacted if he was your son? Would you have supported his interpretation of this strange dream, or would you have instructed him to pack his things and then hauled him back to your family compound in order to start rebuilding your lives afresh?

How do the scriptures record Joseph's response? Prepare yourself for another famous biblical understatement. Matthew 1:24 simply states, "When Joseph woke up, he did what the angel of the Lord had commanded him and took Mary home as his wife."

What are we learning about Jesus's earthly father thus far? First, we have learned that he was a righteous man. We will look deeper at the meaning of righteousness later in this book, but for now, suffice it to say that the original meaning of the Hebrew concept of righteousness simply meant any action that makes better a relationship between two people or between a person and God. With that simple understanding, we see that Joseph was relationally (righteously) driven. Not only does the Bible call him righteous, but we see that specific virtue lived out in his decisions regarding Mary. Even before the angel speaks to him in his dream, the Bible states that Joseph did not want to publicly disgrace Mary, which would have destroyed her life and maybe cost her life. He chose to sever the betrothal quietly, as to not sully her reputation further than it already would be, once the community realized that she would give birth to a child out of wedlock.

That alone speaks volumes about the character of young Joseph. But our understanding of him doesn't stop there; we also learn that he was immensely sensitive to God's voice. For as we just discussed, which of us would have honestly believed that dream to be anything more than our brains processing a horrific day, and even if we had believed that God was attempting to speak with us, who among us would have woken up and, on that day, taken an unfaithful woman as our wife, despite almost certain opposition from family.

Take a moment and ponder the following questions. How sensitive are you to God's voice? Do you hear His gentle nudges? If so, do you respond willingly, regardless of how your obedience might be perceived by those around you? Do you help the oppressed? Do you live beneath your means so that you can secretly meet the needs of others? How is your prayer life, really? If you pause to think about your family, your coworkers, your finances, and how you use your time, what is the gentle whisper of God's Spirit calling you to do? What has the Spirit been calling you to do? What promptings are you silencing or rationalizing away?

Consider what kind of flak Joseph likely received from his family when he informed them of his decision—based only on a dream— which would bring shame on his family, since neighbors and friends could easily calculate the timing between the wedding and the birth.

It is possible that as a result of this decision, Joseph and Mary were disowned by their families. That may be why the new couple traveled alone to Bethlehem to comply with the census, why none of their Bethlehem relatives was willing to take them in, and, therefore, why were they were alone for the birth of their first child in nothing more than a shelter that housed livestock.

It was a ninety-six–mile journey to get from Nazareth to Bethlehem. Ladies, how many miles per day do you think you could reasonably hike in sandals and over rugged terrain in the third trimester of pregnancy? Given the length of the journey, they would have needed to carry food, a tent or tarp, supplies, and water. Although it is possible that they were traveling with Joseph's family, there are no indications of such in the scriptures. Assuming they were alone, how deep the division between Mary and Joseph and their parents must have been that they would avoid traveling together for the birth of their grandchild and a census requirement to which they were all subject. Given these conditions, how many of us would have felt justified in blowing off the census requirement and staying home? The Bible says that Joseph was faithful to the law, and boy, do we see that here.

You know the story. Once in Bethlehem, Mary goes into labor. Why not stay in their tent? Maybe it was winter and too cold for a newborn. Maybe the tent offered no protection from wind or blowing dust. They knocked on door after door, and no one would take them in. If this happened to my wife and me, I would grow in frustration, anxiety, and fear. I can imagine asking, "How is this possible?" and "How can people be this selfish and uncaring?" My blood would begin to boil. Maybe Joseph lamented to himself, "These are my fellow Israelites, and no one will lift a finger to help a young woman in labor?" I know myself well enough to know that my frustration would boil over to God. I can see myself losing self-control and saying things like, "No room in the inn? Not a single compassionate countryman? Are you kidding me, God? Anything else you want to throw at us in addition to being stuck in a barn surrounded by the smell of manure, mildew, and feed?"

Can you relate to this kind of experience? Have you ever had a day where you believed you were doing everything that God asked of you, yet it felt as if He just kept piling on? Do you think Joseph was tempted with these kinds of thoughts? Do you think that he felt like a bad provider? Do you think he was ever tempted to doubt the validity of his dream? Maybe he thought, *What have I done?* while wondering if he had been wrong to conclude that his dream was from God. If so, was God now opposing him for not listening to his family? Do you think he was ever tempted to doubt Mary's story about her still being a virgin? Would you believe a pregnant friend or coworker who claimed that her baby was conceived by God as the father? Which historical precedent did Joseph have to rely on? What family was there to offer guidance or emotional and physical support? Rather, they are alone, desperate, frustrated, scared, and clearly without enough money to buy their way into anything better than a barn.

And it is in that moment of desperation and exasperation, holding their new baby in their arms, that God sends a small amount of encouragement, arguably just enough encouragement to sustain them until the next challenge. A handful of grungy and odorous shepherds show up unannounced and explain to Mary and Joseph that they too had seen an angel and heard about a savior being born (keep in mind that Joseph had not yet named his son). They told them about the great company of heavenly host that had appeared and praised God.

Isn't it interesting that God didn't show the awesome sight of heavenly host to Mary and Joseph but instead to a group of uninvolved shepherds, who had to relay it to Mary and Joseph? Is that not the way God works? He challenges your faith, refines your soul, demands your obedience no matter how steep the climb may be, and then, when you think you are at the breaking point, He gives you just enough encouragement to carry on but in a manner that doesn't remove your need to keep acting on faith. You see, had God showed Mary and Joseph what He showed to the shepherds, they would not have needed faith, for faith is being certain of what you cannot see. Instead, He required of them to trust the shepherds' story in order to find comfort in it. Of course, to carry on the tradition of biblical understatements, the scriptures sum up the entirety of these events with one short statement: "Mary treasured up all these things and pondered them in her heart" (Luke 2:19).

The book of Luke tells us that during the first week of Jesus's life, his parents traveled six miles to Jerusalem to comply with the law regarding circumcision. As first-time parents, did you take your one-week-old baby on a six-mile hike? I know we didn't. On the contrary, as parents of a newborn, we quarantined our child from every possible germ while my exhausted wife was trying to recover from the birthing process, all while feeding and changing our new baby every few hours. But not Joseph, for he was faithful to the law. Now, this may apply only be me, but I find a small amount of humor in the thought that Joseph's faithfulness to the law might have created some friction between him and Mary during these first few weeks, and if so, they certainly would not have been the first new parents to experience marital friction following the birth of a child.

With no shelter and no money, Joseph and Mary likely returned to their home in Nazareth after naming Jesus and circumcising Him in Jerusalem. The book of Luke tells us that in obedience to the purification rites required by the Law of Moses, "Joseph and Mary *took [Jesus] to Jerusalem* to present him to the Lord" (Luke 2:22, emphasis added). This statement makes it clear that they did not stay in Jerusalem following Jesus's circumcision, which is why they needed to return to Jerusalem for the purification rites. In case you are starting a tally, that is a ninety-two–mile journey. Worse, because the direct route was through Samaria, and the Jews hated the Samaritans, it is more likely they would have taken the Jericho Road, which is 120 miles.

So Mary and Joseph most likely traveled ninety-six miles from Nazareth to Bethlehem while Mary was at the end of her third trimester, then six miles to Jerusalem in the first week of Jesus's life for His circumcision, then ninety-two (or 120) miles back to Nazareth following Jesus's circumcision, and then back again to Jerusalem in order to comply with the purification rites required by the Law of Moses. Luke 2:39 tells us, "When Joseph and Mary had done everything required by the Law of the Lord, they returned to Galilee to their own town of Nazareth," another ninety-two (or 120) miles. So, within the first fifty days of Jesus's life, Mary and Joseph likely traveled some 460 miles in order to comply with the Law of Moses and the laws of Rome. When the scriptures state that Joseph was faithful to the law, can there now be any doubt that God is describing a defining aspect of Joseph's character?

How is your obedience to the law? Do you honor the city engineers by adhering to the speed limits they have calculated for your safety? Are you above reproach in how you compute your taxes? Are you obedient to government rules and regulations, corporate rules and regulations, and health and safety regulations, or are you the person everyone can count on to explain why all of these laws are unnecessary, government overreach, and overly burdensome? It is noteworthy that when God was searching for one to raise His Son, a wholehearted adherence to the laws of man was not only an important character trait but one of which God made painstaking note in the scriptures, so much so that it is one of the few things God recorded for us regarding Joseph.

You see, brothers and sisters, as with so many decisions we face in life, there are only two options: to show honor or to give in to pride. Whether you agree or disagree with laws and regulations is irrelevant. What is relevant is whether or not you show honor to others by surrendering your pride and adhering to the societal boundaries placed on us by those in authority and thus display a core virtue of our heavenly Father that we will soon see embodied in Jesus.

Let's take one more momentary tangent and quickly touch on the purification rights mentioned above, for through them, we can discover another gem about this beautiful young family.

Exodus 13:2 and 13:12b-14 state,

> Consecrate to me every first-born male. The first offspring of every womb among the Israelites belongs to me, whether human or animal.

> All the firstborn males of your livestock belong to the Lord. Redeem with a lamb every firstborn donkey, but if you do not redeem it, break its neck. Redeem every firstborn among your sons.

> In the days to come, when your son asks you, 'What does this mean?' Say to him, 'With a mighty hand the Lord brought us out of Egypt, out of the land of slavery.'

Leviticus 12:2-6 and 8 state,

> A woman who becomes pregnant and gives birth to a son will be ceremonially unclean for seven days, just as she is unclean during her monthly period. On the eighth day, the boy is to be circumcised. Then the woman must wait thirty-three days to be purified from her bleeding. She must not touch anything sacred or go to the sanctuary until the days of her purification are over. When the days of her purification for a son or daughter are over, she is to bring to the priest at the entrance to the tent of meeting a year-old lamb for a burnt offering and a young pigeon or a dove for a sin offering.

> But if she cannot afford a lamb, she is to bring two doves or two young pigeons, one for a burnt offering and the other for a sin offering. In this way, the priest will make atonement for her, and she will be clean.

According to Luke 2, Joseph and Mary chose the latter sacrifice, meaning that they could not afford a lamb. This would make sense if they had been cut off from their families after deciding to go through with the marriage. After the chaos of the surprise pregnancy and the fallout from possibly being disowned, Joseph and Mary gave birth in a barn and then traveled hundreds of miles before Jesus was forty days old. Upon arrival in Jerusalem, they could not even afford the nicer of two sacrifices for their son.

Can you relate to the feeling that God keeps asking things from you, and it just seems like too much? Maybe you have wondered "why me?" when everyone else seems to be having an easier time of it. But just as Mary and Joseph approach another possible breaking point—poor, alone, exhausted, facing an uncertain future and maybe even some friction in their own relationship—God sends them another small but timely encouragement. While at the temple, they meet Simeon, also recorded as a righteous and devout man, whom the Holy Spirit was upon. Simeon had been promised that he would not die before seeing the Messiah. Prompted by the Spirit, he went to the temple on the day that Mary and Joseph arrived, took the child in his arms, and stated aloud,

> Sovereign Lord, as you have promised, you may now
> dismiss your servant in peace. For my eyes have seen
> your salvation, which you have prepared in the sight
> of all nations: a light for revelation to the Gentiles,
> and the glory of your people Israel. (Luke 2:29–32)

As did the shepherds, Simeon also refers to Jesus as "your salvation" and the Bible states that Joseph and Mary marveled at what was said about Jesus.

Then God sent them Anna, who had lost her husband after only seven years of marriage and had spent every day since in the temple courts. She too encouraged these new parents with news about how their son would bring the redemption of Jerusalem. What a wonderful God we serve! He is loving and disciplined enough to refine us through challenge and trial but never leaves our side. He is always there to provide just enough encouragement to sustain us until the next challenge, yet without ever crossing a line that negates our free will. As for Mary and Joseph, their next challenge was soon to come.

Sometime after returning home to Nazareth following the purification rites, Mary and Joseph appear to have settled into a home and were enjoying some semblance of normalcy. They had heard nothing more about their son being the Messiah and no additional dreams with orders from angels for the better of two years, when out of nowhere, very wealthy advisers to Eastern kings arrive with their entourage and present expensive but not very useful gifts to Jesus.

Although Mary and Joseph must have been appreciative, this unexpected visit could not have made a whole lot of sense. But little did Mary and Joseph know that as soon as the Magi left, Joseph would have another strange dream, in which an angel would tell him that they must immediately leave for Egypt in order to protect their son from King Herod. If the dream to disregard Mary's perceived unfaithfulness and to take her as his wife, despite family opposition, wasn't challenging enough, now he was prompted in another dream to leave everything—his home, his income, and his relationships— and flee to a foreign land with a language he likely did not speak. Can you imagine how that conversation went with Mary or with his parents, provided they were on speaking terms? It is also worthy of note that unlike the pregnancy, Mary had no similar dream to confirm that of her husband.

But true to his nature, Joseph listens to the Spirit's gentle whisper and is obedient. He packs up his family and begins the three-hundred–mile journey to Egypt. There, they stayed until Herod's death in 4 BC. Although we cannot know precisely how long they stayed in Egypt, it was long enough to make the journey, wait until Herod's execution order had been carried out, and then return. It is also not unreasonable to surmise that it very well may have been proceeds from the sale of the Magi's expensive gifts that sustained them financially during this period. If that was the case, wouldn't that be just like God? I cannot begin to recall the number of times I have come into extra money just days before I have incurred an unexpected expense that was equal to the amount of my extra funds. This has happened so frequently that my wife and I have come to call our budget the manna budget, for it appears that God has decided to provide us with exactly what we will need and not any more. And while many around us have been successful in packing away extra savings for their future, is it really a bad thing if our heavenly Father chooses to mete out to us only what we need in order to foster trust in and keep us reliant on Him?

The story of Joseph comes to an end in the scriptures with two more dreams, both of which Joseph attributes to God and then acts upon with full obedience. The first is found in Matthew when Joseph is told. "Get up, take the child and his mother and go to the land of Israel, for those who were trying to take the child's life are dead" (Matthew 2:20). The second occurs while on that journey, when Joseph is told to divert to Nazareth because Herod had been succeeded by Archelaus.

Upon their arrival in Nazareth from Egypt, it appears that the family was finally able to settle down and have additional children. Family relationships seem to be repaired over time, at least in part, for by the time Joseph and Mary lost twelve-year-old Jesus at the temple, the scriptures note that they were again traveling with relatives and friends.

And this, brothers and sisters, was the environment in which Jesus was raised.

THE HISTORY

Before we continue, take just a moment to consider Joseph's lineage and the oral traditions and family faith stories young Joseph heard, Sabbath after Sabbath, during family worship. If you are looking for an interesting Bible study for your prayer times, take time to research some of the people listed in the lineage recorded in the first chapter of Matthew, keeping in mind that each story you learn was one that Joseph would have heard week after week from his direct descendants. With that knowledge, contemplate the oral traditions and family faith stories that young Jesus heard from his earthly father during their family Sabbath worship times. Not only was Jesus raised hearing the faith stories of all the men and women in his own lineage, but He witnessed, firsthand, numerous other faith stories as his father and mother lived them out in front of Him.

According to Luke 2:39–40, Joseph and Mary returned with Jesus to Galilee to their own town of Nazareth. "And the child grew and became strong; he was filled with wisdom, and the grace of God was on him." I love this scripture because it clearly tells us that Jesus had an upbringing during which He grew and became strong, and it was during this upbringing that He was filled with wisdom, and God's grace was on Him. When did this occur? After the Spirit came upon Him at baptism? Nope. According to Luke, this filling up of wisdom occurred while He was still growing physically, at the feet of His parents, with whom He lived until He was ready to begin His ministry at age thirty. Mark 1:9 states, "At that time Jesus came from Nazareth in Galilee [where his parents had settled] and was baptized in the Jordan." Matthew 4:13 tells us that Jesus left Nazareth, indicating that He was with His family until that time.

I would like to highlight one other interesting scriptural note regarding Joseph before we get into some analysis. Luke 3:23 states, "Now Jesus himself was about thirty years old when he began his ministry. He was the son, so it was thought, of Joseph…" We have learned quite a bit about Joseph by taking time to contemplate and personalize the stories behind the scriptures. But in reality, the earthly father of the Son of God is mentioned in the scriptures very few times, and we know nothing of his death. The man who raised Jesus not only simply disappears from any further scriptural account, but those who met Jesus were not entirely sure who His father was. Let me ask you: are you satisfied with a background role? Is it acceptable to you if you exist only for your children to stand on your shoulders? Does your use of time display overwhelming proof that the spiritual and moral growth of your children is more important to you than your career? Your entertainment? Your rest? Your dreams and ambitions? If not, what steps can you take today to begin reprioritizing?

One important note of encouragement: Luke says that the "grace of God was upon him" as a growing child. Do you know why that was? First Corinthians 7:12–14 answers this question for us in the following manner: as a result of your faith, you have sanctified your children because they are under the umbrella of God's grace poured out on you. Therefore, if you are in a right relationship with God, then your children are starting from a place of sanctification.

Our job as Christian parents is to not drop the ball. Many of us are overwhelmed by the thought that we need to bring our children to a full and complete knowledge of God. Although true, one's perception of how that is accomplished is pivotal. It is of utmost importance to understand that the primary means through which children will come to a complete knowledge of God is by observing their parents' faith in action—in their relationships, at home, at work, how mom and dad respond to both suffering and blessings, and how they resolve conflict and seek and offer forgiveness.

We will discuss our role in the salvation of others shortly. But as it pertains to our children, the *most important* thing we can do for them is live in such a manner that we don't misrepresent the beauty and majesty of God, which He tries to display through us in our everyday life circumstances.

THE REFLECTION

Before we conclude this chapter, we have a few more things to learn from Jesus's earthly father. We have gleaned as much about Joseph as we can by looking at the scriptures directly related to him. To learn anything more about Joseph, we need to turn to that which Jesus learned from his earthly father. But bear with me for a little longer—for us to effectively see Joseph through his son Jesus, I must first draw your attention to a few other scriptures.

Hebrews 2:17–18 states:

> For this reason He [Jesus] had to be made like them, fully human in every way, in order that He might become a merciful and faithful high priest in service to God, and that He might make atonement for the sins of the people. Because He Himself suffered when He was tempted, He is able to help those who are being tempted.

Paul tells us here that Jesus had to be made like us, fully human in every way. What does that mean? Well, when the scriptures leave us with a question, I have learned that it is always better to allow scripture to answer it.

> During the days of Jesus' life on earth, He offered up prayers and petitions with fervent cries and tears to the One who could save Him from death, and He was heard because of His reverent submission. Although He was a son, He learned obedience from what He suffered and, once made perfect, He became the source of eternal salvation for all who obey Him and was designated by God to be high priest in the order of Melchizedek. (Hebrews 5:7–10)

What do we learn here? Jesus had fears. He had anxieties. He had his own dreams and ambitions, and they were not always aligned with God's. He had to learn obedience. Why would He have to learn obedience if He was born perfect? What if He wasn't born perfect? Did you ever consider that Jesus might have been as the scriptures say—exactly like us, "fully human"? Maybe He cried when His mom told him no, threw temper tantrums, and pushed or lashed out at His siblings when He was mad. But His parents trained Him and modeled for Him spirituality, faith, and a relationship with God that was infectious. Maybe Jesus had to figure out that He was the Son of God, rather than having a preexisting knowledge of this fact.

Before you get too caught up on the theology of this point, please keep in mind that for the purpose of this discussion, we do not need to solve the question of from which point Jesus did not sin. Just consider the possibility that Jesus was not born perfect with a supernatural ability to see the future but instead was exactly like you and me. Hebrews 5 continues with the words in verse 9, "once made perfect, he became the source of eternal salvation." Why would Jesus need to be made perfect if He was perfect from birth? Equally important is *how* the scriptures say that He was made perfect—from what He suffered.

Then, there is Luke 2:52, which states, "And Jesus grew in wisdom and stature, and in favor with God and man." Why would Jesus need to grow in wisdom if He was born with all wisdom?

Additionally, Isaiah 7:14–16 states:

> The virgin will conceive and give birth to a son, and will call him Immanuel. He will be eating curds and honey *when he knows enough to reject the wrong and choose the right*, for before the boy knows enough to reject the wrong and choose the right, the land of the two kings you dread will be laid waste. (emphasis added)

It seems pretty clear from scripture that there was a definitive time in Jesus's life when He knew enough to reject what was wrong and choose what was right. If we can wrap our minds around Jesus's being fully human, then we must set aside our own excuses for choosing differently.

> For we do not have a high priest who is unable to empathize with our weaknesses, but we have one who has been tempted in every way, just as we are— yet he did not sin. (Hebrews 4:15)

Is it reasonable to believe that Jesus could be tempted in every way if He had been born with the security of knowing that He was God, with a fully formed faith, with all wisdom and all knowledge without the bounds of time? And if that is true, then how could He be fully human in every way? Why did He have to learn obedience if He was always obedient? Why did He have to be made perfect if He was already perfect? Is it not possible that the scriptures mean what they plainly say, and Jesus was made like us, fully human in every way, heard by God due to His submission, had to learn obedience through suffering, needed to be made perfect, and had to grow in wisdom? If so, then where did all of this preperfection training occur? It must have occurred before He reached the age of accountability, as Hebrews 4:15 states, "[He] was tempted in every way, just as we are—yet he did not sin." Brothers and sisters, if true, then all of this learning occurred under the protection, comfort, training, and molding of two young parents named Joseph and Mary.

And with that context, we can now move into our analysis of what Jesus learned from His earthly father, Joseph.

Luke 2:41 states, "Every year Jesus' parents went to Jerusalem for the Festival of the Passover." We see here an example of what we have already surmised—that Jesus grew up watching His father's obedience to the law.

After His parents realized that Jesus was not traveling with them, "They began looking for him among relatives and friends" (Luke 2:44). We see here that they were again traveling with extended family. When Jesus's parents found Him, Mary asked, "Son, why have you treated us like this? Your father and I have been anxiously searching for you" (Luke 2:48).

An interesting side note, which we will not expand on here, is that Joseph and Mary confronted perceived sin by addressing the impact that Jesus's actions had on their relationship. In other words, they addressed what they perceived as unrighteousness, rather than focusing on the action itself. (This is an aspect of righteousness that we will address later in this book.)

Can you visualize this scene? Jesus has now reached the age of accountability, and Hebrews 4:15 makes it clear that from that point forward, Jesus does not sin. It is with a clean conscience that He sits at the rabbi's feet and absorbs the scriptures. When His panicked parents find Him, He doesn't understand why they had been looking for Him. He is genuinely baffled and asks, "Didn't you know I had to be in my Father's house?" (Luke 2:49).

Could you hear it more clearly if Jesus had said, "Dad, I don't understand. Isn't this what you taught me? We have traveled to Jerusalem in obedience to the law every year. You taught Me to listen to the Spirit's whisper. Is this not where I should be?" Jesus is in the process of transferring His allegiance from His earthly father to His heavenly Father, and He is confused by His earthly father's surprise and exasperation.

"Then He went down to Nazareth with them and was obedient to them" (Luke 2:51). And this is where the scriptures reveal that Jesus grew in wisdom and stature and in favor with God and man, long before His baptism and receipt of the Holy Spirit.

Where did Jesus learn to be instructed by the scriptures? Where did Jesus learn to listen to the gentle whisper of the Spirit? Where did He first feel the affirmation of these traits? What is your attitude toward being an avid student of the scriptures? How do you feel about pursuing scriptural knowledge by sitting at the feet of those farther along the Christian experience? Are your answers to these questions supported by how you currently live? Are you characterized as being a student of God's Word, or do you have a desire to have Jesus's and Joseph's passion for God's Word, but, in truth and in practice, it is an unfulfilled desire?

How about Matthew 4:1, which states, "Then Jesus was led by the Spirit into the wilderness to be tempted by the devil"?

Where did Jesus learn to hear the Spirit? What about you? Are you sensitive to the Spirit's prompting? Are you hearing the Spirit, or are you characterized as always being busy, never quiet, and routinely filling silence with entertainment? Do you act when the Spirit prompts you to share your faith with someone, or are you no longer even hearing that prompting? What about when the Spirit nudges you to assist someone by holding open a door, retrieving a dropped item, or assisting with a broken-down vehicle, or is your life too loud to even notice these things? Can you hear God speak at all, or is the entirety of your relationship (righteousness) with Him defined by only your voice being heard by Him? If the latter, then it's time to reevaluate the pace of your life and create the time to listen.

Matthew 5 contains Jesus's first recorded sermon after leaving His family to fast and pray in the wilderness. Where did Jesus learn the godly virtues with which He opens His sermon, and where did He learn the blessings that result from embodying them? Take a minute and read Matthew 5:1–11, with Jesus's upbringing in mind. This brings an entirely new light to what was going on in Jesus's heart as He was teaching this, as He had seen each one of these virtues lived out in the lives of His parents. Is there any doubt that their submission to God had both modeled for and solidified in Jesus's heart the magnificence of living by virtue, rather than by fear? Joseph was pure in heart; he received his comfort from God when mourning. He defined meekness, yet he inherited the earth. And just for clarification, the Greek word that is translated as *meekness* is not akin to shyness and weakness; instead, the same word is used to describe an untrained horse that submits itself to a trainer so that it may be broken and trained.

Joseph exemplified hungering and thirsting for righteousness. He was the embodiment of mercy toward Mary, yet still a peacemaker with the family. Was he not persecuted because of the decisions he made that were rooted in righteousness? Ponder for a moment Jesus's conclusion in Matthew 5:11–12, which states, "Blessed are you when people insult you, persecute you, and falsely say all kinds of evil against of you because of me." Is that not exactly what had happened to His earthly father, Joseph? Jesus continues, "Rejoice and be glad, because great is your reward in heaven, for in the same way they persecuted the prophets who were before you." Can there be any question that at least some of the inspiration for Jesus's first sermon was the life and faith of His earthly father? Ask yourself, as Jesus's blood brothers and sisters: do you want Jesus to look upon you with the fondness with which He saw Joseph, or do you want Jesus to see you as one who protects self, stores up treasure on earth, is blind to the needs of others, and is deaf to God's gentle whisper? If the former, then what steps can you take today to become more like Joseph?

Luke 14 records Jesus saying that in order to be His disciple, you must hate your family. Consider that if a Jewish son or daughter accepted Jesus as the Messiah, they were deemed to have disowned not only the family religion but the entirety of their Jewish heritage. Who modeled this for Jesus? Where did Jesus see this lived out? Might it have been that as a child, Jesus had watched Joseph and Mary attempt to repair their relationships with their own families, which were likely strained through Joseph's decision to listen to a dream rather than listen to his parents? Might it have been that Jesus was an illegitimate child whose adoption by Joseph brought shame on Joseph's and Mary's lineage, yet Jesus witnessed his parents' faithfulness to God and their unconditional love for Him at the cost of their own family relationships?

What about when Jesus fed the five thousand in Matthew 14, Mark 6, and Luke 9? The scriptures record that Jesus noticed they were hungry and helpless, like sheep without a shepherd. Where did Jesus learn that spiritual encouragement and meeting physical needs are interrelated and that one without the other can be perceived as condescension and pity, rather than genuine love and concern? Might He have learned about the impact that the shepherds' encouragement had on His mom and dad during one of their scariest moments? Might it have been the stories of how God provided physical gifts through the Magi before His parents were aware that they would need them for economic survival? Might it have been when He learned the impact that Simeon and Anna's words had on His parents during one of their loneliest times and largest faith challenges?

What about Jesus's reaction to the suicidal leper of Matthew 8? You see, it was punishable by death if a leper entered a populated area. It is therefore logical to surmise that this individual was so distraught that he was wagering his life on Jesus. He concluded that he would either be healed by Jesus or be stoned by the crowd, and either outcome was better than his life situation. Why would people stone lepers? Because leprosy was believed to be transmitted by touch. Visualize the scene with me: Jesus comes down from the hillside into a crowd of people who are fixated on Him. Out of nowhere come the gasps, the loud warnings, and the screams of "get out of here," as the parting crowd scrambles to get away from this infectious man. People begin grabbing stones in order to protect themselves and their children. The mob mentality sets in. Fear is driving behavior. And what does Jesus do? He reaches out and publicly touches the man. Maybe Jesus placed a hand on his shoulder. But I like to imagine that Jesus cupped the man's scarred face in both of His palms and lifted his eyes to meet His own. And with a gentle, kind, and loving smile, He answered the man's question with, "I am willing," before healing the man.

Where did Jesus learn this kind of compassion—that sometimes doing what was most repulsive to all those around was the exact thing that would minister to the person in need? By touching the leper, Jesus did something viewed as impure, just as His father, Joseph, had done when he took a woman perceived to be unfaithful as his wife, disregarding the opinions of those around him because it was exactly what Mary needed. Do you realize that this leprous man had likely not felt the touch of another human since he had contracted his disease? He had been separated from his loved ones and cast out of his society. He now resided in the area outside of the city gates called Hades, where trash was strewn and all of the human waste from the city would pool. This was where those infected with diseases and cast out of society would search for anything edible. What if Jesus had lifted the man's face with His palms so that their eyes could meet and said, "It is not the time for Me to heal you, but I see you, and I love you." Consider the needs that Jesus was meeting, irrespective of the physical healing. Does that sound like you? Is this how you live your life at work? At school? In the grocery store? In line at the Department of Motor Vehicles? Is there anything stopping you from looking for needs, listening to the Spirit's prompting, and then acting to meet both spiritual and physical needs around you? If not, then what is stopping you?

Consider the woman described in John 8. Here, it is recorded that a woman is dragged before Jesus, having been caught in the act of adultery. If she was caught in the act, then she was likely unclothed, terrified, horrified, humiliated, and at her most vulnerable state. And how does Jesus react? Well, He refuses to add to her shame and humiliation by looking at her nakedness; instead, He squats down to doodle with His finger in the dirt. And rather than publicly address the woman's choices, He chooses to address those in the crowd who were self-righteousness. Once the crowd disperses, Jesus elects to put off addressing her behavior and instead reassures her that neither the crowd nor He will condemn her to death that day. Instead, He freely offers her a second chance without an ounce of condescension.

Where did Jesus learn not to judge someone's alleged impurity at face value? Where did Jesus learn to respect women and to show them honor by not leering at them when they were dressed immodestly? Are you beginning to see the theme here? God chose Joseph and Mary and then orchestrated for them a life journey that was intended to both refine them and allow them to model virtue for His Son, therefore instilling that virtue in Jesus, not though words alone but by witnessing virtue and its blessings lived out in His earthly parents, day after day, over the normal course of life.

In Matthew 6:25–34, Jesus tells us to seek first the kingdom and His righteousness, and God will meet our needs. Where did Jesus learn that God would provide daily necessities? Where did Jesus learn that each day will worry about itself? Where did Jesus learn how God the Father clothes even the lilies of the field and daily feeds the birds of the air? Have we not already become convinced that Jesus had a front-row seat to God's meeting Joseph and Mary's needs in ways they never could have orchestrated on their own?

In Mark 12:17, Jesus commands us to "give to Caesar what is Caesar's and to God what is God's." Where did Jesus learn to honor the law without compromising His convictions?

> No one can serve two masters. Either you will hate
> the one and love the other, or you will be devoted to
> the one and despise the other. You cannot serve both
> God and money. (Matthew 6:24)

Where did Jesus learn that God would provide for Him financially? Where did Jesus learn that the security that comes from money is in direct opposition to building one's faith in God's sovereignty? I am convinced that, by now, you know this answer.

Brothers and sisters, we are looking at the convictions of Joseph lived out in Jesus! Joseph imparted these virtues to his son, not through church summer camp or by setting Him up in a top-notch, hip teen ministry. Rather, the scriptures provide us with three clear lessons. Joseph was defined by his sensitivity to the Spirit's voice, his obedience to God's instructions, and his commitment to righteousness. Given all people in existence at that time or any two people that God could have created to perfectly suit His needs, God chose, as earthly parents, two individuals who lived what they believed in the face of consequence and who loved God more than they loved themselves, which was overwhelmingly evident through action.

Joseph and Mary, through their own lives, showed Jesus how to hear when God speaks, what it looks like when one responds to God's instructions, despite earthly consequence, and what it means to consider others better than oneself. Jesus's earthly parents were defined by virtue, and that virtue was so overwhelmingly beautiful that it painted an image for Jesus of an invisible God so attractive that from the age of His own accountability, Jesus chose not to sin.

I decided to open this book with the story of Joseph and Jesus because I can think of no other scriptural story that displays the premise of this book so beautifully and majestically. And that premise is simple: God's virtuous way is always more beautiful than anything the world has to offer. If we can learn to anchor our faith in virtue, then we will be like a man who built his house on a rock. The rain will come down, the streams will rise, and the winds will blow and beat against the house, yet it will not fall.

Who among us doesn't want our faith anchored in the same manner by which Jesus's faith was anchored? Who among us thinks the servant can be greater than his master? God handpicked Joseph and Mary and orchestrated every aspect of their lives to paint for Jesus a more beautiful and complete picture of Him, and He foresaw that they would be willing to become less so that God could become greater. I see in Joseph a young man who wrestled year after year to faithfully accept God's lot, surviving on the crumbs of encouragement he found along the way. But by doing so, he embodied and modeled a more beautiful way for his son. As a direct result, God was able to provide—through the young man Joseph and the young woman Mary—the parenting foundation for the Savior of the world.

On whose shoulders will your children stand? What picture of God are you painting for them? God has given you everything you need to be a Joseph. All He asks of you is to trust Him, to act justly, to love mercy, to walk humbly with your God (Micah 6:8). If you have any interest in anchoring your faith in virtue, then please join me by beginning that journey in the following prayer:

Father, it is so clear from the scriptures that You want a relationship with us that is built on mutual trust, includes a daily dialogue, and is anchored in Your virtues. Thank you for loving us flawlessly, despite our utter lack of deserving. Thank you for modeling for us what a life of virtue looks like so that we can be free to commune in relationship with You, rather than be stuck in the legalism that results from obedience to the law without relational context. You are the perfect Father, and we want to do everything we can to return to You as a bride who has chosen Your love over anything the world had to offer.

Please bless our study of the virtues that define You so that we can become like You. Please help us to get out of our own way and to learn to care more about what You think than what others think. Help us to learn, through the following pages, what a relationship with You actually looks like so that we can successfully transition from spiritual milk to solid food, from elementary teachings to righteousness. We have no way to adequately thank you for this opportunity, but we pledge to spend our lives trying. Amen.

Chapter 2

FAITH

IN CHAPTER 1, WE LOOKED AT THE LIFE OF JOSEPH AND THE INDELIBLE impact he made on Jesus. We learned how a life anchored in virtue is the single most important element we can add to our faith. We saw how the story of Joseph displays our premise that God's virtuous way is always more beautiful than anything the world has to offer. Now, it is time to further confirm that premise with scripture.

Paul writes,

> In fact, though by this time you ought to be teachers, you need someone to teach you the elementary truths of God's word all over again. You need milk, not solid food! Anyone who lives on milk, being still an infant, is not acquainted with the teaching about righteousness. But solid food is for the mature, who by constant use have trained themselves to distinguish good from evil. (Hebrews 5:12–14)

This passage makes it clear that part of the Christian experience is to transition from elementary teachings to more mature understandings. Paul uses the analogy of an infant transitioning from milk to solid food. An infant needs milk because its digestive system is not yet ready to process solid foods, and mother's milk contains very specific enzymes that are needed for the newborn's nutrition and to help establish its digestive biome and immune system. This is true of the Christian experience. We need to ingest the type of foundational teachings Paul references in Hebrews 6 (repentance from sin, faith in God, cleansing rites, laying on of hands, the resurrection of the dead, and eternal judgment) in order to prepare ourselves to move on to the "teaching about righteousness." It is noteworthy that in Hebrews 5, milk is equivalent to an assortment of elementary teachings but that solid food is a much more specific reference to teaching about righteousness.

In order to have a fuller understanding of what this verse is telling us, it is essential that we first understand what is meant by "righteousness." Fred Faller has done a masterful job of defining this Hebrew term in his paper "Right or Righteous,"[1] so I will not try to duplicate that here. Suffice it to say that the original Hebrew word for "righteousness" did not necessarily originate with religious connotations. Rather, it can be defined in its simplest form as "anything that makes a relationship better." When the Bible speaks of righteousness, it is not speaking of religiosity, being right, or even doing right. Instead, it is speaking specifically of making decisions and behaving in a manner that betters your relationships with others and with God. Let me reiterate this concept because this theme is critical for understanding the entire Bible, let alone this book. *Righteousness is anything that betters a relationship between two people or between someone and God.*

With that definition in mind, consider the behaviors the Bible defines as sinful. Hate is the opposite of bettering relationships. Stealing damages relationships. Lust damages relationships. Lying damages relationships. Yes, even white lies or lies intended to encourage, once exposed, damage relationships by damaging trust. In fact, the reason something is a sin is because it damages relationships

---

[1] Fred Faller, "Right or Righteous?" Published in the *Boston Church of Christ Bulletin*, Boston, MA (May 28, 2015); *Discipleship Magazine*, (1991); and *The Revised Disciple's Handbook*, DPI.

and is therefore unrighteous. For those who tend to view God as prohibitive and authoritative, this understanding alone can help to transform that perspective to a God who desires our lives to be full of pure and boundless relationships, most importantly with Him. Hebrews 5 explains that an essential part of the Christian experience is the need to move from elementary and foundational doctrinal teachings into building robust relationships with each other and with our heavenly Father.

Let's look at another essential point in our understanding of transitioning from milk to solid food or from elementary teachings to righteousness. Proverbs 9:10 states, "The fear of the Lord is the beginning of wisdom and knowledge of the Holy One is understanding." The fear of the Lord is intended to be a core foundational element in our conversion, but it is *not* intended to define our lifelong relationship with God. You may feel that you have moved on from milk to solid food because you have a daily prayer and Bible-reading time or because you are unshakable in your scriptural knowledge of sin, repentance, and conversion (all great things, I might add). But if, in your heart, you largely perceive your Christian life as a living sacrifice, and you find that your primary motivator in resisting temptation is the fear of consequence, then too much of your diet remains milk. There is a better, more mature way, and if we fail to become well versed in that better way, we will be handicapped in our relationship with God, while also being unable to model for our hearers (both children and neighbors) the magnificence of a solid-food relationship with God.

Please imagine for a moment what your relationship with your spouse would be like if you confessed to him or her every evening that there are other things you would rather do than be with them and other people you would rather have married. Then you followed that nightly confession by reassuring your spouse that you had resisted the temptation and were committed to him or her, regardless of how intensely you were tempted to be with someone else. How many times do you think you could have this conversation before your spouse would grow weary of your lack of love for him or her?

One could say, "Wait a minute! Look at how faithful and committed I was," but it doesn't take a trained marriage counselor to figure out that a marriage relationship is doomed if you don't find a way to fall in love with your spouse in a manner that surpasses the desire to be with another. Does that mean that you will never be tempted? Not at all. But please honestly consider which of the following more accurately characterizes your relationship with God: Is it defined by a passion for Him and all that He encompasses, or is your Christian experience more defined by your gut-level commitment to never quit, no matter how much you desire something else? Are you defined by loving every aspect of your current relationship with God or do you mostly rely on the promise of your heavenly reward to make up for how difficult you perceive the Christian life to be? If you consistently view sacrifice in a negative light or as hardship, rather than an investment that pays dividends, or you view God's boundaries as prohibitions rather than beautiful lines that fall in pleasant places, then your diet consists of too much milk and not enough solid food.

Now let's contrast that mentality against what the disciple, whom Jesus loved, said:

> And so we know and rely on the love God has for us. God is love. Whoever lives in love lives in God, and God in them. This is how love is made complete among us so that we will have confidence on the day of judgment: In this world we are like Jesus. There is no fear in love. But perfect love drives out fear, because fear has to do with punishment. The one who fears is not made perfect in love. (1 John 4:16–18)

According to John, we need first to rely on the love God has for us. But what about mercy, forgiveness, and redemption? Although these are essential components of how God's love is played out in your life, if the overwhelming focus of your relationship with God is fixated on your need for mercy, forgiveness, and redemption, then you are missing the reason why God granted you mercy, forgave you, and redeemed you, which is that He is head over heels in love with you! If we live in love, then we live in God and God in us. The goal of resisting temptation and denying self is to live in an ever-increasing love relationship with God *in this life.* In fact, verse 17 states that if love is made complete among you, then you will have confidence on the day of judgment. Wow! What a bold promise! But let's be frank; the only way we are going to have this kind of confidence on the day of judgment is if we come to see ourselves the way God sees us, believe the plans He has for us, and accept the fact that He has given others in exchange for us (see Isaiah 43:4). Never forget that on the day of your conversion, the only being in existence who was acutely aware of every sin you committed up to that point _and_ every sin you would commit until your dying breath is the heavenly Father, who knowingly forgave you for every single one of those sins that very day and welcomed you back into His family with open arms (Luke 15:23–24) with full knowledge of the growing pains you would encounter (2 Corinthians 3:18).

John concludes his thoughts in verse 18 by stating, "There is no fear in love"; "The one who fears is not made perfect in love"; and "Perfect love drives out fear, because fear has to do with punishment." How much of your relationship with God is defined by fear? Remember that fear of the Lord is not bad—it is the beginning of wisdom—but John makes it clear that although fear is a starting point, it is not the goal. If your relationship with God is characterized by the fear of losing His love or a low-level but ever-present anxiety over being punished for yesterday's sin, then too much of your spiritual diet is milk, and it is time to introduce more solid food. We now know that solid food refers to the teaching about righteousness, which, as we just learned, means anything that improves our relationship with God and with others. This is different from your standing with God or others, for those who are redeemed are already clothed in Christ (Galatians 3:27), meaning your standing is secure. It is the relationship that needs to be developed.

If anyone had reason to remain in fear, it would have been

Peter, who, contrary to his personal promise to Jesus that he would never deny Him, *did* deny knowing the Messiah three times. Even worse, Jesus witnessed Peter's third passionate denial; it was the last impression with which Peter left Jesus before His death. But despite that relationship-shattering (unrighteous) failure, Peter didn't remain in fear; he ultimately discovered solid food and, thankfully, began to define that very transition for us in when he stated:

> For this very reason, make every effort to add to your faith goodness; and to goodness, knowledge; and to knowledge, self-control; and to self-control, perseverance; and to perseverance, godliness; and to godliness, mutual affection; and to mutual affection, love. For if you possess these qualities in increasing measure, they will keep you from being ineffective and unproductive in your knowledge of our Lord Jesus Christ. (2 Peter 1:5–8)

Second Peter 1:5–8 will be our theme scripture for the remainder of this book as we explore together the virtues of goodness, knowledge, self-control, perseverance, godliness, mutual affection, and love. There is a reason why Peter chose these seven virtues and instructed the disciples to make *every effort* to add them to their faith. He tells us that if you possess these qualities in increasing measure, then they will keep you from being ineffective and unproductive in your knowledge of our Lord. This sentence can be misinterpreted to mean that growth in these areas will keep you from being ineffective and unproductive in your Christian life, evangelism, or godly works. But that is not what Peter said. Rather, growth in these specific areas will keep you from being ineffective and unproductive in your *knowledge of our Lord.*

Remember our discussion of Proverbs 9:10 above, which revealed that knowledge of the Holy One is the foundation of righteousness (relationship), just as falling in love with someone occurs as you get to know that person. Physical attraction, infatuation, and curiosity incentivize you to get to know someone but cannot sustain a lifelong love relationship. Similarly, fear of God initiates a seeking of Him, but we must all move beyond the trigger and into the stage where we grow in our love for God by getting to intimately know Him through the revelation of the virtues that compose His character.

For the remainder of this chapter, we will focus on the virtue from which we anchor all others. According to Peter, that foundational virtue is *faith*. In the original Greek, the word used here is πίστει (*pistei*), which translates as trust, confidence, and faith in the active sense. Its particular usage in 2 Peter indicates faith is a virtue that is to be coupled with other virtues of similar nature. Let's look at the same Greek word used in other scriptures:

> But you, man of God, flee from all this, and pursue righteousness, godliness, faith, love, endurance and gentleness. (1 Timothy 6:11)

> You, however, know all about my teaching, my way of life, my purpose, faith, patience, love, endurance, persecutions, sufferings. (2 Timothy 3:10–11a)

> Teach the older men to be temperate, worthy of respect, self-controlled, and sound in faith, in love, and in endurance. (Titus 2:2)

I mentioned above that faith (pistei) in the scriptures is, more often than not, combined with other virtue or action. In these three passages, not only do we see an interconnectivity between faith and other virtues but, more importantly, we see an expectation for Christians to embody virtue. In 2 Timothy 3, we see Paul exemplified by these virtues. In 1 Timothy 6:11, we see Paul instruct Timothy to pursue these very virtues. In Titus 2:2, we see Paul direct that these same virtues be expected of older men in the church.

But let's take it even deeper.

> Because you know that the testing of your faith produces perseverance. Let perseverance finish its work so that you may be mature and complete, not lacking anything. (James 1:3–4)

Here in the book of James, not only do we see that interconnectivity between faith and virtue, but we begin to see an inter-reliance between the virtues. (We will further pursue this concept in our study of 2 Peter 1.) Brothers and sisters, we all know nonbelievers who exemplify certain biblical virtues. We love to watch documentaries of historical figures or top athletes who personify perseverance, self-control, patience, diligence, selflessness, etc. It seems clear that embodying these specific virtues is not reliant on a having faith in God, yet the scriptures indisputably connect virtue to faith. It is, therefore, important for us to diagnose and understand this perceived disconnect and answer the two following questions: How can those without faith exemplify virtue, and how does virtue rooted in faith differ?

Let's begin by ensuring that we understand what the scriptures really mean by (pistei) faith.

Two of the most famous passages on faith are:

> "Truly I tell you, if you have faith as small as a mustard seed, you can say to that mountain, 'Move from here to there,' and it will move. Nothing will be impossible for you." (Matthew 17:20b)

> He replied, "If you have faith as small as a mustard seed, you can say to this mulberry tree, 'Be uprooted and planted in the sea,' and it will obey you." (Luke 17:6)

Modern interpretations of these two verses are wide-ranging. On one end, they have become the foundation of the prosperity gospel—that if you just believe, anything is available to you, from healing physical ailments to accruing wealth, and from gathering abundance to obtaining a nirvana-esque comfort in this life. On the other end of the spectrum, some are taught that joy, peace, spiritual productivity, and comfort are not as the world defines. Rather, they are entirely separate from physical circumstance and therefore may only be found through faith in God's love, plan, and sovereignty. Rather than looking for the truth in one of these teachings or somewhere in between, consider the possibility that we are missing Jesus's point altogether.

If we are to understand what Jesus actually may have communicated, we need to understand four common metaphors that would have been familiar to Jesus's audience. First, in scripture, the concept of the mountain (ὄρει; *orei* in English) was more often than not a symbolic reference to kingdoms of man or the kingdom of God. Hebrews 12:22–24 is an example of this:

> But you have come to Mount [ὄρει] Zion, to the city of the living God, the heavenly Jerusalem. You have come to thousands upon thousands of angels in joyful assembly, to the church of the firstborn, whose names are written in heaven. you have come to God, the Judge of all, to the spirits of the righteous made perfect, to Jesus the mediator of a new covenant, and to the sprinkled blood that speaks a better word than the blood of Abel.

Another example of this symbology is found in Isaiah 2:2-3a, which states,

> In the last days, the mountain of the Lord's temple will be established as the highest of the mountains; it will be exalted above the hills, and all nations will stream to it. Many peoples will come and say, "Come, let us go up to the mountain of the Lord, and the temple of the God of Jacob."

We also know that at this point in Jesus's ministry—and largely from the scripture in Isaiah just referenced—His disciples were still wrestling with the societal belief that the Messiah would come to usher in a physical kingdom, such as had been experienced under the rule of King David, which would cause all other kingdoms to kneel before it, in particular the kingdom of Rome.

Second, the mulberry tree was native to Israel and produced an enormous amount of fruit.

Third, the sea (θαλάσσῃ, *thalassē* in English) was perceived as a dark and deep unknown, the depths of which could not be seen or explored. It took the life of many and, absent intervention, one could survive in the sea only for a short time before succumbing to exhaustion and descending into it. You may recall that Jonah was rescued from the sea by divine intervention. Only Jesus could tame it and God had held back its waters and used them to wipe an army from the face of the earth.

Lastly, we should understand that a mustard seed is one of the smallest seeds, with a width of only one to two millimeters. Once grown, it turns into a massive plant that can exceed nine feet in height. In a short time, this aggressive plant can overtake an entire field or hillside.

With these contextual understandings in mind, let's consider what Jesus actually may have been describing. There is a distinct possibility that Jesus was using metaphoric language, as He often did, to describe three concepts. First, faith is a journey, during which the amount of faith we possess at any given time will vary. Second, the smallest amount of faith in God has the ability to move kingdoms and to uproot and replant one of the earth's most fruitful trees right into the center of Satan's stronghold. Third, the faith of which Jesus speaks in these passages may have less to do with determining our spiritual productivity and more to do with the core foundational element in our *relationship* with God.

Consider the following verse:

> And without faith it is impossible to please God, because anyone who comes to him must believe that he exists and that he rewards those who earnestly seek him. (Hebrews 11:6)

Humor me for a moment as we consider the possibility that faith is not some mysterious and nebulous spiritual concept. Instead, maybe it simply means, as the scripture states, that in order to have a relationship with your heavenly Father, you must first believe that He exists. Logical, is it not? How can you have a relationship with someone who does not exist or with whom you don't believe exists. You may dream of a relationship with someone who is nothing more than a figment of your imagination, but you cannot have an actual relationship with that person. Since we cannot see God or hear His physical voice, how can we come to faith so that we may know that He is more than a figment of our imagination? Let's let the scriptures answer that for us. Romans 10:17 states, "Faith comes from hearing the message, and the message is heard through the word of Christ."

It is interesting that this type of faith does not come from the entirety of scripture. Instead, it comes from hearing the actual words of God while He was inhabiting our flesh and living among us. We therefore can logically deduce that seeing God interact relationally with humans while in the form of Jesus is sufficient to produce enough faith on which to build our relationship with Him. In fact, it is more than sufficient; it is the only way to create the type of faith of which Jesus speaks.

This is such a pivotal element in Christianity that it bears further exploration. God created man so that He could have a relationship with one like Him, created in His own image. But the fall of man brought about a great chasm that stifled man's relationship with God. Therefore, God provided the law—the same kind of structure that is provided to small children; that is, rules without understanding. But it was not possible to have a relationship with the law. So God provided His people with their own nation. Unfortunately, that resulted in men who saw obedience to religion as a mechanism for national success and for obtaining power and self-importance. As was true with the law, one could not have a relationship with a nation. God then withdrew His voice and placed His people into a four-hundred–year period of silence.

In fact, God's last recorded words before this period of silence warn Israel that if they do not turn their hearts back to their children and their children's hearts back to the parents, that He will strike the land with a curse. The inference can not be missed. God is all about relationships, starting with familial relationships, as they are a physical representation of the spiritual relationship He wants to have with His children. But still, Israel failed to comprehend. So God became a man and allowed humanity to witness firsthand what it looked like when God interacted with man—what made Him laugh, what made Him cry, what met His needs, what made Him indignant, and how He withheld judgment and condemnation in order to lavish unconditional love on the fallen. It is this firsthand witnessing of the person of God that creates the foundation for a relationship with Him. Absent Jesus, we would still be trying to have a relationship with the law and/or using religion for national or personal advancement.

Let's evaluate our relationship with God, shall we? If you were sitting beside Jesus and lamenting about your spiritually lost friend, would you say, "Jesus, save him!" or would you say, "Jesus, how can I help You reach him?" You see, to those around Jesus, it was clear that He wanted to save the lost more than they did. Therefore, they didn't need to command Jesus to do what He had already set out to do; rather, they needed to act as a friend and determine how they could be helpful. If you were sitting beside Jesus, would you ask for more money, or might you ask how you could better serve Him with what He had already loaned you? If you were sitting beside Jesus, would you beg only for healing, or would you also ask that He help you learn from the condition He had allowed you to endure? You see, brothers and sisters, the single greatest failing of humans is that we don't understand that having a relationship with God means having an actual *relationship* with God. How often do you speak with God in prayer? How much of your prayer time is devoted to understanding God's perspective, how He feels about the issues you are currently facing? Are you getting to know God through your prayer life or is your prayer time largely a one-sided dialogue?

You may recall the words that Jesus says will be used on the day of judgment: "Then I will tell them plainly, 'I never knew you. Away from me, you evildoers!'" (Matthew 7:23). What Jesus will plainly state should be plain to us. We need a restored, two-way, functional relationship with our Creator. This relationship will not magically come to be upon our deaths. It needs to be established now.

What have we learned thus far? Faith is not just belief in the supernatural. It is confidence that the God of the Bible exists. Hebrews 11:1–3 confirms this:

> Now faith is confidence in what we hope for and assurance about what we do not see. This is what the ancients were commended for. By faith we understand that the universe was formed at God's command, so that what is seen was not made out of what was visible.

Surprisingly, that confidence emerges not from scientific proofs or the study of apologetics but from watching God interact with men while in human form. Once obtained, even a mustard seed of faith becomes the foundation of your relationship with God, and that relationship with God allows you to participate in the ushering in of God's kingdom and the bearing of abundant fruit, even when swimming in the surrounding waters of spiritual abyss.

But faith must not remain a confidence in the reality of God that does not result in a relationship. If that is the case, then we will be included only among a group with which we best not associate. James 2:19 states, "You believe that there is one God. Good! Even the demons believe that—and shudder." Remember that Hebrews 11:6 makes it clear that not only do we need to be confident in His existence but that we must earnestly seek Him. Let me ask you a question. Can anyone honestly say that they are earnestly seeking a relationship with someone with whom they refuse to converse? Imagine waiting in line for hours after a professional sporting match to meet your favorite player, or at a book signing to meet your favorite author, or after a rally to meet your favorite politician, and when your opportunity finally arises, you stand there, unable to get out a word. Would you walk away from that interaction believing that you had initiated a relationship? Certainly not. In fact, to initiate an actual relationship, most of us would try to get into a one-on-one conversation, where we could make a connection over similar thoughts or interests.

Brothers and sisters, if we are going to earnestly seek God, we must acknowledge that the most basic element of relationships is regular communication. God speaks to us through His Word and we speak to Him through prayer—and I am not speaking of reciting scripted prayers but actually speaking with God, as people spoke to Him while He was in human form. We must first believe that He exists, and then we must earnestly seek Him in the pages of the Gospels. We must earnestly seek Him by learning how He reared the Israelite nation as a parent raises a child. We must earnestly seek Him by regularly conversing with Him because that is how relationships work. It is why Jesus lived among us—to show us how to have a functional, relational walk with the living God.

One of my most significant spiritual challenges is self-reliance. I was raised to believe that I could accomplish just about anything that I set my mind to, and, in many significant areas of my life, that seemed to prove accurate. But the older I become, the more I realize the fallacy of that thinking. For in truth, virtually everything I have ever accomplished was with the assistance of others. The skill set necessary for what would become my career was largely funded by the financial flexibility of my parents, which included the gift that I did not need to work to support myself through college. The longevity of my marriage largely has been due to a great amount of help that my wife and I received in learning the skills of biblical conflict resolution. The success I've had in child-rearing has been almost entirely due to the work of other individuals, who took the knowledge and understanding that the Lord had gifted them and made it available to others. My ability to choose to act in a manner that keeps me out of trouble was largely due to the countless hours of effort that my parents put into developing self-control in their children. And so much of my standard of living is due to the fact that I was born in a first-world country. Did I work hard? Certainly. Did I set goals? Often. Can I take some credit for the state of my life? Some. But this deep-rooted self-reliance constantly gets in the way of my desire to develop a relationship with God because so many of the areas He wants to discuss with me are areas I would rather gloss over because they are areas in which I need His help.

I am aware that I can likely get through life comfortably with my current level of discipline. I can maintain most of my relationships with my current level of compassion and empathy. I am comfortable with my current level of self-sacrifice. But, brothers and sisters, God has not called me to standards with which I am comfortable. God has called me to earnestly seek Him and to make every effort to add to my faith a list of virtues that He is modeling for us. And this level of discipline, compassion, empathy, moral excellence, self-sacrifice, vulnerability, and unconditional love requires me to remain in a daily relationship with Him, through which I receive strength from His Spirit and motivation from my relationship with the Father of us all.

I am too sinful to pull myself up by my own bootstraps to meet the standards set by God. The self-reliance that has functioned in other areas of my life is actually an impediment to righteousness, for it creates a barrier in my relationship with God that runs counter to reliance and surrender. And therein lies the difference between the world exhibiting a godly virtue and a disciple becoming Christlike. True biblical virtue cannot be obtained, absent a relationship with God.

This concept is so very well explained in Matthew 5:43–48. Midway through His Sermon on the Mount, Jesus states:

> "You have heard that it was said, 'Love your neighbor and hate your enemy.' But I tell you, love your enemies

and pray for those who persecute you, that you may be children of your Father in heaven. He causes his sun to rise on the evil and the good, and sends rain on the righteous and the unrighteous. If you love those who love you, what reward will you get? Are not even the tax collectors doing that? And if you greet only your own people, what are you doing more than other? Do not even pagans do that? Be perfect, therefore, as your Heavenly Father is perfect."

Jesus states here in a few sentences what it took me multiple paragraphs to say. Settling for a level of biblical virtue that suits you makes you no better than a pagan. Instead, Jesus calls us to embody virtue *as He displays it*. While we were still His enemies, He left heaven and became a man and endured hardship, poverty, and scorn. As the whole world mocked Him, He laid down His own life so that the few who would later pursue a relationship with Him would have the ability to be forgiven and welcomed into an eternal bliss that they could never earn. Quite the opposite of our own homes, God's home will be full of those who were once His enemies, living among Him as if they deserved it, when, in fact, the only reason we will be with Him in heaven is that He pursued us, He died on our behalf, He found us, He wooed us, He forgave us, He protected us, and He restored us to Him. And He now expects us to imitate His level of virtue, which He describes as "perfection." Brothers and sisters, absent a daily relationship with our Father, that is simply impossible.

If a man remains in me and I in him, he will bear much fruit, apart from me you can do nothing. (John 15:5b)

For the remainder of this book, we will endeavor to understand the virtues that Peter instructs us to make every effort to add to our faith. In doing so, we will develop with our heavenly Father the type of daily relationship that He seeks; the kind of relationship that will cause Him to know us on the day we meet face-to-face; the type of relationship that will compel Him to welcome us home with open arms and the words, "Well done." The embodiment of these virtues is impossible if we do not have a faith that results in a functional, conversant, daily relationship with the God, from whom we derive our strength. Commit with me today that you will spend time each day looking at how God in the flesh interacted with humanity and discussing openly with Him where you need help to become more like Him. Absent that, this book will become nothing more than a transfer of knowledge that, as Paul states, does nothing more than puff up one's ego, unless combined with heart.

We will conclude this chapter in the second chapter of James, which is pivotal to our understanding of the purpose of faith and how it ties in to our theme scripture of 2 Peter 1:5-8. To connect the teachings from these two important brothers, let's look first at 2 Peter 1:1-4, which states,

> Simon Peter, a servant and apostle of Jesus Christ, To those who through the righteousness of our God and Savior Jesus Christ have received a faith as precious as ours: Grace and peace be yours in abundance through the knowledge of God and of Jesus our Lord. His divine power has given us everything we need for a godly life through our knowledge of him who called us by his own glory and goodness. Through these he has given us his very great and precious promises, so that through them you may participate in the divine nature, having escaped the corruption in the world caused by evil desires.

This absolutely phenomenal passage bears breaking down. First, Peter writes to those who "through the righteousness of our God and Savior Jesus Christ have received a faith as precious as [that of the apostles]." So, it is through witnessing the righteousness (relationships) of God with men, while He was in the form of Jesus, that we have received a precious faith. And with that faith comes a divine power that provides everything we need for a godly life. But this godly life isn't motivated by fear. Rather, it is motivated by the knowledge of God, which we gained while watching Him in human form.

We will delve into the concept of knowledge two chapters from now. For now, suffice it to say this word refers to an intimate knowledge of another person that is intertwined with a relationship. I ask you to also store away the concept that God has called us by His own glory and goodness—two more concepts that we will discuss in depth later in this book. It is through His glory and goodness that He has given us His very great and precious promises so that, through them, we may participate in the divine nature. Participating in the divine nature is called godliness, which is another concept we will soon address.

Now back to James:

> What good is it, my brothers and sisters, if someone claims to have faith but had no deeds? Can such faith save them? Suppose a brother or sister is without clothes or daily food. If one of you says to them, "Go in peace; keep warm and well fed," but does nothing about their physical needs, what good is it? In the same way, faith by itself, if it is not accompanied by action, is dead … You foolish person, do you want evidence that faith without deeds is useless? Was not our father Abraham considered righteous for what he did when he offered his son Isaac on the alter? You see that his faith and his actions were working together, and his faith was made complete by what he did. And the scripture was fulfilled that says, "Abraham believed God, and it was credited to him as righteousness," and he was called God's friend. You see that a person is considered righteous by what they do and not by faith alone. (James 2:14–17, 20–24)

Confidence that God exists is faith, but that faith by itself is without effect. We must add to that faith by pursuing a relationship with Him, whom we believe exists, and that includes behaving in a manner that fosters a relationship. Consider that, as young adults, we hope and believe that our future spouses exist, so much so that we put ourselves out there and date. But getting another person to agree to go on a date is insufficient. We must behave in a manner that fosters a relationship if we want that relationship to result in a marriage, let alone a successful marriage. Is faith all that different? In order to pursue a relationship with Him, you must believe that He exists. You must then "date" and get to know your heavenly Father by sitting across from Him while He was in human form (through the words of Christ). And it should go without saying that we must behave in a manner that fosters a relationship, which is insightful as to why faith is more often than not included among virtue—one without the other leaves us in a similar condition as the demons who believe God exists, yet have no relationship with Him and, instead, await eternal condemnation.

Too many of us view faith only as a type of biblical magic that opens doors to answered prayers and miracles. Although faith has many layers—one having to do with answered prayer and another with miracles—I would challenge you, for the purposes of 2 Peter 1, to consider a much more basic definition of faith. Faith, in its simplest form (the mustard seed), means that we believe God exists and that He rewards those who earnestly seek Him. To obtain this entry-level faith, the prescription is to witness God interacting relationally with humans while He Himself was in human form. Once obtained, we are to begin adding virtue to this faith. Failure to do so will guarantee our inability to move on from milk to solid food, and we will forever be unproductive in our knowledge of our Lord. But a decision to do so will result in the beginning the most important relationship we will ever experience, the one for which we were created. The size of one's faith will vary, and there will be bumps along the road, as there are in every true relationship. But the reward of this relationship is the core of satisfaction in this life and the next. For those of you willing to take this journey with me, let's read on. I am excited and grateful to have you with me.

Chapter 3

GOODNESS

I N CHAPTER 2, WE DISCUSSED THE MOST IMPORTANT ELEMENT OF faith; that is, its most basic meaning that faith is confidence that God exists and that it is the foundation on which we are to build a relationship with our Creator. James 2:23 states, "And the scripture was fulfilled that says, 'Abraham believed God, and it was credited to him as righteousness,' and he was called God's friend. You see here that a person was considered righteous by what he did and not by faith alone."

Let's take a moment with this incredibly important verse. It is first helpful to know that this is believed to have been written by Jesus's physical brother. If anyone understood the different facets of a relationship with Jesus, it was James, for they had been together since infancy. James understood the familial aspect of a relationship with Jesus, as well as balancing the spiritual aspect of a relationship with God in the flesh, who was also his physical brother. And how does he choose to describe it to us? First, James wants us to know that it was Abraham's confidence in God's existence that formed the basis of his relationship with God. At this particular point in Abraham's life, his faith was of such a high confidence that he was willing to sacrifice his only son upon God's command.

We also know that God, in His perfect judgment, perceived

Abraham's faith as righteousness. In other words, Abraham's belief in God, combined with his acting upon that belief, was perceived by God as bettering their relationship, so much so that God calls him "friend." So many of us consume ourselves with whether or not our faith results in our definition of spiritual productivity. It is not my intention to diminish any personal spiritual goals, only to put before you that the most important element of your faith should be whether or not it produces relationship-forming behaviors that result in a friendship with God. Isn't this why we were created in the first place?

The word for *friends* found here in James 2:23 was φίλος (*philos* in English) and means a friend with whom one associated with familiarity. In other words, an actual friend, not simply an acquaintance. As we know, friendship is a two-way street; it requires both people to be committed to each other. Recall our short recap of the Genesis creation story. God wanted other beings, created to be like Him, who freely chose a relationship with Him. That must be our ultimate goal. Evangelistic success, church involvement, obedience to scripture, etc., are all important elements of the Christian life, but if our most important goal is not seeking and fostering a relationship with God, then where does that leave us? Recall Jesus's words:

> "Many will say to me on that day, 'Lord, Lord, did we not prophesy in your name and in your name drive out demons and in your name perform many miracles?' Then I will tell them plainly, 'I never knew you. Away from me, you evildoers!'" (Matthew 7:22–23)

This is one of the most sobering yet encouraging scriptures in the Bible, for Jesus makes it clear that the things we most often deem important, which are actually important, are subordinate to a relationship with God. You see, Jesus is not welcoming people into His eternal home based on their "spiritual productivity" but instead on a singular item: do you have a relationship with Him? Brothers and sisters, the most important thing in this life is to live and die with a functional relationship with our heavenly Father. Those who have a relationship with God will live with Him. Those who reject a relationship with Him in this life will not magically have a relationship with Him in the next.

Imagine if I had shown up at the door of my now-wife, having never met her before, and said, "Hi, I'm Dave. I just wanted you to know that I've been behaving in a manner to which you certainly would be attracted, and I have learned all about you from afar. I've just never taken the time to introduce myself and build a relationship with you. Sound good? OK. Here's an engagement ring. Bet you can't wait to marry me!" This scenario is utterly ridiculous, yet those of us who do not avidly pursue a relationship with our heavenly Father will tragically experience Matthew 7:23. It is not a punishment. It is a consequential result of our choosing. What makes this passage so awesome is the obvious inference that God desperately wants a relationship with you, and anything that stands in the way of that relationship is on your end, not His.

It is my deepest prayer that the following pages of this book will effectively walk you through the biblical process of getting to know your heavenly Father and developing a lasting relationship with Him, in which your life's purpose is fulfilled, and His goal of entering into a relationship with one created like Him is brought to eternal fruition. This is exactly where Peter intends to take us when he writes,

> For this very reason, make every effort to add to your faith goodness; and to goodness, knowledge; and to knowledge, self-control; and to self-control, perseverance; and to perseverance, godliness; and to godliness, mutual affection; and to mutual affection, love. For if you possess these qualities in increasing measure, they will keep you from being ineffective and unproductive in your knowledge of our Lord Jesus Christ. (2 Peter 1:5–8)

If you are interested in pursuing or deepening your relationship with God, such that He calls you friend, then let's start by looking at the first virtue that Peter implores us to add to our faith. That virtue is *goodness*.

In the original Greek, the word used here by Peter is ἀρετὰς (*aretas*), and it most often means moral excellence and virtue. It is also used less frequently to mean glories or praises.

This is the very same word used in 1 Peter 2:9–10, but is translated as praises.

> But you are a chosen people, a royal priesthood, a holy nation, God's special possession, that you may declare the praises [ἀρετὰς] of him who called you out of darkness into his wonderful light. Once you were not a people, but now you are the people of God; once you had not received mercy, but now you have received mercy.

Let's reread that verse with the entire definition of aretas included:

> But you are a chosen people, a royal priesthood, a holy nation, God's special possession, that you may declare the *goodness, moral excellence,* and *virtue* of him who called you out of darkness into his wonderful light. Once you were not a people, but now you are the people of God; once you had not received mercy, but now you have received mercy.

What is really being communicated here? Just like Israel, you too are chosen by God to be not only a priesthood but a royal priesthood—because you are children of both the High Priest and also of the King—to bring God's lost children constantly before Him in prayer and, in turn, adequately represent God to His lost children. We are to declare the goodness, the virtue, and the moral excellence of our heavenly Father, such that the world can see Him through us and be drawn back into a relationship with Him, a relationship that will result in their receiving God's mercy and having God's name placed upon them, as it has been placed on us.

Brothers and sisters, we will look at a few more verses to solidify this conviction, but please let this sink in for a moment. You are specifically chosen by God. He saw your misery, heard your cries, and was concerned over your suffering. His *goodness* compelled Him to send a physical representation of Himself so that you could be wooed back to Him. Before you chose to return, He poured out mercy by choosing the death you deserved and placing the punishment upon Himself, while in human form. Then, like an adoptive parent, He placed His name upon you and claimed you as His own, giving you an inheritance that can never spoil or fade. And finally, He provided you with instructions on how to live so that you might have a relationship with Him, through which you become like Him and then adequately represent Him to a lost world. I cannot think of a better way to sum this up than Paul, who stated,

> But whatever were gains to me I now consider loss for the sake of Christ. What is more, I consider everything a loss because of the surpassing worth of knowing Christ Jesus my Lord, for whose sake I have lost all things. I consider them garbage, that I may gain Christ and be found in him, not having a righteousness of my own that comes from the law, but that which is through faith in Christ—the righteousness that comes from God on the basis of faith. (Philippians 3:7–9)

Now, ἀρετὰς (aretas) is also the same word used earlier in 2 Peter in the verses that precede our theme scripture. In verses 3–4, Peter states,

> His divine power has given us everything we need for a godly life through our knowledge of him who

called us by his own glory and goodness [ἀρετῇ]. Through these he has given us his very great and precious promises, so that through them you may participate in the divine nature, having escaped the corruption in the world caused by evil desires.

What do we learn here? First, goodness is akin to moral excellence and living by virtue. In fact, God's goodness (or moral excellence) is the specific virtue He possesses that motivated Him to act on His compassion and call us out of darkness into His wonderful light, for "by them," we were called, and "through them," we participate in the divine nature. Thank goodness (literally), for we would have no chance at salvation without it. Second, it is that goodness that we are to declare to a lost world so that they too can begin to see a glimpse of the One who formed them, and perhaps they may reach out to Him and find Him. In addition, God's goodness motivated Him to want to be known by us, and it is that intimacy through which we access His divine power, which gives us *everything* that we need to live a godly life. Now that very goodness (that motivated the death of Jesus for our forgiveness) and motivated God to reveal intimate elements of Himself to us is the exact same goodness that Peter says that we should make *every effort* to add to our faith. That is a high calling, is it not?

What would goodness look like if it were lived out in us? One great personal Bible study is to look through the Gospels at how Jesus embodied goodness in every one of His interactions. Look at Jesus's excellence, both morally and also in life (Mark 7:37). The fact that God became a man so that we could meet Him in person, rather than introduce Himself solely through the law, is, by itself, the embodiment of goodness. Look at how Jesus's love for the lost motivated His own personal life sacrifice so that we could have a chance at salvation. Look at how Jesus elected to withhold judgment and condemnation so that He could display God's unconditional love for people who were wracked with the deep insecurity that comes from being in a broken relationship with God. Then take some time to visualize what this might look like in your life. How would you reflect God to a lost world if you set aside critical thinking and judgment and loved people based on how God values them? How would your relationships differ if you were compelled to action based on your compassion and desire to understand the challenges others are facing? How would your countenance differ if you were daily consumed with pursuing moral excellence in every area of your life?

I find this calling very challenging yet extremely rewarding, for we live in a world that is consumed with judging others and placing them in categories based only on things such as accomplishment, race, socioeconomics, looks, intelligence, or behavior. It is difficult not to get caught up in that thinking because it feeds the part of my brain that seeks self-esteem through contrast and comparison. But that is not reflective of our Father. God is goodness, which displays itself in understanding our innermost parts, responding to our cries, weeping over our hurts, and taking action to alleviate our suffering by the ultimate sacrifice of daily laying down His own life.

One beautiful example of goodness lived out in the life of a man is captured in the movie, *The Secrets of Jonathan Sperry*.[2] Jonathan was a widower who continued to reside in the home where he and his wife had raised their children to maturity and godliness, but those children were now residing in other cities, raising their own children, and making their own ways. Since the passing of his wife four years earlier, Jonathan had, as far as the community was concerned, settled into the role of the kind elderly man who lived down the street. Despite the absence of his wife and the passing of most of his friends, Jonathan continued to monitor the state of his community and prayed daily for all of his neighbors, even those who no longer paid him any attention.

One afternoon, Jonathan offered to pay one of the neighborhood boys to mow the lawn of the elderly gentleman across the street, who was known to be a crotchety old man with no tolerance for human

---

[2] *The Secrets of Jonathan Sperry* (2008) is available via Amazon Prime or may be purchased on Amazon.com. It is a wonderful movie for your family's collection and is appropriate for all ages.

interaction or perceived charity. The boy accepted what seemed to be an easy offer but only because he was unaware of the mistreatment he would endure by the owner of the lawn he was hired to manicure. And although the verbal abuse seemed unbearable, each difficult encounter afforded Jonathan an opportunity to mentor this boy on the virtues of compassion, understanding, servanthood, and many other important life lessons.

Over time, Jonathan developed a relationship with the boy and his friends that went beyond a business arrangement. The boys began to open up to him about being bullied at school, their romantic interests, and other intimate life details. By God's grace, the lessons the boys learned by serving the older gentleman across the street, combined with Jonathan's guidance, equipped them to deal with their own life challenges.

Day after day, Jonathan mentored these boys and watched as they came to the realization that absent a relationship with God, they were simply not equipped to make it through life while remaining on a virtuous path. It wasn't long afterward that, one by one, Jonathan helped the boys to seek God's forgiveness and restore their relationships with their heavenly Father. As time passed, not only did these boys witness the impact that choosing virtue over vice had on their peer and family relationships, but little by little, the crotchety man across the street began to soften as he was won over by the moral changes and servitude displayed by them.

Imagine, if you will, how this conviction was seared within the hearts of these boys when they discovered that the elderly man whom Jonathan had been paying them to serve was the very man who had taken the life of Jonathan's wife years earlier by driving while intoxicated. Not only had Jonathan not asked anything of them that he had not already asked of himself, but he had, in fact, set the bar much higher than any of them were currently being called to. Little by little, the older man across the street had his protective outer shell broken by the virtue displayed in the boys' behavior. The movie ends with a scene in which the man weeps as he seeks forgiveness from Jonathan.

The impact of a widowed elderly man on the community around him was astounding. But more than that, his impact was directly attributable to the godly virtues embodied within someone who wore the name Christian. In this movie, we see what goodness looks like in the life of a modern man. He was driven to be morally excellent. His pursued a life above reproach. He was motivated to help those around him find their way back to God, and he was willing to sacrifice himself to bring about the salvation of the one who had done him great harm. The story of Jonathan Sperry is also a great example of how the virtue of patience will reap a harvest, provided we continue to make every effort to be like God.

Another suggested viewing in an effort to see the virtue of goodness lived out is a *60 Minutes* segment titled "Predicting Murder." Although the title can be off-putting, the segment follows an outreach program in South Chicago and the impact it has on those who otherwise see no way out of their life situations and surroundings. The URL to this segment is https://www.cbsnews.com/video/predicting-murder

Let's recap some important takeaways:

1. Milk is the equivalent of foundational biblical teachings, often motivated by fear of consequence and punishment, whereas solid food is ever-increasing righteousness.
2. Righteousness is anything that makes better a relationship between people or between people and their God.
3. As we focus on the indescribable beauty of God's virtue (His more beautiful way), we will begin to fall in love with Him (transition to solid food).
4. Virtue lived out is beautiful and highly motivating and stirs the heart to listen to the Holy Spirit's prodding for how we can reveal God's virtue to those in our lives.
5. On the contrary, one who demands virtue from those around him but fails to model it will not be able to move on from being motivated by guilt and fear of consequence. This leads

first to discouragement, and ultimately to bitterness and a critical view of others.

6. Goodness—the first of the virtues stacked upon faith—is moral excellence of such a degree that it caused God to sacrifice Himself to provide His enemies a path to salvation, while spurring us to know more about Him.

As we begin to embody the seven virtues listed in 2 Peter 1:5–7, we will not only get to know our heavenly Father on a more intimate level, but we will begin to see the more beautiful way with which He wants to entice us during this life. As a result, the temptations of this world will begin to lose their power. In addition, we will model these virtues for those around us, including our children, which was part of God's plan when He placed them into our care. Embodying virtue will allow us to more accurately represent an invisible God to those who cannot yet see Him (see "Christ's ambassador" in 2 Corinthians 5:20) until they have reached an age or understanding where they can be handed back over to Him.

In the following chapters, we will spend one chapter on each of the remaining six virtues. There is a lot of material in these chapters, and much of it calls for deep thinking, reflection, and meditation. Consider breaking them up in order to read them in a manner conducive to your learning style. Whatever that is, please give yourself the time to meditate on these concepts and questions so that you may deepen your understanding and become inspired by the virtue we are studying.

I want to encourage you to keep a journal of whatever inspires you and elements you are committing to work on, and then discuss these impressions and commitments with your spouse and those closest to you. Your life situation or current challenges may influence how much you connect with each of these lessons or which elements you take away from them. Do not give up, however, for Peter admonishes us to "make every effort" to grow in these areas. Let us not give in to Satan's temptation to be overwhelmed or be shallow in our thinking or study. Instead, break this into digestible morsels and savor the insight the Spirit provides. I am convinced that understanding these seven virtues can have the single greatest impact on changing our motivations, transitioning us to solid food, and allowing us to experience life to the fullest that Jesus promised in John 10:10.

Chapter 4

KNOWLEDGE

IN CHAPTER 3, WE DUG INTO THE BIBLICAL VIRTUE OF GOODNESS and learned how the fullness of this virtue encompasses moral excellence that results in very specific actions. When God acts on His goodness, it compels Him to provide a way of salvation to the lost; to end the rule of those who oppress the poor, helpless, and downtrodden; and to reveal Himself so that He may be known by those of us who are pursuing Him. And since God is goodness, He *always* acts on this virtue.

I referenced the movie *The Secrets of Jonathan Sperry* and a *60 Minutes* documentary on a Chicago outreach because both of these videos help us to see what the virtue of goodness looks like when it is lived out in the life of a person or people.

If you watched these videos, did you notice how the person(s) who embodied goodness

- provided a way of salvation to the lost,
- acted to stop the oppression of the poor, helpless, and downtrodden, and
- helped someone by allowing intimate knowledge of themself to those they were trying to help?

My fervent prayer is not only that you connect with goodness on a deeper level and are motivated by the beauty of this virtue but that you catch a vision of what God can do through you if you choose to embody the virtue of goodness. What could your neighborhood be like if you prayed for the specific needs of your neighbors every day? What could your impact be like if you quietly served and loved those around you and were inspired to be the spiritual anchor for those whom God has placed near you? What about at work? At school? Yes, it is true that you might be perceived as strange or judged as self-righteous when you politely excuse yourself instead of participating in gossip or inappropriate discussions, but those very coworkers, neighbors, and fellow students—though they might speak disparagingly about you when they are succumbing to peer pressure—will know in their hearts that you are the one person to whom they can turn when they genuinely need help and are desperate for a trustworthy confidant. You stand as a shining light on a hill and provide an avenue for those around you to seek help and to find God. The more you strive to embody goodness, the brighter God's light shines through you.

Most of us view our Christian experience through one of two primary perspectives. The person living with the first perspective is rife with deeply held worries that if he is not a good disciple throughout the day, then God will punish him and hold him accountable for every one of his failures. This is a prohibitive perspective, fixated on punishment and avoiding sin, and rooted in fear. On the opposite end of the spectrum, the person living with the second perspective is genuinely inspired to become the example of goodness in his neighborhood, at his school, and in his job because he wants to be a "Jonathan Sperry" to those around him. He wants to embody the magnificence of God's character so that others can catch a glimpse of their heavenly Father through him. He is motivated by the opportunity to embody such a beautiful virtue and to witness firsthand the impact it has on the community in which God has placed him.

Ask yourself honestly which of these perspectives more accurately describes your underlying motivation. Take time to meditate on which of these two perspectives is more compelling, which perspective is "milk" and which is "solid food," and ask yourself which perspective God would rather you have as your primary motivation.

Which of the following is the healthier marriage? In one marriage, the husband spends much of his time fretting about not having an affair. Every decision he makes regarding his marriage is rooted in and motivated by the fear that if he were to have an affair, his life would crumble. In another marriage, the husband spends every chance he gets thinking about how much he loves his wife, remembering the laughter that came with the good times and the growth in their relationship that accompanied the challenging times. He constantly considers how he can make his wife feel special, honored, and loved by him above all others. Which marriage do you think is healthier? Which marriage do you think a wife would prefer? Which marriage do you think God intended? Which marriage more accurately resembles your relationship with God?

In this chapter, we will look at the biblical virtue of *knowledge*. Our theme scripture in 2 Peter 1:5–7, states,

> For this very reason, make every effort to add to your faith goodness; and to goodness, knowledge; and to knowledge, self-control; and to self-control, perseverance; and to perseverance, godliness; and to godliness, mutual affection; and to mutual affection, love.

Isn't it interesting that we are instructed to add knowledge to goodness? Why this progression? Why not simply work on both, rather than build one atop the other?

We are already familiar with Proverbs 9:10, which states, "The fear of the Lord is the beginning of wisdom, and knowledge of the Holy One is understanding." The fear of the Lord is a godly trait because it is the beginning of wisdom. But knowledge, not fear, is the beginning of understanding God. In the mind of a little child, fear of Mom and Dad's punishment is what motivates him or her to make right decisions. But we were not intended to live our entire adolescence in fear of our parents. Instead, we were intended to grow in our knowledge of who Mom and Dad are so that a relationship will blossom in which the children make decisions that are considerate of their parents.

I witnessed an example of this at a parenting conference I attended many years ago. One of the breakout sessions was hosted by two teenage children of families who had helped to facilitate the conference, but their parents were not in the room. The purpose of the breakout session was to get an unvarnished perspective from these teenagers regarding the parenting style they were under. One of the teenage hosts was asked the curfew his parents had set for him, and his answer put me back on my heels. He replied, "I didn't have a curfew because I knew what time range my parents thought was appropriate, and they knew that I was responsible and considerate of them. If something was happening that was causing me to run late, I would always call them to keep them in the loop because I didn't want them to worry."

You see, this is the kind of functional relationship based on mutual respect and honor that all parents desire with their children, including God. Because so few of us had this kind of mature, functional relationship with our parents, we can project our dysfunction onto our relationship with our heavenly Father, and it, therefore, can be difficult to relate to God in the manner that He wants us to know Him.

Recall from the last chapter that God's goodness is what motivated Him to make a path to salvation for us, which included revealing His intimate side to us. It would logically follow that God must then make Himself known for us to obtain knowledge of Him. And that knowledge of Him is the foundation for a relationship with Him, which, not coincidentally, is the only path to righteousness. That is why Jesus says in John 14:6 that He is the way, the truth, and the life and that no one comes to the Father but through Him. Based on Thomas's question in the preceding verse, we often interpret this passage to mean that we need Jesus's sacrifice in order to have a pathway to heaven. Although that is true, it is not what Jesus had in mind when He uttered these words. Instead, Jesus was stating that He was God in the flesh, and the only way to know God is to know Him. In other words, He became flesh so that we could see what a relationship with God looked like. This meaning is confirmed in very next verse:

> If you really know me, you will know my Father as
> well. From now on, you do know him and have seen
> him. (John 14:7)

The Greek word used here in 2 Peter 1:5 is γνῶσιν (*gnōsin*), which means knowledge but does not refer to head knowledge. Instead, it refers to an intimate knowledge of someone, being in a relationship, or having an acquaintance with something or someone else. Said differently, gnōsin is not book or academic knowledge but an intimate knowledge of a person upon which a relationship is established and continues to blossom.

> Husbands, in the same way be considerate as you live
> with your wives, and treat them *with respect* as the
> weaker partner and as heirs with you of the gracious
> gift of life, so that nothing will hinder your prayers."
> (1 Peter 3:7, emphasis added)

The actual Greek word translated here as "with respect" is *gnōsin*. It is interesting how that changes the meaning of the verse. To treat someone "with respect" in English simply means to consider and respect their differences. But we see here that this verse means much more than this; it means to treat your wife with an intimate knowledge of who she is and what makes her different than you. Imagine if you treated your wife with consideration of the entirety of who she is, where she came from, how she thinks, and how she feels. Although similar, treating your wife with gnōsin is significantly deeper, more personal, and more intimate than simply treating her with respect.

KNOWLEDGE IS THE FOUNDATION OF RELATIONSHIP

> Oh, the depth of the riches of the wisdom and *knowledge* of God! How unsearchable his judgments, and his paths beyond tracing out! Who has known the mind of the Lord? Or who has been his counselor? (Romans 11:33–34, emphasis added)

Regardless of the quality of your relationship with your parents, if you grew up with them, then you know (gnōsin) them like no other. In fact, that intimate knowledge of them resulted in your inheriting a number of their behavioral traits and perspectives. This often becomes more obvious when you see your parents' propensities in the way you are inclined to parent your own children. Do you realize that as Christians—children of God redeemed by the blood of our only perfect brother, Jesus—you have the opportunity to know God in ways that no non-Christian ever has or can ever hope to? Not only non-Christians, but you have the opportunity to know God in a way that even the Old Testament prophets could neither comprehend nor even knew to be an option (Matthew 13:17; Luke 10:24). But in order to get to know God, we must endeavor to fully understand His traits; we need to see Him clearly. In the previous chapter, we spent time looking at and meditating on God's goodness, through which salvation was made an option for us. Now, we will look at what it really means to know God and to make ourselves known to God *and* to those God has placed in our lives.

BECOMING THE KNOWLEDGE OF GOD

Before we look at some examples, let's explore a few more scriptures that just scratch the surface of this incredibly important virtue.

> But thanks be to God, who always leads us as captives in Christ's triumphal procession and uses us to spread the aroma of the *knowledge* of him everywhere. For we are to God the pleasing aroma of Christ among those who are being saved and those who are perishing. To the one we are an aroma that brings death; to the other, an aroma that brings life. And who is equal to such a task? Unlike so many, we do not peddle the word of God for profit. On the contrary, in Christ we speak before God with sincerity, as those sent from God. (2 Corinthians 2:14–17, emphasis added)

Wow! If your pursuit of goodness has inspired you to make yourself known to those around you, then *you can become* to someone the aroma of Christ and therefore a part of their road to salvation. Could there be a greater honor than to be individually selected by the Creator of the universe to be His ambassador (2 Corinthians 5:20)? Recall the moment in the *60 Minutes* segment in which a young man, caught up in a life of crime, said that no one had ever offered him hope and that he could not comprehend a way out of his lot in life. He then went on to describe how the single difference between a life of hopelessness and crime versus a life of normalcy and maturity was the aroma of an older gentleman who chose to act on goodness by making himself known to this young man. The result was that someone became the aroma of goodness and hope, and that aroma was so enticing that it provided sufficient motivation to change the trajectory of this young man's entire life *and* equipped him with sufficient hope to resist future temptation.

Did you catch that? Seeing goodness in someone who opens themselves up to you (i.e., gnōsis) is a lifeline that not only inspires change but also provides sufficient motivation to begin fighting back one's own demons. Brothers and sisters, God wants to make us the aroma of Christ to a lost world that wanders aimlessly in the dark with no hope of ever finding a way forward. It is *not* the words you choose to say to your coworker or classmate that create the aroma; it is your commitment to embodying goodness and a willingness to make yourself known. In doing these things, you will have taken the first two steps to becoming more like your heavenly Father, and by doing so, you will get to know Him on an ever-increasing level of intimacy, which is why He made you in the first place. If you feel unproductive evangelistically, it may not be that you failed to invite enough people to church but rather that you are not yet embodying goodness and knowledge in a manner that reflects how God models those two virtues for us.

THE HIDDEN TREASURE THAT YOU CAN OPEN OR CLOSE

> My goal is that they may be encouraged in heart and united in love, so that they may have the full riches of complete understanding, in order that they may know the mystery of God, namely, Christ, in whom are hidden all the treasures of wisdom and *knowledge*. (Colossians 2:2–3, emphasis added)

Here, Paul beautifully describes how understanding opens the vault to comprehending the mystery of God and all of the hidden treasures of wisdom and knowledge. Do you view the knowledge of God as a hidden treasure? Think back to when you first pursued a relationship with a person to whom you were romantically drawn. Do you remember how every time they revealed to you another hidden side of themselves, you felt more and more special because you were allowed access to intimate details of who this person was that were only made known to a chosen few? Do you realize that the Creator of the universe—the one who sustains the earth in its place among the galaxies, the one to whom Moses, Abraham, David, and Jesus prayed—has chosen to reveal intimate aspects of His character to you, the very aspects that will remain a mystery to all who do not have salvation? There simply is no greater privilege than being invited into an intimate relationship with God, founded in an ever-growing knowledge of who He is, a knowledge that He is choosing to reveal to you. For God tore open the curtain of secrecy and allowed you into the most holy place upon your redemption through the sacrifice of His Son (Matthew 27:50–51). And thank God that revelation of Him (gnōsin) is rooted in goodness, from which we derive our salvation. For those He has not chosen, that revelation will not occur until the day of their judgment, and how horrible to find out how magnificent God is only after the chance to restore one's relationship with Him has passed.

> Woe to you experts in the law, because you have taken away the key to *knowledge*. You yourselves have not entered, and you have hindered those who were entering. (Luke 11:52, emphasis added)

In light of what we are studying, this is a stinging rebuke. Jesus specifically states that these men not only are failing to embody gnōsis but are actually inhibiting others from coming in contact with God's revelation of Himself. Contrary to everything we just looked at, hypocrisy inhibits the knowledge of God because it masks His virtue. When we live lives of hypocrisy by masking sin, compromising to fit in, or hiding our true selves due to insecurity and fear of reprisal, then the magnificent revelation of God cannot be fully shown through us. Worse, if we claim to represent God to those around us but live hypocritical lives, then not only do we inhibit God from being shown through us, but we misrepresent God entirely and create an additional impediment to those around us from finding Him.

KNOWLEDGE CAN BE MASKED BY JUDGMENT

> We demolish arguments and every pretension that sets
> itself up against the knowledge of God, and we take
> captive every thought to make it obedient to Christ.
> (2 Corinthians 10:5)

I love this verse because it highlights how pervasive thoughts are that are contrary to God's truth. Fixing one's eyes on embodying virtue (imitating Jesus) is the only true way to counter Satan's subtle lies. You cannot become like God by fixating on the law (Romans 4:13–15; 7:4–8) or on extra-scriptural tradition (Mark 7:13). Rather, we are commanded to fix our eyes on Jesus, the author and perfecter of our faith (Hebrews 12:1–3) because doing so allows us to throw off every sin that hinders and entangles and to run without growing weary or losing heart. Why? Because rather than spout the law, Jesus was the *perfect embodiment* of God's virtue. And godly virtue lived out is so beautiful, so inspiring, so motivating, and so rewarding that its aroma is attractive to even the most lost and desperate of souls.

If you would like further encouragement on whether God wants us to fixate on His law or His virtue, take a moment to read 2 Corinthians 3:7–12; then continue reading verses 13–18 to see how God reveals Himself to us and how we then are expected to reveal ourselves to the lost.

The single greatest way that Satan tricks us with pretenses is when we succumb to making judgments on others without knowledge (gnōsin) of them. Think of the *60 Minutes* episode mentioned earlier, featuring young men and women who found themselves caught up in violence in South Chicago. Consider how you might feel toward these youth if your judgment was formed only from the perspective of their victims and absent any knowledge of the person who committed the crime. When we have intimate knowledge of the sinner, that knowledge opens the door to empathy, compassion, and understanding, even when we don't approve of their choices.

So much of God's compassion and mercy is rooted in His

knowledge of who we are, where we came from, what we have been taught, and what we are struggling with (Matthew 9:36; Mark 6:34; Hebrews 4:15–16), and if you are beginning to understand this, then you are also beginning to understand how goodness and knowledge are intertwined.

Obeying God's expectation that we withhold judgment (John 3:17; 12:47) and are quick to listen and slow to anger (James 1:19) creates a protective barrier that allows God's truth to be exposed and Satan's lies to be demolished. (We will discuss this further in a later chapter.)

If you are interested in truly putting knowledge (gnōsin) to the test, you might consider watching the following special on Jeffrey Dahmer, titled *Confessions of a Serial Killer: Jeffrey Dahmer Talks to Stone Phillips* (https://youtu.be/APqq1Pvvqbs).[3] I do not recommend this for everyone, as Jeff's crimes were very dark, and this interview (although it does not focus on his crimes) can be disturbing. The interview was conducted while he was in prison, about a decade before a fellow inmate took Dahmer's life. Unlike any other available interview of a serial murderer, Jeff exhibits an unusual level of vulnerability while recounting his upbringing and his behavior.

If you are interested in watching this video, I would encourage you to see if the knowledge you gain of Jeff produces any empathy or compassion within your heart. If it does, then you have experienced the spiritual law of gnōsin; you have seen how the receipt of intimate knowledge of who someone truly is and where he came from produces understanding, empathy, and compassion, even for those whose behavioral choices are abhorrent. We therefore can have a minuscule glimpse into the understanding, empathy, and compassion God must have for His lost children, since He knows every detail of their lives, every insecurity of their hearts, and every data point of the matrix through which they process thoughts.

---

[3] The video I have refenced was an interview conducted in February 1994 by Stone Phillips and included Jeffrey Dahmer's father, Lionel and his step-mother, Shari. This video is available via a number of YouTube postings in addition to the link provided above.

We have seen that there are three sides of gnōsin for us to digest and internalize.

- First, God revealing Himself to you is the most intimate gift you could ever receive (similar to your spouse revealing intimate details to you while you were dating).
- Second, knowledge of sinners is so powerful that it can produce empathy and compassion, even toward the most sinful among us.
- Third, revealing ourselves to others throws them a lifeline that provides both motivation to change and access to borrowing faith, with which they can resist temptation.

With this understanding, meditate on the power of the virtue of knowledge and how magnificent it is when it is added to goodness. Consider as well how the virtue of knowledge (gnōsin) led Jesus to make His statement:

> Do not judge, or you too will be judged. For in the same way you judge others, you will be judged, and with the measure you use, it will be measured to you. (Matthew 7:1–2)

Different Greek variants are used for the words translated as *judge* and *judged* in this passage. If scholars were to use a lengthier translation, it would more accurately read, "Do not pass human judgment, or you too will be judged by the divine. For in the same way that you make human judgments of others, you will be judged by the divine." You see, God is the *only being* capable of making a wholly accurate judgment on individuals because only God can know everything that makes up those individuals, their mindsets, their pasts, their hurts, their belief systems, etc. And so, Jesus—the only human to ever possess the ability to make accurate judgments of the heart—embodies for us an example of this magnificent quality of God by making Himself known to us, while also showing us how to exercise the self-control to withhold making judgments of others. Let me ask you: would you rather have your heavenly Father judge you with the measure you use to judge others or with His full *gnōsin* of who you are, rooted in his goodness? If the latter, then it is time that we work diligently on setting aside our judgments of others and replacing that with the pursuit of gnōsin.

As you meditate on this virtue, ask yourself who you allow to truly know you. Do you have relationships with other brothers or sisters, to whom you have revealed your most intimate thoughts? Similarly, with whom are you sharing your faith by revealing yourself, beyond simply an invitation to a church event? Intimate details about yourself are pearls that should not be thrown to swine (Matthew 7:6), but too many of us think that in order to impact a non-Christian, we need only to show them the side of us that has it together. In truth, the most powerful influence you have in leading others to Christ is when they see how Christ is fixing you, not when they see the filtered image that you are most comfortable putting on display.

The Christian life is not easy; in fact, just when we think we are pulling ourselves together, God peels back an additional layer of the proverbial onion and reveals another side of us that we need to work on. When non-Christians are allowed to see how God is working in our lives, it creates a lifeline for them, as they become encouraged that if God is working in our lives, then maybe He will work in theirs. Please don't misunderstand; I am not saying that you should reveal intimate details of yourself without consideration and discretion. We know that some will misuse that knowledge to puff up themselves and hurt you. But if you are not practicing gnōsin with non-Christians in your life, then you are missing a huge component of imitating God and are handicapping your effectiveness in leading others to Him.

A coworker of mine once shared that he had been assigned to work a few days with a gruff and overtly arrogant coworker. After a few days of verbal abuse, my friend lost self-control and curtly answered the question of why he wasn't doing something a particular way by stating, "Because I don't want to become like you!" He later confessed this outburst to some brothers over breakfast and was challenged to apologize to the coworker, both for passing judgment without knowledge and for losing self-control. After returning to work, it took two days for him to gather the courage, but ultimately, he said to his coworker, "The other day, I lashed out at you in frustration. Please accept my apology and forgive me for my lack of self-control. That is not the person I want to be, regardless of circumstance." The shocked coworker tried to dismiss the event as not having been a big deal. But my friend continued, "You may not need to offer forgiveness, but I could really use it because I am genuinely trying to behave more like Jesus." In response, the coworker uncomfortably uttered, "OK," and moved on. But from that moment on, the coworker who had previously exhibited a gruff, unkind, and arrogant demeanor changed and began to treat my friend with respect. Even after their time working together had concluded, the previously gruff coworker would often reach out to my friend for advice.

What happened? Gnōsin happened. By revealing an intimate part of himself through humility, he won over the heart of a non-Christian who had learned to protect himself with a harsh demeanor. The exhibition of gnōsin was so beautiful and embracing that it broke through a lifetime of defenses and sparked a friendship. That, brothers and sisters, is what the God of all is doing for us. He is compelled by His goodness to reveal Himself to us so that our newly discovered knowledge of Him can become the foundation for healing in an otherwise fractured relationship.

SUMMARY

And you, my child, will be called a prophet of the Most High; for you will go on before the Lord to prepare the way for him, to give his people the knowledge of salvation through the forgiveness of their sins, because of the tender mercy of our God, by

which the rising sun will come to us from heaven to
shine on those living in darkness and in the shadow
of death, to guide our feet into the path of peace.
(Luke 1:76–79)

This is a great way to conclude our study on gnōsin, as it correlates
the things we have learned in a beautiful summation. This verse
references the role of John the Baptist as the prophet and foreteller
of the Most High (Jesus), who would prepare His way by giving His
people the knowledge of salvation through the forgiveness of their
sins. This salvation is only available because of the "tender mercy of
our God," which we have learned is the direct result of His goodness.
The light of the world (the rising sun) comes through God's goodness
to us and shines on the lost so that we can guide them to the path of
peace. What a concept!

Do you see the theme here? Knowing (gnōsin) God by studying
and understanding His virtues must be our primary goal. People
were unable to get to know God through the law. For through the
law, God became to Israel the punisher of acts of disobedience—
the ultimate enforcer. That perspective led to rote obedience out of
fear of consequence. Such a limited paradigm leads to one of two
outcomes—either outright rebellion or a feeling of inadequacy that
results in a prohibitive consequence. God sent Jesus to be our ultimate
sacrifice, right? Yes! But if you only see Jesus as the sacrifice for our
sins, then you have missed the greater picture. God became flesh and
made His dwelling among us (John 1:14). When Jesus opened His
mouth, we heard the very words of God (John 12:49–50). Jesus wasn't
focused on judging others. He was focused on saving others (John
3:17; 12:47). God became, for twelve men, what He had been trying to
show every previous generation—that He wanted a personal, intimate
relationship with them. He wanted a relationship that displayed how
failure couldn't surprise an all-knowing partner, where forgiveness was
poured out like a waterfall, and where God would carry the burden of
complete understanding and mete out to us what we needed to know
as we gained the moral understanding and maturity to handle it.

But whatever were gains to me I now consider loss for the sake of Christ. What is more, I consider everything a loss because of the surpassing worth of knowing [γνώσεως—gnōseōs] Christ Jesus my Lord, for whose sake I have lost all things. I consider them garbage, that I may gain Christ and be found in him, not having a righteousness of my own that comes from the law, but that which is through faith in Christ—the righteousness that comes from God on the basis of faith. I want to know [γνῶναι—gnōnai] Christ—yes, to know the power of his resurrection and participation in his sufferings, becoming like him in his death, and so, somehow, attaining to the resurrection from the dead. (Philippians 3:7–11)

Brothers and sisters, too many of us are passing our days in this life by spending an inordinate amount of time trying not to let God down, rather than focusing on how we can show Him love by deepening our knowledge of Him, by understanding and pursuing His virtues. As a result, we can be plagued by a prohibitive conscience and a feeling that God is constantly displeased with us. Instead, those who grasp the magnitude of God's goodness and connect with how He has chosen to reveal His intimate side to them are falling deeper in love with Him, while simultaneously becoming the conduit through which the world has its first face-to-face contact with God.

This is exactly what Peter meant by moving on from milk to solid food. It is time to mature our relationship with God. A relationship cannot become mature until your fear of losing the person you are pursuing is supplanted by mutual devotion to each other and the confidence that comes from a commitment to meet each other's needs (1 John 3:21–24). As we have already discussed, there are two primary means for getting to know God relationally. First, we need to intently study how God interacted with us while inhabiting our flesh. Second, we need to use the Bible to explore the virtues that make up His magnificent character. We scratched the surface of how God in the flesh interacted with man in our first chapter. The remaining chapters will explore the additional virtues that Peter deems the most important aspects of God's character for us to understand and then embody.

Chapter 5

SELF-CONTROL

W HEN I FIRST BEGAN STUDYING THE VIRTUES LISTED IN 2 PETER 1:5–7, I will confess that self-control elicited in me the most negative reaction. There was something innately prohibitive in my understanding of this concept, for it inferred that I had to control myself from doing things that entice me and live in a state of self-denial. But I will tell you truthfully that, as I write this chapter, I am more excited about this virtue than any of the others, not because it has a higher importance than other virtues but because my perspective has changed so vastly that it is having the most notable impact in my life.

Thus far, we have studied faith as the basic building block to relationship, God's goodness (His moral excellence, from which flows the forgiveness necessary for our salvation), and God's knowledge (His intimate revelation of Himself to us). In light of these virtues, we also have taken some time to look into what currently defines our personal relationship with God—what really motivates us, whether relational insecurity, fear of consequence, or an ever-deepening and personal relationship with our heavenly Father.

If you have made progress in these areas, then you likely are beginning to feel a freedom in your relationship with God, a freedom to be more conversational, a freedom that comes with a conviction that you exist to meet God's desire for a personal and intimate relationship with you, and that is what He most desires from you each day. Yet in the midst of this relational honeymoon, here comes the demand for *self-control*—the command to steer clear of temptation and to reject sin. What can flood back into our hearts is the negative feelings associated with prohibition and punishment. If this is what the thought of self-control produces in you, as it did with me, then I put before you that we are missing a massive part of what Peter is imploring us to add to this newly recharged relationship with our heavenly Father. Our propensity toward punishment and consequence masks one of God's biggest blessings.

Let's start by defining self-control and see if we can't expand our understanding together. The Greek word used in 2 Peter 1:6 is ἐγκράτειαν (pronounced *enkrateian* in English), and it means to control oneself, to abstain from something, especially in matters of sexual purity, personified as a virtue. Well, there you have it; abstain from what your sinful nature wants to do, resist the temptations that attack you from every corner of the world in which you live, and keep turning away from what others seem to be enjoying.

We have already highlighted the fact that because we tend to think prohibitively, we largely limit the definition of self-control to the resistance of temptation and avoiding sin, and that seems to be confirmed by its definition. But you will see in the remainder of this chapter that resisting temptation only scratches the surface of this beautiful virtue, and there is much more here for us to explore.

I want to start by sharing with you an excerpt borrowed from Eric and Leslie Ludy's book on God's more beautiful way of biblical courtship. In it, the Ludys paraphrase Homer's *The Iliad* and *The Odyssey*, which may sound like a strange segue, but its application will make sense shortly:

> **The Siren Allurement**—Greek mythology tells of a certain group of evil, conniving mermaids— the Sirens. These mermaids, though spectacular in beauty, were devilish and diabolical. Their weapon

was the intoxicating song that they sang. Sitting atop their rocks, the Sirens would sing their tempting tune as ships passed. It was a powerful enticement that no hot-blooded man could resist. With their lustful melody, the sirens could control the wills of men. Their song could woo even the most steely-hearted ship captains to turn their vessels toward the Siren's rocky coastline. Their music lured ship after ship into a watery grave.

Enter Ulysses—a ship captain of great renown whose noble mission forces him to pass those terrible Siren shores. But Ulysses is determined that he will not fall victim to their allurements as many others have done. So as he approaches the deadly Siren coastline, he commands his crew to stuff beeswax into their ears so they won't be overcome by the haunting songs.

Ulysses himself is intrigued to hear the music that has sent so many mighty sailors to their death. But he knows he cannot withstand the temptation. So he commands his crew to tie him to the mast of the ship, and tie him tight. He reasons that he can safely listen to the Sirens' song while bound to the mast since the ropes will render him unable to steer his ship in the wrong direction.

As the intoxicating Siren melody fills the air, Ulysses is overcome with uncontrollable longing to steer his ship toward the dangerous shore. His knees buckle and his mind swoons under the sway of the Siren sounds. He screams for his crew to turn the boat toward the singing, but his crew is already under orders not to heed his voice while he is under the mermaids' spell.

Ulysses curses, writhing in agony, consumed with only one thought—"I must get closer to the music!

I must quench this insatiable thirst for more of the Siren's song!" He furiously seeks to untie the ropes that bind him. But his efforts are useless, and he shakes in misery until finally the mermaid music fades to nothingness and his ship sails beyond its terrifying reach.

When danger is past, Ulysses is untied. He falls to the deck of the ship, exhausted and humiliated by the entire episode.

And yet, Ulysses is a hero. He did what few had ever done before him—he made it past the temptation. He escaped death upon the rocks.

His crew applauds their strong and noble captain for his amazing feat. He succeeded in escaping danger in spite of the fact that he was miserable the entire time.

Singing a Sweeter Song—Greek legend has it that there was another noble captain who braved the lurid waters of the Sirens. In fact, he wasn't far behind Ulysses. His name was Orpheus. And his approach to the Siren threat was very different than that of Ulysses. He didn't use beeswax, and he didn't use a rope. He wasn't afraid of the Sirens. He looked upon the dangerous coastline as an opportunity.

As his ship approached the Siren enticement, his crew let out a shout of joy.

"The Sirens! The Sirens! Captain Orpheus, it is time!"

While Ulysses' crew had been filled with dread as they approached this legendary danger, Orpheus's crew was buoyant with excitement. Some, in fact, had joined Orpheus's crew just for this very occasion.

"Bring me the case!" boomed Orpheus, as the sailors cheered.

A beautifully adorned case was brought to Orpheus. He smiled as he opened it. The crew surrounded him, their eyes filled with eager anticipation. Orpheus slowly removed from the case a lovely musical instrument, studded with jewels and plated with precious metals.

"Play it, Captain!" roared the crew, as their eyes transfixed upon their hero. "Play us your song!"

As the Sirens' sweet melody began to fill the air, Orpheus began to play his own instrument. It was the most perfect music human ears had ever heard. Each crewman became lost in the grandeur and the majesty of the song.

All too soon the Siren coastline was out of sight and the master musician concluded the song that he himself had composed. Not a single man aboard ship had been tempted by the Sirens' melody. In fact, no one even noticed it. Though the mermaids' music was alluring and sweet, Orpheus played for his crew... a sweeter song.[4]

You may already sense my intent in including this excerpt. For the vast majority of us, the Christian experience most closely resembles Ulysses's journey. We trudge through life tied to the mast of self-denial, purity, integrity, tithing, commanded humility, required evangelism, and the obligatory serving of others. We pray that God will reward our efforts on His behalf and beg Him to overlook our daily failures. We know the Bible's teaching on God's forgiveness, but we wonder if He's really forgiven us for our deepest and darkest thoughts and desires. When we have a spiritually focused day, we feel saved and approved, and when we have a spiritually challenging day, we feel condemned. When we suffer, we feel punished, and although

[4] Taken from *Teaching True Love to a Sex-at-13 Generation* by Eric and Leslie Ludy. Copyright © 2005 by Eric and Leslie Ludy. Used by permission of Thomas Nelson. www.thomasnelson.com.

people can feign excitement when they speak of meeting God in sermons and at memorial services, the thought of our own death and ultimate day of judgment can bring to the surface our deepest fears. The atmosphere of our journey is prohibitive and fear-driven, and while we long for something better, we have trouble visualizing what *better* is.

Before you feel judged while reading this, please understand that the paragraph above describes the things with which I have wrestled over my thirty-three years as a Christian. I am sharing them only because I see this mindset of prohibition in so many other Christians, and I therefore am convinced that many of you also will see yourself in the description above. If you can relate, do not be discouraged, for it is noble that you have resisted temptation by tying yourself to the mast! That is more than 99 percent of the world is willing to do on behalf of their heavenly Father. We are to be praised for helping our "crew mates" protect themselves by willfully blocking out the world. You have nothing to apologize for and nothing to be ashamed of, but you have everything to look forward to.

Ask yourself the following questions: Do I think Ulysses's story describes the Christian experience that God created for me? Do I believe that depicts the tenor of the relationship God wants with me? Was that what God had in mind when He envisioned making man in His image, sons and daughters with whom to share His innermost being and His inheritance? Is this His vision of the bride He composed of those who have chosen to love Him?

Yet I put before you that the Christian experience, for a large portion of believers, does not resemble the experience of Orpheus's crew, for we have not yet learned how to hear God's more beautiful song. Nowhere is that more evident to me than in our understanding of the virtue of self-control. Some time ago, I attended a men's service where we studied 1 Peter 4:7, which instructs us to be alert and of sober mind so that we can pray. After the message, a number of brothers publicly responded to the lesson, and in their responses, every one of them interpreted that verse to mean that we must stay away from sin and temptation. One brother said that he felt that he was walking through life on the lip of a vortex and one wrong step would cause him slip into a downward spiral. Another shared that, to him, the verse meant that he needed to constantly clear his mind of temptation. What awesome brothers we have! These men live valiant lives for God and are willing to share publicly with great vulnerability. Nothing negative can or should be said about these men, but what struck me was that no one shared the side of sober-mindedness that encompasses having the mind of God.

Have you ever experienced a day on which you were clear-minded and sharp in your thinking, where wisdom was heightened and spiritual concepts made sense? Do you recall how good that felt? We enjoy being clear-minded and sharp, but when this phrase is placed into a biblical context, we immediately default to the concepts of temptation, sin, and punishment. Why is that? I put before you that it is because many of us are living our entire Christian lives tied to the mast, having no idea that we are missing the better song. As a result, our entire perception of the Christian life is viewed through the lens of prohibition, and the hope of heaven is our only solace.

This is one reason why Christian parents often can appear to be different people at home than in public. It is not that they are necessarily hypocritical Christians (although this is something we all need to guard against). Instead, being tied to the mast saps the strength from our bones. When we get home, we loosen those ropes a bit, and our true nature is exposed. Then, the next morning, we pray that God will provide sufficient strength so that we can make it through one more day, all the while we live with a low level of anxiety because we believe that we are always one sin away from slipping into *the vortex*.

This is *not* the Christian experience that God designed. This is not His dream for you. Jesus came so that you could have "life to the full" and to renew your strength so that you could soar like an eagle, not be trapped like a caged animal. The difference between the two experiences is that we have not yet learned to hear God's more beautiful song. He is loudly playing it, but Satan is masking it. Self-control is all about ripping that mask from our eyes so that we can see and hear God's most beautiful song. My passionate prayer is that by the time we finish studying self-control, you will have a different outlook on this beautiful virtue and will have started or bolstered your journey on the path of the more beautiful way.

What does self-control look like? In order to make this very practical and applicable, we will break down self-control into three simple categories. These are by no means exhaustive, and the Spirit likely will lead you to see much more in this beautiful virtue than possibly could be placed on these pages. Nonetheless, this will be sufficient to start us along the way of discovering this magnificent aspect of our Christian journey.

1. We need self-control in order to make ourselves second.

Not long ago, I attended another men's discipleship group, during which a friend of mine shared with the group how he had a long-time broken relationship with an older child and that recently, they had begun to mend that relationship. In fact, he shared with the group that his child had said that she loved him for the first time in many, many years. The father could barely get through his sharing as he choked back the deep emotion of years of despair mixed with glimmers of hope. Over time, I likely will forget the purpose of that men's group and what else was shared, but I will never forget the raw emotion expressed by my friend, rooted in his indescribable love for his wayward daughter. All I could think about in that moment was that we massively underestimate the depth of God's love for us, the hurt He feels over our broken relationship, and the mustard seeds of hope to which He clings to that we will not only return to Him but enter into the eternal, ever-deepening relationship with Him for which we were created (see Luke 15:11–32).

When we come in contact with God's goodness through His revelation of Himself to us (gnōsis), we can easily misinterpret God's lavishing of love to think that it's all about us, our salvation, our happiness, our future. It is here, brothers and sisters, that we encounter the first area in which we need to control ourselves. *It is not about us; it is all about God.* We exist only because He chose to make us. He has loved us through all of our filth, horrible decisions, and the depths of our depravity because we are His creation, created for His pleasure. He hurt and wept when we were proud, boisterous, sarcastic, unforgiving, entitled, and harmed others with our callous hearts. He sacrificed His only faithful Son on our behalf while we were still enjoying the short-term pleasures of utter self-focus. If we are going to "walk humbly with our God," as He requires in Micah 6, then the first element of self-control that we must exercise is to stop thinking about ourselves and realize that this is all about God.

I recently read an article that described three suicide notes written by one California teenager just before he took his life. The first was a love note to his parents, telling them that it wasn't their fault. In that note, he reassured them that they had done their best and that there was nothing else they could have done that would have changed this outcome. The second letter was to his friends, conveying a similar theme. But the third letter was to his school, blaming the teachers for their lack of compassion and the intensity of the scholastic atmosphere that created too much pressure for him to handle. He took the time to place his suicide squarely on the back of the school and its administration.

I am aware of chemical imbalances in the brain and the intensity of untreated clinical depression and do not want to minimize any of those influences on this young man's decision to take his own life. But let's set aside, for one minute, any mental illness he may have experienced and look simply at this young man's logic. He was so consumed with himself that he couldn't see the lifelong pain that he would inflict on his friends and family through his action, which he masked as martyrdom. Yes, the school may have responded by providing on-campus grief counseling and adding a suicide prevention hotline and associated posters to its walls, but the all-consuming selfishness of this young man's mindset kept him from seeing the utter lack of logic in his thinking, and the number of lives he destroyed by taking his own was masked by his inability to see beyond himself.

While we can feel critical of this young man's justifications, I put before you that he is not that different from us. We spend virtually every waking moment thinking about our finances, our careers, our stress, our problems, the imposition of others on our lives, our health, our mortality, our children, our marriages, our salvation, our happiness, our savings, our retirement plans, our dreams, our giving, our philanthropy, our talents, and the list goes on and on. I am not categorizing these things as good or bad, just highlighting the overwhelming amount of daily thought we put into ourselves. On the contrary, there is an incredible freedom that comes from realizing that the world does not revolve around us and our daily decisions. As long as we put God first and prioritize Him in our lives, then His Spirit will move and use both our weaknesses and strengths to accomplish His more perfect will, which is indescribably bigger and more encompassing than ours could ever be.

Imagine for a moment what your life would be like if you were convinced that you existed solely to meet God's relational needs and that He would take care of *everything* in your life, as parents do for their children. Do you remember the reckless abandon with which you played as a child, the uninhibited dreams you contemplated for yourself, the deep and peaceful sleep you experienced when you implicitly trusted that your parents had everything under control? For those of you who did not have this type of childhood experience, I am confident you can still comprehend what I am communicating.

What would your life be like if you fully trusted that the Creator of the universe had already orchestrated your entire life on this earth and arranged every detail in such a way as to maximize your relationship with Him? What if you really believed that God not only forgave you for every sin you had ever committed but every sin that you would commit until your dying breath, including sins that would later surprise and embarrass you? How different would you feel if you could see with your eyes that you were surrounded by angels and hear with your ears that you were cheered on by the multitude of saints who had gone on before you? What if you believed that absolutely everything in your future and your past was part of God's perfect plan to refine you to become like Him and to ready you to meet Him face-to-face? What if you believed that you would never meet anyone whom God didn't send, and you never would suffer any pain that God didn't allow? What if you were sure that you literally never were alone because the Creator of the universe continually walked alongside you and understood you, even better than you knew yourself. Do you believe that He has placed His all-powerful Spirit inside you to aid you with every thought, emotion, and temptation; to rejoice with you in your victories and to comfort you in your defeats; to acknowledge your failures and to remind you to get back up, take the focus off of yourself, and to feed His sheep?

What if your prayers sounded something like this: "Father, thank you for making me so that I can know You. I cannot describe the privilege and the honor of getting to know You or being able to speak directly with You since You have cleansed me and restored me to You. I want to do everything in my power to get to know You better. Please help me daily to want to know You, even when the feelings wane or I am distracted by life's challenges. I look forward to seeing how you have orchestrated my day to further refine me and to better our relationship. Help me to see both sufferings and victories as things that help me fall deeper in love with You, rather than as rewards or punishments. Help me take everything that I know about You and put it into practice so that others can see a glimpse of You through me and experience a glimmer of hope that there is something better for them. I cannot believe that I am allowed to know Your thoughts and to speak directly with You since You have cleansed me."

Do you see the difference? It is subtle, but when we realize that our existence is all about God and not about us, it changes our perspective, it orders our relationship, it adds confidence to our outlook, and it produces a biblical peace and true joy in our hearts, regardless of circumstance.

Brothers and sisters, gaining and keeping this mindset throughout each day takes an enormous amount of self-control, for since the day we came into this world, we have been fixated on our own needs and desires. Meeting the emotional and physical needs of our own children requires from us such a high level of selflessness that we parents can feel justified and even balanced, but in truth, virtually all of our thoughts remain about ourselves. It is not possible to find pure joy until we do what Jesus commanded in Luke 9:23—that anyone who would come after Him must deny themselves, pick up their crosses, and follow Him. To those of us who are coming after Him, the question is whether or not we resemble Him. The first step of self denial is to accept that none of this is about us. It is all about God (Philippians 1:21). The self-control required to maintain that focus with every thought on every day is a challenge, but that is why God gave us a Spirit of power and self-control, for we could not do it without Him (see 2 Timothy 1:7).

2. **We need self-control to take captive our thoughts and surrender them to God's truth.**

Take a moment to meditate on the following verses:

> We do, however, speak a message of wisdom among the mature, but not the wisdom of this age or of the rulers of this age, who are coming to nothing. No, we declare God's wisdom, a mystery that has been hidden and that God destined for our glory before time began. None of the rulers of this age understood it, for if they had, they would not have crucified the Lord of glory. However, as it is written: "What no eye has seen, what no ear has heard, and what no human mind has conceived"—the things God has prepared for those who love him—these are the things God has revealed to us by his Spirit. The Spirit searches all things, even the deep things of God. For who knows a person's thoughts except their own spirit within them? In the same way no one knows the thoughts of God except the Spirit of God. What we have received

is not the spirit of the world, but the Spirit who is from God, so that we may understand what God has freely given us. This is what we speak, not in words taught us by human wisdom but in words taught by the Spirit, explaining spiritual realities with Spirit-taught words. The person without the Spirit does not accept the things that come from the Spirit of God but considers them foolishness, and cannot understand them because they are discerned only through the Spirit. The person with the Spirit makes judgments about all things, but such a person is not subject to merely human judgments, for, "Who has known the mind of the Lord so as to instruct him?" But we have the mind of Christ. (1 Corinthians 2:6–16)

Are you letting that sink in? Think about each one of these statements:

- We alone have a message of wisdom among the mature.
- We have a message that those without the Spirit of God cannot conceive.
- No one knows God's thoughts except the Spirit of God, and we have received that Spirit.
- When we speak from the Spirit, we speak God's thoughts, for we have the mind of Christ.

And for context, consider that *Christ is God in human form*, so when Jesus speaks, you are listening to the very words of God.

It is hard to know where to begin here, but let me try to capture my thoughts with the following summary. Because God's Spirit resides inside of you and because you have the mysteries of the scriptures unveiled, you have the opportunity to take captive the thoughts generated by your human and sinful nature and, instead, make them subject to the very thoughts of God. You, disciple of

Christ, have the ability to see things as God sees them. Can you imagine a better way to go through life than with God's perspective?

Oh, how we limit the magnificent virtue of self-control when we restrict our understanding to resisting sin. While turning from sin is certainly a component of self-control, I put before you that biblical self-control is more about capturing your earthly thoughts, making them your slave, and replacing them with the very thoughts of your heavenly Father.

To further explore this, it helps me to put this concept into practical application. So let's see what it might look like if we were to take captive our earthly thoughts and subject them to the mind of God by imitating Jesus in the wilderness.

- When tempted to find your value in who others think you are, your performance, or your accomplishments, what if you exercised the self-control to remember from where your value truly flows? Consider the following:

The Creator of the universe has chased after us (Matthew 18:12–14) and has plotted our course back to Him (Acts 17:26–27). We were like lost sheep (Matthew 10:6), but the God of heaven took on the form of a man (Philippians 2:7) in order to save us (Luke 19:10), and we were purchased for a steep price (1 Corinthians 6:20). But He appeared in person for more than that. He came also to leave us an example (John 13:15) that we should do as He did, love as He loved (John 13:34), and become His ambassadors (2 Corinthians 5:20) who correctly deliver His message (2 Timothy 2:15; John 13:16). We have been restored as children of God (John 1:12), and on the day we were restored to Him, there was great rejoicing in heaven (Luke 15:7). As a result of that salvation, we have been given an inheritance that can never spoil or fade (1 Peter 1:4), which includes a liberation from bondage and decay that is replaced with the freedom and glory of the children of God (Romans 8:21). This inheritance is kept for us in heaven, where we will soon see God's face (Revelation 22:4) and hear those welcoming words, "Well done, good and faithful servant"

(Matthew 25:23). Until that time, we are shielded by God's power (1 Peter 1:5) and indwelled by His Spirit (2 Corinthians 1:22), and we can be confident (Philippians 1:6) that we are receiving the goal of our faith—the salvation of our souls (1 Peter 1:5).

- When you are tempted to be busy with life, what if you exercised the self-control to say, "No. First, I am going to spend time with the one who created me for His pleasure, because my Father, who has already planned out my entire life, says the following"?

  > "For I know the plans I have for you," declares the Lord, "plans to prosper you and not to harm you, plans to give you hope and a future. Then you will call on me and come and pray to me, and I will listen to you. You will seek me and find me when you seek me with all your heart." (Jeremiah 29:11–13)

  > I rise before dawn and cry for help; I have put my hope in your word. My eyes stay open through the watches of the night, that I may meditate on your promises. Hear my voice in accordance with your love; preserve my life, Lord, according to your laws. (Psalm 119:147–149)

- When praying about your needs, what if you exercise the self-control to stop and first meditate on God's needs—His hurts, His lost children, His desire to enjoy walking with you—just as Jesus did when acknowledging the pain that life brings those who don't recognize God's presence?

  > As he approached Jerusalem and saw the city, he wept over it and said, "If you, even you, had only known on this day what would bring you peace—but now it is hidden from your eyes. The days will come upon you when your enemies will build an embankment

against you and encircle you and hem you in on every side. They will dash you to the ground, you and the children within your walls. They will not leave one stone on another, because you did not recognize the time of God's coming to you. (Luke 19:41–44)

- When someone behaves in a manner you perceive as rude (e.g., cuts you off while driving), instead of fixating how that person's action affects you and judging his or her intentions, what if you exercised self-control by capturing that thought and praying something similar to the following?: "God, I don't know which of Your children is driving that car and whether they are experiencing an emergency that is causing them to drive in such a manner or whether they are simply giving in to sin. Either way, that is Your child, and You alone know what is in their heart. Whatever help they need, please provide it to them."

  Do not judge, or you too will be judged. For in the same way you judge others, you will be judged, and with the measure you use, it will be measured to you. (Matthew 7:1–2)

- When someone wears something immodest or overly revealing, do you look down on them for making clothing choices based on insecurities, or do you exercise self-control by capturing that thought and praying, "Father, help me not to be critical of their choices or to judge their motives and intentions but instead to treat them with the honor and value You place on them so that they can see You through me"?

  I counsel you to buy from me gold refined in the fire, so you can become rich; and white clothes to wear, so you can cover your shameful nakedness; and salve to put on your eyes, so you can see. (Revelation 3:18)

At dawn he appeared again in the temple courts, where all the people gathered around him, and he sat down to teach them. The teachers of the law and the Pharisees brought in a woman caught in adultery. They made her stand before the group and said to Jesus, "Teacher, this woman was caught in the act of adultery. In the Law Moses commanded us to stone such women. Now what do you say?" They were using this question as a trap, in order to have a basis for accusing him. But Jesus bent down and started to write on the ground with his finger. When they kept on questioning him, he straightened up and said to them, "Let any one of you who is without sin be the first to throw a stone at her." Again he stooped down and wrote on the ground. At this, those who heard began to go away one at a time, the older ones first, until only Jesus was left, with the woman still standing there. Jesus straightened up and asked her, "Woman, where are they? Has no one condemned you?" "No one, sir," she said. "Then neither do I condemn you," Jesus declared. "Go now and leave your life of sin." (John 8:2–11)

- When someone is struggling with a spiritual challenge that you either overcame many years ago or simply cannot relate to, do you give in to the temptation of thinking less of them or becoming frustrated with them, or do you exercise self-control by capturing that thought and instead try to get to know them as God knows them—where they came from, what their background is, what led to that way of thinking, how they were parented (or not parented), who has hurt them, and who has taken advantage of them? In doing so, you can become God's spokesperson to them. If you choose judgment, however, you no longer speak for God but become another obstacle for them to overcome.

For we do not have a high priest who is unable to empathize with our weaknesses, but we have one who has been tempted in every way, just as we are—yet he did not sin. Let us then approach God's throne of grace with confidence, so that we may receive mercy and find grace to help us in our time of need. (Hebrews 4:15–16)

The purposes of a person's heart are deep waters, but the one who has insight draws them out. (Proverbs 20:5)

- When your spouse doesn't do something the way you have requested that it be done many times before, do you allow feelings that are rooted in judgment to fester, or do you exercise self-control and capture those thoughts by looking for all of the good your spouse brings to the relationship in areas where you are weak? That does not mean that you don't respectfully convey to your spouse how something may have hurt your feelings or left you feeling disrespected, but what do you do with your attitude? How do you manage the temptation to place judgment on your perception of someone's actions?

> Catch for us the foxes [the everyday unresolved hurts], the little foxes that ruin the vineyards, our vineyards that are in bloom. (Song of Songs 2:15)

> Above all, love each other deeply, because love covers over a multitude of sins. (1 Peter 4:8)

> If your brother or sister sins, go and point out their fault, just between the two of you. If they listen to you, you have won them over. (Matthew 18:15)

(It is noteworthy that Matthew 18:15 is followed by the story of the unmerciful servant.)

- When one financial hit after another keeps coming in your direction, and you toss and turn at night under the stress of your role as a provider, do you get angry at God, or do you exercise self-control and let God know that you're being tempted with anger and seek His help (and the help of others) in righting your perspective that you are a steward of what is God's, not an owner of anything?

> Therefore I tell you, do not worry about your life, what you will eat or drink; or about your body, what you will wear. Is not life more than food, and the body more than clothes? Look at the birds of the air; they do not sow or reap or store away in barns, and yet your heavenly Father feeds them. Are you not much more valuable than they? Can any one of you by worrying add a single hour to your life? And why do you worry about clothes? See how the flowers of the field grow. They do not labor or spin. Yet I tell you that not even Solomon in all his splendor was dressed like one of these. If that is how God clothes the grass of the field, which is here today and tomorrow is thrown into the fire, will he not much more clothe you—you of little faith? So do not worry, saying, 'What shall we eat?' or 'What shall we drink?' or 'What shall we wear?' For the pagans run after all these things, and your heavenly Father knows that you need them. But seek first his kingdom and his righteousness, and all these things will be given to you as well. Therefore do not worry about tomorrow, for tomorrow will worry about itself. Each day has enough trouble of its own. (Matthew 6:25–34)

> Two things I ask of you, Lord; do not refuse me before I die: Keep falsehood and lies far from me; give me neither poverty nor riches, but give me only

my daily bread. Otherwise, I may have too much and disown you and say, 'Who is the Lord?' Or I may become poor and steal, and so dishonor the name of my God. (Proverbs 30:7–9)

- When God takes from you what is most important, including your health or the health of a loved one, do you burn with rage, or do you exercise self-control and learn to lament in a godly way, surrounded by friends who will listen, empathize, and provide godly encouragement, rather than commiserate with sinful thoughts?

> There is a time for everything, and a season for every activity under the heavens: a time to be born and a time to die, a time to plant and a time to uproot, a time to kill and a time to heal, a time to tear down and a time to build, a time to weep and a time to laugh, a time to mourn and a time to dance. (Ecclesiastes 3:1–4)

> During the days of Jesus' life on earth, he offered up prayers and petitions with fervent cries and tears to the one who could save him from death, and he was heard because of his reverent submission. Son though he was, he learned obedience from what he suffered and, once made perfect, he became the source of eternal salvation for all who obey him and was designated by God to be high priest in the order of Melchizedek. (Hebrews 5:7–10)

I would be remiss in continuing without confessing that I am guilty of failing to exercise self-control in every area above on too many occasions to remember. I spent the first half of my Christian life tied to the mast of prohibition, hoping that day's prayer time or a good sermon would provide me with enough incentive to be godly until I could find my next injection of spiritual motivation. It wasn't until I saw the need to instruct my own children in virtue that I realized how ill-equipped I was to paint for them God's more beautiful way, the magnificence behind His moral laws.

Sadly, brothers and sisters, we don't inherit this prohibitive mindset from God but often from our own parents, who spend our formative years telling us what is right and what is wrong but rarely providing us with the beautiful reason behind the instruction. The result of a lack of training in moral reasoning is that we come to categorize behavioral requirements as prohibitions, and once out from under our parents' influence, we toss off their instructions and experiment with that from which we were prohibited.

Because the child has never received the privilege of understanding the beauty behind God's moral instructions, sin becomes too enticing to withstand, once out from under the enforcer of consequence. This is the most frequent behavior we witness when children leave home for college. Even if those children later attempt to repair their relationship with God, as I did, their psychological makeup still can view behavioral requirements as prohibitive, and those same feelings of prohibition, consequence, and punishment become the filter through which they view biblical commands.

Let me give you an example from Gary Ezzo, executive director of Growing Families International, of what it means to think morally rather than prohibitively. Gary tells the story of conducting an interview of a young girl for acceptance into a private elementary school, in which he asked the following question: "If you were sitting on a bus and an elderly woman boarded the bus, but there were no seats available, what would you do?" The young girl put her head down and thought for a while, long enough that the Gary began to wonder if she knew this basic moral courtesy at all.

The little girl then lifted her head and said, "If there was no sign instructing me to remain seated, I would stand up and offer my seat to the woman so that I could honor her, but if there was a sign telling me to remain seated, I would move over and offer to share my seat with her." What we see here is the magnificence of learning to subject our thoughts to God's thoughts. You see, what Gary didn't know was that in the girl's experience, a sign to remain seated was on every school bus. That complicated the question as it caused her to consider how to reconcile the sign on the bus with the desire to show honor to the elderly woman.

Ultimately, this young girl was able to harmonize the commands of Leviticus 19:32—"Stand up in the presence of the aged, show respect for the elderly and revere your God. I am the Lord"—and Romans 13:1—"Let everyone be subject to the governing authorities, for there is no authority except that which God has established. The authorities that exist have been established by God"—because she understood the intent behind the command, rather than seeing the command as nothing more than a mandate that required rote obedience.

Brothers and sisters, it is not just our privilege but also our duty to adopt the mind of our heavenly Father. Can you imagine what Jesus envisioned by a "light shining on a hill" when He foresaw a time where the world would be full of true Christians (little Christs) who were "making every effort" to rely on the Spirit of self-control that resided within them *to see every area of their lives from His perspective*? If you lack joy, it is likely because you are not adopting the mind of Christ. If you feel unable to overcome sin, it may be that you are focusing too much on avoiding the sin and not enough on God's more beautiful way (the more beautiful song). If you lack peace, then you need to come in closer contact with the thoughts of God, who holds the unfathomable universe in one hand while orchestrating every detail of the lives of nearly eight billion humans in the other.

For further conviction, please meditate and journal on the following verses:

> We demolish arguments and every pretension that sets itself up against the knowledge of God, and we take captive every thought to make it obedient to Christ. (2 Corinthians 10:5)

> Therefore, I urge you, brothers and sisters, in view of God's mercy, to offer your bodies as a living sacrifice, holy and pleasing to God—this is your true and proper worship. Do not conform to the pattern of this world, but be transformed by the renewing of your mind. Then you will be able to test and approve what God's will is—his good, pleasing and perfect will. (Romans 12:1–2)

> You were taught, with regard to your former way of life, to put off your old self, which is being corrupted by its deceitful desires; to be made new in the attitude of your minds; and to put on the new self, created to be like God in true righteousness and holiness. (Ephesians 4:22–24)

3. **We need self-control in order to resist temptation and to flee sin.**

Yes, brothers and sisters, in addition to everything we have looked at thus far, it remains true that we need to resist temptation and flee from sin. I hope you do not hear me minimizing that important aspect of self-control. But my prayer is this: if you are convinced that it takes exercising the virtue of self-control to keep at the front of your mind that it is all about God and practicing self-control to subject all of your thoughts to the mind of God, then you will no longer see resisting temptation and fleeing from sin as a prohibition but as a natural extension of the relationship you have with God. Then, you will be empowered to resist sin because, for you, sin will run a distant second to the more beautiful song that is playing in your ears and filling your head.

Sin is the equivalent of unrighteousness, and unrighteousness is the opposite of righteousness. We know from our previous discussion that righteousness is anything that makes relationships better. Who on earth would want to do something that would hurt the very relationship that they are so intent on protecting and enhancing? Ulysses avoided sin by tying himself to a mast and enduring a miserable journey so that he could receive the prize. Odysseus realized that he was in possession of the prize and played the more beautiful song, a song so much more enticing than anything the Sirens had to offer that temptation was put back in its rightful place. The world's "siren song" is so much less than what God offers that the scriptures say the disparity is as wide as the heavens are above the earth. In short, we are so much better equipped to resist temptation and flee from sin when we have the mind of Christ, and we listen to God's more beautiful way.

Thankfully, the Bible gives us a clear guide when it comes to equipping ourselves and developing the mind of Christ. Consider Ephesians 6:10–20, which states:

> Finally, be strong in the Lord and in his mighty power. Put on the full armor of God, so that you can take your stand against the devil's schemes. For our struggle is not against flesh and blood, but against the rulers, against the authorities, against the powers of this dark world and against the spiritual forces of evil in the heavenly realms. Therefore put on the full armor of God, so that when the day of evil comes, you may be able to stand your ground, and after you have done everything, to stand. Stand firm then, with the belt of truth buckled around your waist, with the breastplate of righteousness in place, and with your feet fitted with the readiness that comes from the gospel of peace. In addition to all this, take up the shield of faith, with which you can extinguish all the flaming arrows of the evil one. Take the helmet of salvation and the sword of the Spirit, which is the word of God. And pray in the Spirit on all occasions with all kinds of prayers and requests. With this in mind, be alert and always keep on praying for all

the Lord's people. Pray also for me, that whenever I speak, words may be given me so that I will fearlessly make known the mystery of the gospel, for which I am an ambassador in chains. Pray that I may declare it fearlessly, as I should.

There is a week's worth of personal Bible study in Ephesians 6, but I want to focus on two elements of God's armor in the context of God's virtues. First is the breastplate of righteousness. God wants us to wrap all of our vital organs in our relationship with Him. That is what I have spent this entire chapter trying to describe. Prohibition and fear do not protect our vital organs. A loving, ever-increasing intimate relationship with God protects our vital organs. As we discussed in the last chapter, a husband fixated on avoiding an extramarital affair is guaranteed a much-more-challenging road than a man who spends his energy choosing to fall deeply in love with his wife. Second is the sword of the Spirit, the Word of God. Knowing God, knowing God's more beautiful song, and knowing how to use God's words to counter Satan's temptations, as Jesus did in the wilderness, is the essential component in our being able to embrace this life that God has gifted us, rather than living a life of fear and insecurity.

We are the most blessed people on earth because we alone have been given the spirit of self-control, and we have been given access to the mind of Christ. Our entire earthly lives are about getting to know God and getting to know ourselves. It is about becoming goodness, as our heavenly Father is good, and about pouring ourselves out for others, as our heavenly Father pours Himself out for us. It is about learning our place in our relationship with God, as well as among those who make up His bride. And ultimately, it is about learning to surrender everything we think is ours to Him, to whom it actually belongs, including, at some point, our very last breaths.

The more we learn to trust, the more we learn to surrender, and the more we learn to surrender, the more we experience life to the fullest that Jesus describes in John 10:10. But, brothers and sisters, surrender does not mean that you no longer care about your desires or that you will be fine with any outcome. Instead, surrender means that you choose to believe that God's plan is best and that you are going to continue to obey His will, even when it is painful. It is the decision—rooted in self-control—that you will not let your desires or fears inhibit your ability to grow in your relationship with God or to use them as an excuse to stop displaying Him to a lost world.

In conclusion, why does Peter instruct us to add self-control to knowledge, which is to be added to goodness? Because self-control is the gateway virtue to a balanced and ordered relationship. It facilitates growth, understanding, surrender, and truth.

The benefit of relational intimacy is that it is the key to removing limits on a relationship (righteousness), but the consequence of intimacy is that it breeds familiarity, which breeds complacency. That is precisely why Peter places the addition of self-control right after knowledge. We, who are tasting God's goodness and who are developing an ever-increasing intimacy with Him, must daily exercise self-control in our thoughts, lest we become complacent in our thinking and allow God's perfect filter to be replaced by our worldly filter.

SUMMARY

Back to 1 Peter 4:7—"The end of all things is near. Therefore practice self-control and keep your minds clear so that you may pray." Does self-control encompass resisting temptation? Absolutely. But I pray that we have come to realize or have strengthened our convictions that self-control encompasses much more than resisting temptation. It also means to redirect our paradigm to believe that everything we know and see is about God, and we accept that we are created for His pleasure. And it means to capture every thought and surrender it to God's perspective. This is one of the most practical ways you can honor God throughout your day—surrender your every thought to Him.

You see, the order in which Peter tells us to add these virtues makes perfect sense. God's goodness opens the door to a relationship with Him. His choice to exercise gnōsis with us creates the foundation of an intimate relationship with Him. But that very confidence that comes from knowing that God accepts us, understands us, and loves us unconditionally allows us to become lazy in our treatment of Him. Once we allow this complacency to enter our relationship with God, then the virtue of intimacy loses its effectiveness, and we are left with little motivation other than fear of consequence and punishment. It is with great wisdom that Peter says to those who are experiencing gnōsis that they must make every effort to add self-control.

FOR FURTHER STUDY

> But the fruit of the Spirit is love, joy, peace, forbearance, kindness, goodness, faithfulness, gentleness and self-control. Against such things there is no law. Those who belong to Christ Jesus have crucified the flesh with its passions and desires. Since we live by the Spirit, let us keep in step with the Spirit. Let us not become conceited, provoking and envying each other. (Galatians 5:22–26)

> Do you not know that in a race all the runners run, but only one gets the prize? Run in such a way as to get the prize. Everyone who competes in the games goes into strict training. They do it to get a crown that will not last, but we do it to get a crown that will last forever. Therefore I do not run like someone running aimlessly; I do not fight like a boxer beating the air. No, I strike a blow to my body and make it my slave so that after I have preached to others, I myself

will not be disqualified for the prize. (1 Corinthians 9:24–27)

Chapter 6

PERSEVERANCE

THIS CHAPTER MARKS THE HALFWAY POINT OF OUR STUDY OF 2 Peter 1:5–8. My sincere prayer is that you are growing along with me in our understanding of the relationship God longs to have with us, while also increasing in confidence as we equip ourselves to act and think like our heavenly Father and become more attuned to His more beautiful "song."

What have we learned thus far? Faith in God's existence is the foundation of a relationship with Him and the fertile soil from which virtue grows. God's goodness is the wholeness of His moral excellence, from which flows our salvation. As we strive to embody the goodness that we see in our heavenly Father, others will be able to see glimpses of God through us and be drawn to a relationship with Him. Although God's goodness is so magnificent that it is largely indescribable, He offers us something greater than just the privilege of seeing His goodness from afar. He offers us an intimate knowledge of Him through a day-in/day-out relationship with Him that is not predicated on our actions, for we do not need to prove ourselves to the One who knows us better than we know ourselves. The natural result is that we who are experiencing an ever-deepening intimacy with God will be compelled to open our lives to others so that He can become more visible as we become less (John 3:27–30).

We then studied how controlling ourselves is an essential ingredient to maturity, for God cannot become more visible to those around us if we are not becoming more like Him. We learned that controlling ourselves is much more than simply turning from evil. Self-control encompasses placing God's passions ahead of our own, capturing every thought and subjecting it to the mind of Christ, and resisting temptation and fleeing from sin with appropriate armor and a *virtue-based perspective.*

If you took the challenge and have been working daily on those three aspects of self-control, then it will come as no surprise why Peter now says to add *perseverance,* which is the virtue we will study in this chapter. But don't hang your hat on the obvious definition of perseverance because, once again, there is much more to this biblical virtue than meets the eye.

The Greek word for *perseverance* is ὑπομονήν (pronounced *hypomonēn* in English), which in that specific form means patience, endurance, fortitude, and steadfastness.

In this lesson, we are going to look at these four aspects of hypomonēn so that we may have a more complete understanding of this magnificent virtue and therefore can make every effort to embody it, as we are doing with goodness, knowledge, and self-control. Let's begin with the side of perseverance that is patience.

1. Patience: Scripture seems to home in on three specific areas of patience in which we must grow if we are to successfully persevere until the end of our earthly lives. Let's spend some time with each.

    a. We must learn to be patient with ourselves.

Do you expect your toddler to behave like an adult? To think like an adult? To reason like an adult? I would venture to say that none of us has those expectations. What we do expect is age-appropriate behavior, a teachable heart, and a devotion to family. With those things in place, we know that we can mold a young heart into a well-reasoned, thoughtful, and moral adult. Why would God's expectation be any different from those whom He calls His children? In fact, I put before you that as young Christians, we are more challenging than newborns because we come with baggage, whereas our biological children come with a clean slate. If you are anything like me, you have already experienced numerous failures just since we began studying 2 Peter 1:5–8 together. In fact, if you have been 100 percent successful in capturing every one of your thoughts and subjecting them to the mind of Christ, please come speak with me because we may be experiencing the Second Coming. After all, John reminds us that pure sinlessness is neither possible nor expected.

> This is the message we have heard from him and declare to you: God is light; in him there is no darkness at all. If we claim to have fellowship with him and yet walk in the darkness, we lie and do not live out the truth. But if we walk in the light, as he is in the light, we have fellowship with one another, and the blood of Jesus, his Son, purifies us from all sin. If we claim to be without sin, we deceive ourselves and the truth is not in us. If we confess our sins, he is faithful and just and will forgive us our sins and purify us from all unrighteousness. If we claim we have not sinned, we make him out to be a liar and his word is not in us. (1 John 1:5–10)

It is noteworthy that God expects us to strive for perfection (see also Matthew 5:48), yet He knows that we will not achieve perfection in this life. So while we strive for perfection, God provides us the privilege of walking in the light. A good metaphor I once heard regarding this verse is that walking in the light is akin to living under a waterfall. As long as you remain under the waterfall, the mud slung at you and the dirt you get on yourself is immediately and continually washed away. But if you choose to leave the protection of the waterfall (the light), your inability to cleanse yourself becomes evident, since you are leaving behind the very relationship that pours out forgiveness.

What does God expect of us, from a practical perspective? For starters, we are to "remain in Him" through prayer, Bible study, and commitment to His people; "to make every effort" to adopt God's character; "to confess our sins" to each other; and to be an open book (gnōsis) so that we may bear much fruit. But He also expects us to have failures, many of them, and when we do, we are to dust ourselves off, confess our sins, and get right back to business.

Unfortunately, many of us mishandle our mistakes. Sometimes, we hide them out of embarrassment, which is rooted in the prideful thought, "I'm better than this and don't want to sour my reputation." Other times, we fail to progress beyond worldly sorrow. We hide our sin out of fear of facing the consequences, but this reveals that we are still focused on ourselves and not on the one we sinned against. Similarly, we can become downcast and feel that we are failures, which is rooted in self-pity and the belief that God is no longer able or willing to use us, despite the reality that He had foreknowledge of this sin before He saved us. Sometimes, we get angry at ourselves for sinning and then try to use that anger as the fuel of conviction. But anger, self-pity, and pride are not godly fuels; they are worldly deceits. Instead, we were created to be open books, acknowledging our strengths as God-given, and accepting our weaknesses so that we can rely on the one who perfects us (2 Corinthians 11:30; 12:9–10).

I know that I have said this before, but it bears repeating: There exists only one being who knew every sin that you committed before the day of your salvation *and* also knew every sin that you would commit until your dying breath, even those sins that would later surprise you. That being was the God who forgave you for every single one of those sins on that very day. You cannot surprise God; you can only surprise yourself. Don't give up on the one who already knew. Rather, imitate Paul's attitude, captured in the following scriptures:

What a wretched man I am! Who will rescue me
from this body that is subject to death? Thanks be to
God, who delivers me through Jesus Christ our Lord!
(Romans 7:24–25a)

But he said to me, "My grace is sufficient for you, for
my power is made perfect in weakness." Therefore I
will boast all the more gladly about my weaknesses
so that Christ's power may rest on me. (2 Corinthians
12:9)

Let us not become weary in doing good, for at the
proper time we will reap a harvest if we do not give
up. Therefore, as we have opportunity, let us do good
to all people, especially to those who belong to the
family of believers. (Galatians 6:9–10)

Jesus once told a parable about a man who cleaned a demon
out of his house but did not fill up the newly emptied house. His
failure to do so left room not only for that demon but also for other,
more wicked demons to return to the man. In fact, Jesus specifically
stated that the final condition of the man was worse than if he
had never removed the demon in the first place (Luke 11:24–26).
What an amazing insight. If we clean out our sinful thoughts but
do not replace them with a love and pursuit of godly virtue, a new
habit of acknowledging our weaknesses, and a gratitude for God's
help, then we leave gaping holes in our thinking for Satan and his
demons to repopulate. Remember the story of Ulysses who made it
past the Siren's song, only to live with the memories of their sinful
enticement inside his head for the remainder of his life. On the
contrary, Odysseus's crew filled their minds with a more beautiful
song and, by doing so, never gave the Sirens a foothold.

Similarly, in Galatians (above), Paul instructs us in what not to
do—become weary in doing good—but more than that, he tells
us how to fill our home so that the demons have no place in us

to inhabit. Paul makes it clear that there are two components to perseverance. The first is a decision to not become weary, but the other is an action to do something specific instead. And what are we to do? We are to do good to all people, especially our brothers and sisters.

In chapter 5, we discussed how self-control requires us to take the focus off ourselves and place it on God and others. Here is another example of the *why* behind the command. Those who consistently train to put God and others before themselves are filling their head with acts of selflessness that squeeze out the thoughts that sprout from self-focus. Contrary to the world's understanding of patience, we can see here that biblical patience does not mean inaction.

We need to be patient with ourselves, but doing so requires us to redefine patience to align with God's expectation, which is not to sit around "being patient" with the things that happen to us while we grind out this life. Instead, we are to be patient with ourselves as we strive for perfection, while remaining in the light, and doing so as open books before our Creator and our spiritual family.

b.   We need to learn patience in suffering.

Consider this: if God suffers, then how can we ever truly know (gnōsis) God, until and unless we also experience suffering? Let's look once again at Hebrews 5.

> During the days of Jesus' life on earth, he offered up prayers and petitions with fervent cries and tears to the one who could save him from death, and he was heard because of his reverent submission. Although he was a Son, he learned obedience from what he suffered and, once made perfect, he became the source of eternal salvation for all who obey him and was designated by God to be high priest in the order of Melchizedek. (Hebrews 5:7–10)

Let this verse sink in for a moment. Jesus, a human in every way, had to learn obedience, but learning obedience simply through His parents' instruction was insufficient. He had to learn a level of obedience that was only obtainable through suffering. During His life on earth, Jesus saw the lost die. A close friend left the faith. It is possible that Joseph and Mary lived excommunicated from their own families as a result of their marriage and Mary's "illegitimate" child. He had no similar-aged male playmates. And worse, it was because of Him that none existed. He was a refugee in Egypt, and His family did not speak the language. There was nothing in His appearance that would cause anyone to desire Him (Isaiah 53:2). He lacked the companionship that only a spouse can provide. Once He started His ministry, He was rejected by those in His own hometown (Mark 6:1-6). He was lied about, gossiped about, and continually slandered. He likely lost His dad at a fairly young age. He was betrayed for thirty pieces of silver by a close friend. He was disowned by Peter for free. He was falsely imprisoned. He was given an unfair trial, and the presiding judge was a coward who succumbed to the desire for popularity over justice. He never tasted wealth. He never experienced romantic love. He was tortured and suffocated, and those who imposed these horrors upon Him mocked Him, incessantly and publicly, while He died.

And in every one of those instances, Jesus became one step closer to understanding His heavenly Father. This does not mean that He enjoyed what He had to experience but that He did not let His own desires and fears interfere with God's will for His life. He allowed His experiences to shape Him into the image of God. Is that how you view suffering? One step closer to God with every trial? A good friend once told me that our lives on this earth are all about learning to surrender everything, up to and including our very last breaths. Whether we are speaking of surrender or suffering, patience is made possible only through our faith in an all-knowing, just, and perfect God, who loves us enough to become one of us, live among us, and sacrifice Himself for us. That is why Peter says that perseverance comes after self-control, which comes after knowledge, which comes after goodness. For faith precipitates understanding God's goodness, from which flows an intimacy with Him that motivates us to make our thoughts subject to His thoughts. Only then can we find true peace and joy in suffering. This is an irreplaceable component of knowing Him and becoming His ambassador.

> For those who are led by the Spirit of God are the children of God. The Spirit you received does not make you slaves, so that you live in fear again; rather, the Spirit you received brought about your adoption to sonship. And by him we cry, "Abba, Father." The Spirit himself testifies with our spirit that we are God's children. Now if we are children, then we are heirs—heirs of God and co-heirs with Christ, if indeed we share in his sufferings in order that we may also share in his glory. I consider that our present sufferings are not worth comparing with the glory that will be revealed in us. For the creation waits in eager expectation for the children of God to be revealed. For the creation was subjected to frustration, not by its own choice, but by the will of the one who subjected it, in hope that the creation itself will be liberated from its bondage to decay and brought into the freedom and glory of the children of God. We know that the whole creation has been groaning as in the pains of childbirth right up to the present time. Not only so, but we ourselves, who have the firstfruits of the Spirit, groan inwardly as we wait eagerly for our adoption to sonship, the redemption of our bodies. For in this hope we were saved. But hope that is seen is no hope at all. Who hopes for what they already have? But if we hope for what we do not yet have, we wait for it patiently. (Romans 8:14–25)

This is one of the most amazing verses in the New Testament. First, it explains that sharing in God's sufferings is a prerequisite to sharing in His glory. God's *glory* is a term used to describe the manifestation of God's presence, as perceived by humans. While we groan for the redemption of our bodies, God groans for the revelation of Himself to His lost children who are wandering in the darkness. How and where will that frustrated creation first be introduced to God? When it encounters the freedom and glory of the children of God. When we think of firstfruits, we usually think of tithing. But when God thinks of firstfruits, He thinks of what He has given to you. He has given the best of Himself so that His lost children can find Him. And what is the best of Him? You are! If that doesn't motivate you to make every effort to embody the character of God by pursuing His virtues, I don't know what will. And if you can get your head wrapped around the fact that *you the embodiment of God to His lost children*, then waiting patiently for your present suffering to end will become a worthwhile sacrifice.

Brothers and sisters, suffering hurts. Health challenges, financial challenges, relational challenges, loss, work stress, rejection, seclusion, and segregation all hurt. But for us, suffering has a purpose. God is teaching us to trust in Him, to rely on Him, and to obey Him. He is protecting us from becoming too comfortable in a world that is not our home, and He is perfecting us so that we can become a conduit for the salvation of others who will see the Spirit of an almighty God through us. Lament when necessary. Cry, shout, and groan when needed. Vent to and confide in reliable brothers and sisters, but be grateful that you have spiritual brothers and sisters in whom you can confide, while the world lacks any godly counsel.

When the lost suffer, they suffer in vain. They have no hope, no future, no salvation, no remedy, no forgiveness, and no answers— that is, until they meet you. As the song says, this world is not our home; we are just passing through. The home that awaits us cannot be described in words, and after a few "days" there, all of our present sufferings will evaporate and be placed in the right perspective. We spend so much energy in wanting and pursuing immediate comfort, and so much of our fatigue and disappointment is rooted in our efforts to make this world our home. We would be so much more at peace and have so much more joy if we truly believed that this life is just temporary and that the best use of our time and energy is to reflect God to a lost world. If you are going to store up treasure, store it up where thieves cannot steal, and moths cannot destroy. Consider Peter's plea:

> Praise be to the God and Father of our Lord Jesus Christ! In his great mercy he has given us new birth into a living hope through the resurrection of Jesus Christ from the dead, and into an inheritance that can never perish, spoil or fade. This inheritance is kept in heaven for you, who through faith are shielded by God's power until the coming of the salvation that is ready to be revealed in the last time. In all this you greatly rejoice, though now for a little while you may have had to suffer grief in all kinds of trials. These have come so that the proven genuineness of your faith—of greater worth than gold, which perishes even though refined by fire—may result in praise, glory and honor when Jesus Christ is revealed. Though you have not seen him, you love him; and even though you do not see him now, you believe in him and are filled with an inexpressible and glorious joy, for you are receiving the end result of your faith, the salvation of your souls. (1 Peter 1:3–9)

When our oldest daughter, Emily, was three years old, and her sister Alex was six months, Emily came down with what appeared to be a flu bug. Since we were leaving on a trip to Los Angeles, we saw a doctor who advised us to give her Imodium before boarding the airplane. When we exited the airport in Los Angeles and stood in the sunlight, it was clear that Emily's skin and eyes were yellowing. We then telephoned her doctor, who advised us to go immediately to a hospital, which we did. Following the completion of a number of tests, a doctor and a nurse entered our room. The nurse said to Emily and Alex, "Why don't you girls come with me while your mom and dad speak with the doctor." That was genuinely our first indication that this was going to be something more serious than the flu. The doctor explained to us that Emily had contracted E. coli and that she needed to be immediately placed into the pediatric intensive care unit. There was no cure, it was potentially fatal, and we had greatly exacerbated her condition by giving her Imodium.

For the next three days, we stayed by her side in her pediatric ICU room. Even while she faded into and out of sleep, we were attuned to her heartbeat racing at 160 beats per minute, as it struggled to provide enough oxygen to her organs with whatever red blood cells she had left. We could not know whether she would make it through the night, and there was no way that we were going to allow ourselves to sleep while she passed away. Our close friends, who are disciples in Los Angeles, rushed to be by our sides, and when I saw them, I broke down. I could no longer hold myself together, and their presence brought all of the emotion out of me. But they were there for us. They turned us back to God. They took care of Alex for us. And slowly, Emily pulled through, at the same time that a little girl in an adjacent room was losing her life.

Years later, we would endure another three-year period of suffering with Emily, when we tried to find what was causing her chronic pain, and then again while she fought cancer as a young adult. Although I get emotional just writing this paragraph, I can clearly see the benefit of those experiences. We are who we are because of them. Emily is who she is because of them. They changed our perspective on life, deepened our reliance on God, and transformed our relationships with our daughters. God did for us through suffering what nothing else in life could have mimicked.

I know that the suffering I have shared here pales in comparison to what some of you have undergone or are currently undergoing. We all have our stories. But the beauty is that the suffering we endure in this fallen world is woven by an all-powerful God into the fabric of our refinement so that we can *know* Him in an ever-deepening way and have our lives defined by and credited to us as righteous. Let's not squander our suffering by becoming bitter—or worse, by giving up.

c. We need to be patient with God.

> We know that the whole creation has been groaning as in the pains of childbirth right up to the present time. Not only so, but we ourselves, who have the firstfruits of the Spirit, groan inwardly as we wait eagerly for our adoption to sonship, the redemption of our bodies. For in this hope we were saved. But hope that is seen is no hope at all. Who hopes for what they already have? But if we hope for what we do not yet have, we wait for it patiently. In the same way, the Spirit helps us in our weakness. We do not know what we ought to pray for, but the Spirit himself intercedes for us through wordless groans. And he who searches our hearts knows the mind of the Spirit, because the Spirit intercedes for God's people in accordance with the will of God. And we know that in all things God works for the good of those who love him, who have been called according to his purpose. For those God foreknew he also predestined to be conformed to the image of his Son, that he might be the firstborn among many brothers and sisters. And those he predestined, he also called; those he called, he also justified; those he justified, he also glorified. (Romans 8:22–30)

Prioritizing God's dreams ahead of our own, capturing every thought and submitting it to the mind of Christ, and resisting temptation and fleeing from sin is tiring. And on top of that, we have Satan, his demons, and our own sinful nature routinely nagging at our thoughts with lies and appeals. It's permissible—in fact, it's expected—that we will groan and have longings from time to time.

But we cannot forget that God's timing is perfect and just. It can be helpful to remind ourselves where we would be if God had allotted us the same amount of patience that we typically allot Him. Although we may groan periodically when things seem overwhelming or feel as if we are running out of steam, we need to fixate on the prize— our adoption as sons and daughters and the redemption of our bodies. We need to remind ourselves that we cannot hope in what we already see, only in what we do not yet have.

God has given us His Spirit to help us in our weaknesses by searching our hearts in order to intercede for us. As heirs, we have the promise that God works all things to the good of those who love Him (Romans 8:28). And we cannot miss that He has predestined us to be conformed to the image of His Son. Isn't that exactly what we have been learning—becoming like God by making every effort to embody His virtue? Consider Peter's words just a few chapters after our theme verse:

> But do not forget this one thing, dear friends: *With the Lord a day is like a thousand years, and a thousand years are like a day. The Lord is not slow in keeping his promise, as some understand slowness. Instead he is patient with you, not wanting anyone to perish, but everyone to come to repentance.* But the day of the Lord will come like a thief. The heavens will disappear with a roar; the elements will be destroyed by fire, and the earth and everything done in it will be laid bare. Since everything will be destroyed in this way, *what kind of people ought you to be? You ought to live holy and godly lives as you look forward to the day of God and speed its coming.* That day will bring about the destruction of the heavens by fire, and the elements will melt in the heat. But in keeping with his promise we are looking forward to a new heaven and a new earth, where righteousness dwells. So then, dear friends, since you are looking forward to this, *make every effort to be found spotless, blameless and*

at peace with him. Bear in mind that our Lord's patience means salvation, just as our dear brother Paul also wrote you with the wisdom that God gave him. He writes the same way in all his letters, speaking in them of these matters. His letters contain some things that are hard to understand, which ignorant and unstable people distort, as they do the other Scriptures, to their own destruction. Therefore, dear friends, since you have been forewarned, be on your guard so that you may not be carried away by the error of the lawless and fall from your secure position. *But grow in the grace and knowledge of our Lord and Savior Jesus Christ.* To him be glory both now and forever! Amen. (2 Peter 3:8–18, emphasis added)

This is the second time Peter instructs us to make every effort. At this point in his letter, he assumes we are now looking forward to the judgment and therefore are making every effort to be found spotless and blameless. But he doesn't end there. He adds "and at peace with Him." Therein lies the difference between a prohibitive conscience that lives in fear of consequence and punishment, and the child of God who pursues spotlessness and blamelessness through the embodiment of godly virtue. We know that patience with God is rooted in faith (as is evidenced by the order outlined in 2 Peter 1:5–7), and we know that the core element of faith is a confidence that God exists and that He rewards those who earnestly seek Him. There is a difference between perseverance without patience and perseverance with godly patience. One requires commitment alone; the other requires commitment with faith. It is simply not possible to exercise a godly patience unless we are developing a belief that God knows better than we do in every instance and every circumstance, that He will do nothing to harm us and everything to save us, and that He is molding us into His vision for us.

Patience is the result of faith in the sovereignty of God and His passionate love, not just for His church but for each of us individually.

That is why we "look forward to the day of God and speed it coming"—because our faith is increasing every time we see God's goodness—demystified by knowledge, accessible though self-control, and given time to blossom through our patience. Look at how Paul views the integral place perseverance has in Christian development:

> We ought always to thank God for you, brothers and sisters, and rightly so, because your faith is growing more and more, and the love all of you have for one another is increasing. Therefore, among God's churches we boast about your perseverance and faith in all the persecutions and trials you are enduring. All this is evidence that God's judgment is right, and as a result you will be counted worthy of the kingdom of God, for which you are suffering. (2 Thessalonians 1:3-5)

It takes time to refine gold. In fact, gold must be heated to approximately 1000 degrees Fahrenheit in order to force the impurities to rise to the surface, where they become visible and can then be removed. Only God knows what He is molding us into, but whatever He has in mind for us after our lives on this earth are over is more than He is willing to describe (or more than we are able to handle) at this point in our spiritual development. The scripture above tells us that God's judgment is right. He knows exactly what He is doing with us. He knows exactly what it will take to get us there. Success in perseverance requires us to "fix our eyes on the author and perfecter of our faith" and also "on the hope set before us." For if we trust Him to get us there, we will be counted worthy of the kingdom. Look at how beautifully Paul addresses this very truth:

> All these people were still living by faith when they died. They did not receive the things promised; they only saw them and welcomed them from a distance, admitting that they were foreigners and strangers on earth. People who say such things show that they are

> looking for a country of their own. If they had been thinking of the country they had left, they would have had opportunity to return. Instead, they were longing for a better country—a heavenly one. Therefore God is not ashamed to be called their God, for he has prepared a city for them. (Hebrews 11:13–16)

Did you catch that? Patience is such a magnificent virtue that our exercise of it causes God to be proud of us and not ashamed. He knows the city He has prepared for us, and He has no regrets. But for now, we need our patience to be motivated by the choice that we will happily reflect God to His lost children. God will reward us in His good timing, and we would do well to grow in our patience. With this understanding of patience, let us continue to examine the other aspects of perseverance.

2. Endurance: Perseverance is a mindset, whereas endurance is built only through exercise.

> Do you not know that in a race all the runners run, but only one gets the prize? Run in such a way as to get the prize. Everyone who competes in the games goes into strict training. They do it to get a crown that will not last, but we do it to get a crown that will last forever. Therefore I do not run like someone running aimlessly; I do not fight like a boxer beating the air. No, I strike a blow to my body and make it my slave so that after I have preached to others, I myself will not be disqualified for the prize. (1 Corinthians 9:24–27)

The second element of perseverance is endurance. Life experience tells us that endurance cannot be purchased with money or obtained through academics. Endurance comes only through repetitive training, which requires commitment and discipline. If you are not characterized by prioritizing daily time with God, then you are not building endurance in the muscles of discipline. If your daily time with God consists only of reading a prayer list, then you are not building endurance in the muscles or relationship. If you are not planning every week to ensure that you are prioritizing that which is most important over those inevitable things that seem urgent, then you are not producing endurance in the muscles of trust. Paul describes this concept in Hebrews 5:14 with the statement, "But solid food is for the mature, who by constant use have trained themselves to distinguish good from evil."

We all know what it feels like when we attempt to do something physical but lack endurance. Our chests hurt, and our muscles ache and pulsate. Our temples pound. We may feel nauseous. Once we feel these physical effects, it becomes increasingly difficult not to fixate on them, and the more we fixate on the pain, the more attractive quitting becomes. On the other hand, those who work daily on endurance obtain two benefits. First, as they grow in their endurance, they can push harder and harder with each passing day, while staying focused on their goals, rather than on their pain. Second, they learn to push through pain rather than become overwhelmed by it. This needs to describe our spiritual commitment. We need to exercise our spiritual habits daily so that we can grow more and more proficient in them while training ourselves to push through the difficult periods without losing our focus.

As we explore more about this aspect of patience, it is important to find motivation—a reason to endure when discomfort vies for our attention. First Thessalonians 1:3 provides some insight when it states, "We remember before our God and Father your work produced by faith, your labor prompted by love, and your endurance inspired by hope in our Lord Jesus Christ."

Endurance needs inspiration. Those who go into training without a goal are often doomed from the outset. We need hope, whether it's winning a competition, achieving a weight-loss goal, readying for an event that requires endurance, or simply wanting to feel better physically. What better goals could exist than knowing that we can enter the most holy place, interact directly with the Creator, and adequately represent and introduce Him to a lost world while we patiently await the renewal of our bodies and our heavenly home? After all, endurance is not just about helping ourselves succeed. It is also about bringing others along with us.

Consider 2 Corinthians 6:3–4, which states:

> We put no stumbling block in anyone's path, so that
> our ministry will not be discredited. Rather, as servants
> of God, we commend ourselves in every way: in great
> endurance; in troubles, hardships and distresses.

Those athletes who lack endurance are incapable of inspiring their teammates because they are constantly running out of steam and hindering the team's performance. But those who practice endurance are capable of encouraging those who lack it, including those who face discouragement over their own mistakes. I want to be the disciple who has practiced endurance so that I can keep my eyes on the prize, while encouraging and inspiring my brothers and sisters. I do not want to be the disciple whose lack of endurance leaves me fixated on myself, and I become the one who needs to be carried by others. We will all have times when we will need to be carried, but let's commit to practicing endurance so that a lack of endurance will not be a self-inflicted wound.

May I speak plainly? Sometimes it feels that some of us are called to persevere more than others and often more than those who seem to be making poor decisions. How do we respond when life hits us disproportionally hard? Let's start that discussion in 2 Thessalonians 1:4, which states, "Therefore, among God's churches we boast about your perseverance and faith in all of the persecutions and trials you are enduring."

Here, we see that endurance during trials is honorable. It is not our role to judge the fairness of our trials. God promises justice, not fairness, and the two are not the same. In short, fairness equalizes everyone's condition so that it levels the playing field. But justice evaluates one's actions, regardless of their condition.[5] For example, sports referees ensure that both teams are given equality in a game and that rules are followed by all players to ensure this level of fairness. God does not promise this. Rather, God promises that the path He designed for you is exactly the right path on which you can find Him and be refined by Him. On the other hand, God does promise justice, in that He alone will evaluate each individual without bias, with full knowledge and complete understanding, and will render an accurate verdict.

If it is true that God has planned the path for our lives, then it is also true that we are guilty of subjecting His plan to our view of what is fair. But God's plan is perfect, and not only do your life's challenges refine your faith, but they create for God a very specific conduit through which He can minister to others through you. If we believe and rely on God's perfect plan, then we can spend less mental energy challenging it. The less energy you spend challenging God's path for your life, the greater your endurance and the more content you become.

> But you, man of God, flee from all this, and pursue
> righteousness, godliness, faith, love, endurance, and
> gentleness. (1 Timothy 6:11)

I love the heart that Paul had for Timothy. I have only included a single verse from 1 Timothy 6, but I would encourage you to read it in context. In Paul's letter, he instructs Timothy that godliness with contentment is great gain and then warns that discontentment can lead to the pursuit of comfort in this life, which has led some to wander from their faith and pierced others with many griefs. But Paul doesn't leave Timothy with a warning. Rather, Paul instructs Timothy to pursue righteousness (i.e., anything that improves our relationship with God and others), godliness (i.e., embodying God's

---

[5] "What does the Bible say about justice versus fairness?", Pastor's Thoughts, August 22, 2010, https://www.hanoverbaptistchurch.org/blogpastor/2010/what-does-the-bible-say-about-justice-versus-fairness/

character), faith, love (which we will get to in a few chapters), and gentleness. I am going to exercise my own self-control here and avoid jumping on a tangent. But a great Bible study, if you are so led, is the inter-reliance between endurance and gentleness.

Brothers and sisters, let's commit to daily practicing those things that increase our endurance so that we can both finish the race and simultaneously inspire those around us to keep running. The Bible states that Jesus endured the cross and scorned its shame for the joy set before Him (Hebrews 12:1–3). Everything that God allowed to happen to Jesus, in addition to the mental and physical discipline that Jesus imposed upon Himself, resulted in sufficient spiritual endurance for Him to finish the race and, in doing so, become the single acceptable sacrifice for our sins. Our salvation rested on His endurance. Let us grow in our endurance so that we can be a conduit for salvation to God's other lost children.

3. Fortitude: inner courage and strength.

> Brothers and sisters, as an example of patience in the
> face of suffering, take the prophets who spoke in the
> name of the Lord. As you know, we count as blessed
> those who have persevered. You have heard of Job's
> perseverance and have seen what the Lord finally
> brought about. The Lord is full of compassion and
> mercy. (James 5:10–11)

There is so much more to say about fortitude, but I will limit my comments to this: Fortitude is the courage of your convictions and a by-product of endurance. It is a brother to the confidence that is built with each spiritual success you achieve, regardless of how small. When you walk by a piece of trash in a neighbor's yard, the temptation is to think, *Well, I didn't leave that there*, or *It's not my responsibility*. But we all have felt the gentle prompting of the Holy Spirit to do what is right, regardless of fault. Those who listen to that prompting and do what is right are rewarded with an unspoken reassurance from the Spirit in the form of a clean conscience and an inner affirmation. Was the trash your fault? No. Was it your responsibility? No. But by picking it up, you were practicing the virtue of honoring the preciousness of others without subjecting them to judgment. Those who spend time meditating on how to honor the preciousness of others are feeding fortitude, while those who do not are left with thoughts of prohibition that sound a lot more like, *If you don't pick up that trash, God will not be happy with you.* Those who live with a prohibitive mentality are doomed to either reluctantly obey or continually justify to their conscience a lack of obedience based on their perception of a lack of fairness.

> You, however, know all about my teaching, my way of life, my purpose, faith, patience, love, endurance, persecutions, sufferings—what kind of things happened to me in Antioch, Iconium and Lystra, the persecutions I endured. (2 Timothy 3:10–11a)

I beg of you to study God's Word with a purpose in your daily quiet times—to discover and meditate on God's more beautiful way. If needed, use these chapters to get yourself into a good habit. Mediate daily on the virtues of goodness, knowledge, self-control, and perseverance so that you can visualize God's more beautiful way (hear His more beautiful song). With each spiritual victory, regardless of how small, you will feel the Spirit's pat on your back, your faith will deepen, your awareness of the spiritual world will awaken, and your fortitude will grow. As long as our convictions are defined by what is prohibitive rather than what is permissible, we will handicap fortitude, but by visualizing the majesty of God's more beautiful way, we increase the fortitude to do what is right, regardless of fairness.

4. Steadfastness: rooted and unshakable.

> Teach the older men to be temperate, worthy of respect, self-controlled, and sound in faith, in love and in endurance. (Titus 2:2)

Assisted-living facilities can be some of the more depressing places on earth because they are largely occupied by people who are awaiting judgment without hope. The elderly are often bitter over what they perceive as the unfair hand that life has dealt them. The majority are often alone, uninspired, unable to repeat failed life stages or mend broken relationships, and destined to live the remainder of their days largely separate from the relationships that mean the most to them.

In contrast, my paternal grandparents spent approximately forty years on the mission field in Cameroon, Africa. When my grandmother entered the final stages of her life, she moved to an assisted-living facility specifically built for retired missionaries. In all of the times I visited, I was struck by the laughter, the voracious conversations between the residents, the stories, the love, and the hope. From that early age, I saw a great contrast between those who had spent their lives in the service of their Savior and those who had lived absent a relationship with Him.

When I am nearing the end of my earthly life, I visualize a few things: faithful children who built their spiritual life on the shoulders of Tami and me, rather than by repeating our mistakes; peace that passes understanding as I await my own judgment; and confidence that I have reflected the character of God more accurately with each passing year. Whether I have a nice house or a shack, a nice car or a clunker, married or a widower, in good health or bad, I want to look more and more like my heavenly Father with each day He grants me. I want Him to be glorified through me while I still have breath in my lungs. I do not know how many more days I have on this earth, but I know that I need to grow daily in my patience, endurance, fortitude, and steadfastness. I know that doing so will require a daily discipline that is inspired by my hope in the One who embodied this virtue more than any other human being who ever walked the earth—Jesus.

A few years ago, I was fortunate enough to visit Rome with Tami and the girls. On one of our last days there, we went to the jail cell in which it is believed that Peter was incarcerated until the day of his death. The cell is subterranean and with a low ceiling, such that an adult could barely stand up. It is dark, dank, and a little smaller than the size of a standard bedroom, with a sloping ceiling on both sides that leaves only the center of the cell for standing upright. There is no toilet or running water, and because the cell is below ground level, it flooded with each rain, causing the sewage that would otherwise be kept in the corner of the room to spread across the floor. Whether it was actually that prison or one similar, I was convicted by the spirit Peter maintained while imprisoned. But what impacted me the most was the location of this jail cell. It sits at the northwest end of the Roman Forum, which extends approximately two thousand feet to the southeast. When we exited the jail and looked to our right, we could see down the length of this enormous forum and visualize the overwhelming majesty it would have had when seen by Peter, with massive colonnades and palaces on each side, the government of Rome operating within, and the whole known world subject to its power.

All that I could think about was the day on which Peter was led from that cell to his own death. I thought about the temptations he must have felt as he was led in chains past this magnificent forum, unnoticed and likely anonymous to anyone but his jailers. I imagine that Satan must have tempted him to think that it had all been for naught as he witnessed the world bustle around him, no one noticing him or caring that he was about to lose his life. It must have struck Peter that the world was going to continue on as if he had never existed. I imagine that, even then, Satan tempted Peter to doubt Jesus and screamed in his head that all Peter had to do to reenter society was to simply deny the lordship of Jesus.

But Peter was steadfast, rooted, and unshakable. His eyes were fixed on the relationship that he had with Jesus, the forgiveness of his previous betrayal, and the gift of conversing directly with the Creator of the universe. Peter may have lacked vision at that moment; he may have wondered what would happen to the church in his absence—we simply do not know. But we do know that he was so in love with Jesus and the beauty of God's virtue that nothing would cause him to betray Jesus now. In fact, history records that Peter did not feel worthy to die like his Lord, and therefore, his last request was to be crucified upside down. But worthiness wasn't the issue, nor was the future of the church. The only thing that mattered to Peter as he passed the Roman Forum on the way to his death was his relationship with the living God. With these thoughts in mind, please take a moment to read Peter's words, likely penned in that very jail cell.

> Peter, an apostle of Jesus Christ, To God's elect, exiles scattered throughout the provinces of Pontus, Galatia, Cappadocia, Asia and Bithynia, who have been chosen according to the foreknowledge of God the Father, through the sanctifying work of the Spirit, to be obedient to Jesus Christ and sprinkled with his blood:
>
> Grace and peace be yours in abundance.
>
> Praise be to the God and Father of our Lord Jesus Christ! In his great mercy he has given us new birth into a living hope through the resurrection of Jesus Christ from the dead, and into an inheritance that can never perish, spoil or fade. This inheritance is kept in heaven for you, who through faith are shielded by God's power until the coming of the salvation that is ready to be revealed in the last time. In all this you greatly rejoice, though now for a little while you may have had to suffer grief in all kinds of trials. These have come so that the proven genuineness of your faith—of greater worth than gold, which perishes even though refined by fire—may result in praise, glory and honor when Jesus Christ is revealed. Though you have not seen him, you love him; and even though you do not see him now, you believe in him and are filled with an inexpressible and glorious joy, for you are receiving the end result of your faith, the salvation of your souls.

Concerning this salvation, the prophets, who spoke of the grace that was to come to you, searched intently and with the greatest care, trying to find out the time and circumstances to which the Spirit of Christ in them was pointing when he predicted the sufferings of the Messiah and the glories that would follow. It was revealed to them that they were not serving themselves but you, when they spoke of the things that have now been told you by those who have preached the gospel to you by the Holy Spirit sent from heaven. Even angels long to look into these things.

Therefore, with minds that are alert and fully sober, set your hope on the grace to be brought to you when Jesus Christ is revealed at his coming. As obedient children, do not conform to the evil desires you had when you lived in ignorance. But just as he who called you is holy, so be holy in all you do; for it is written: "Be holy, because I am holy."

Since you call on a Father who judges each person's work impartially, live out your time as foreigners here in reverent fear. For you know that it was not with perishable things such as silver or gold that you were redeemed from the empty way of life handed down to you from your ancestors, but with the precious blood of Christ, a lamb without blemish or defect. He was chosen before the creation of the world, but was revealed in these last times for your sake. Through him you believe in God, who raised him from the dead and glorified him, and so your faith and hope are in God.

Now that you have purified yourselves by obeying the truth so that you have sincere love for each other, love one another deeply, from the heart. For you have been born again, not of perishable seed, but of imperishable, through the living and enduring word of God. For, "All people are like grass, and all their glory is like the flowers of the field; the grass withers and the flowers fall, but the word of the Lord endures forever." And this is the word that was preached to you. (1 Peter 1:1–25)

Brothers and sisters, what good are goodness, knowledge, and self-control if we fail to persevere? I hope that you see that no one virtue is better than another; they are all inter-reliant (something we will look at more in depth in a later chapter). Each one of these virtues is a quality of your heavenly Father, embodied in Jesus as an example for us. I pray that you see the great wisdom of the apostle Peter when he instructs us to "make every effort" to add these virtues to our faith.

Let's close out our lesson on perseverance in the book of James. To ingest the fullness of these words, I would ask you to remember that they likely were written by Jesus's physical brother. Therefore, James would have known Jesus as a child, watched Him discover God, fall in love with God, surrender everything this life had to offer to God, and endure the greatest possible suffering for God. There are so many elements of Jesus's life on earth over which James could have justifiably been bitter, not the least of which include how the world treated his oldest brother, how his brother was unable to leave behind offspring, or that God allowed his brother to carry the sin of the world on His shoulders. Instead, these are James's words:

Consider it pure joy, my brothers and sisters, whenever you face trials of many kinds, because you know that the testing of your faith produces perseverance. Let perseverance finish its work so that you may be mature and complete, not lacking anything. If any of you lacks wisdom, you should ask God, who gives generously to all without finding fault, and it will be given to you. But when you ask, you must believe and not doubt, because the one who doubts is like a wave of the sea, blown and tossed by the wind. That person should not expect to receive anything from the Lord. Such a person is double-minded and unstable in all they do.

Believers in humble circumstances ought to take pride in their high position. But the rich should take pride in their humiliation—since they will pass away like a wild flower. For the sun rises with scorching heat and withers the plant; its blossom falls and its beauty is destroyed. In the same way, the rich will fade away even while they go about their business.

Blessed is the one who perseveres under trial because, having stood the test, that person will receive the crown of life that the Lord has promised to those who love him.

When tempted, no one should say, "God is tempting me." For God cannot be tempted by evil, nor does he tempt anyone; but each person is tempted when they are dragged away by their own evil desire and enticed. Then, after desire has conceived, it gives birth to sin; and sin, when it is full-grown, gives birth to death.

Don't be deceived, my dear brothers and sisters. Every good and perfect gift is from above, coming down from the Father of the heavenly lights, who does not change like shifting shadows. He chose to give us birth through the word of truth, that we might be a kind of firstfruits of all he created. (James 1:2–18)

Chapter 7

GODLINESS

BROTHERS AND SISTERS, WE HAVE PASSED THE MIDPOINT IN OUR exploration of God's more beautiful way. On a personal note, the years I've spent preparing these lessons on virtue-based Christianity have been transformative for me, and I pray that your relationship with God is making notable strides from prohibition to freedom, from a duty of surrender to a willing sacrifice compelled by friendship (John 15:15). I pray also that you more accurately see Jesus as the same God we will meet face-to-face on judgment day, just while inhabiting our flesh. Although the Bible also confirms that Jesus is God's Son, we will be greatly hindered in our comprehension of God's character if we limit our understanding of Jesus to only that of a son and fail to understand that He is also God in the flesh (John 14:6–7). And that is a good segue for this lesson on *godliness*.

Before we begin this chapter, I ask you to consider the following, which I share in an effort to help us to process what we are learning in a manner that best paves the road for effective and long-term change. Because of our culture's tendency toward prohibition, punishment, and consequence, there is no doubt in my mind that some of you may feel guilty over a lack of matching up in one or more of the virtues we have studied and, as a result, have become overwhelmed. Others may deal with this guilt or feelings of being overwhelmed by justifying reasons why embodying virtue is an unrealistic expectation. And some likely make every effort to add these virtues to their lives but have trouble overcoming the discouragement they feel over repeated failures. None of these is an accurate or productive way to view the journey on which God has us.

How should we process the deficiencies that we identify in our walk with God? It helps to understand that *every spiritual or moral opinion we have falls into one of two categories*. It is either formed in Christ, which means that it accurately reflects God's perspective, or it is "misformed," meaning that it does not align with God's perspective. Areas on which we don't have an opinion are, for the purposes of this discussion, called unformed. Unformed concepts aside, any spiritual opinion we do hold is either formed or misformed.

In the last chapter, we discussed how, as parents, we do not expect perfection from our children because we know that their time with us spans an almost two-decade journey, during which we teach them why right is right and wrong is wrong, how to perceive and process the world around them, how to rebound from mistakes, how to seek and offer forgiveness, how to restore relationships, how to handle failure, and many other essential life skills. Similarly, you too are on a lifelong journey with your heavenly Father. God knows every area where your thinking is not aligned with His. He knows which of your misformed opinions are the result of your upbringing, which is the result of your culture, which is driven by deeply held selfish beliefs and which is simply the result of your trying to figure out how to handle what life throws at you. God also knows each area where you are still unformed (Psalm 103:13-14).

Let me give you a practical example of these terms. Imagine that a young man grows up in a household where his father routinely yells at his mother and throws things across the house when angry, creating terror in the young man and his mother. As a result, this young man decides early on that he will never handle his future marriage in that manner because he knows instinctually that it is wrong, and he sees the hurt his father's behavior causes his mom. But years into his own marriage, this young man finds himself growing more distant from his wife because he has spent his marriage stuffing his frustrations, having committed himself to never act on his anger. As this man begins to study biblical virtue, he realizes that he is misformed on how to handle his anger and unformed on how to effectively communicate with his wife. With this knowledge in hand, he has a number of options. For one, he can give in to feeling like a failure and convince himself that he is incapable of change. Another option is to justify his actions by comparing himself with his own father. On the other hand, he can commit to aligning his misformed thoughts with God's and turn to the Bible for guidance on unformed areas.

If he chooses the third option, he should know that this change won't happen overnight. He will need people to help him to identify the triggers of his anger. He will need to figure out why those triggers result in anger. He will need help learning to communicate with his wife in a godly way, and he must accept that he will mess up many times. It would be helpful if his spouse understood what caused his misformed and unformed thoughts so that she can be his helpmate in making these changes. But in order to be vulnerable with his spouse, he needs to trust her to respect him if he is open with her about these areas. He also needs reassurance that she won't use this intimate knowledge against him or hold it over him.

What God wants from this husband is the commitment to put one foot in front of the other with a singular goal in mind: becoming like God. God already knows about his past and future failures. God knows at which points he will be tempted to quit. God knows every detail about this man's future circumstances. Nonetheless, God wants him to be uncompromising in his goal of becoming like God, while simultaneously accepting that it takes time to learn new ways of thinking and behaving. Missteps and setbacks are acceptable and expected, but quitting is what steps us out of the proverbial waterfall we previously discussed (1 John 1:7–9).

I am asking you to trust God enough to allow Him to reveal the truth regarding how you feel about each aspect of the virtues we are studying and to what degree you honestly embody them. When you see an area of a particular virtue that is misformed or unformed, then I would encourage you to write it down in a journal. Meditate on where your errant thinking originated or developed. Include your spouse in this process. Be open with brothers or sisters you trust, and then make a commitment to go after it. Make every effort to take that virtue as your own, knowing that this kind of change does not come overnight.

The outward sins we put off early in our conversion experience required one process with its own set of challenges, but it is a different process for a more mature Christian who is identifying misformed and unformed thoughts and committing to change behavioral habits and habits of the heart and mind. The former is largely driven out of a fear of eternal condemnation and a desire for God's forgiveness. The latter requires a desire to become like God that is motivated by the security of an ever-deepening relationship with Him that is driven by an increasing knowledge of who God actually is.

You are on a journey on which every step of every day is orchestrated by God. Nothing happens that He has not allowed. No temptation has come upon you without His providing you with a way of escape (1 Corinthians 10:13). No suffering is by accident. *Everything has been incorporated into His plan to draw you closer to Him and for you to become like Him.* None of us knows what God has planned for us in this life or in the next. As we begin our study of godliness, it is time that each of us commits to looking at ourselves intently in God's mirror and committing to tackling any area where we find ourselves reflecting anything other than Him. This is a high calling and an incredible privilege.

Now let's turn our attention to the virtue of godliness. The Greek word for *godliness* is εὐσέβειαν (pronounced *eusebeian* in English). It stems from the word εὐσεβής, which means "pious" and is a combination of two words: εὐ, which means "well," and σέβας, which means "reverence." It means to perform the actions appropriate to God. In addition, the root σέβ- is connected to the concepts of danger and flight and thus the sense of reverence originally described in fear of God. It speaks of the duty that man owes to God. It means sacred awe and reverence, especially in actions.

That is a meaty definition. In order to effectively digest the virtue of godliness, let's begin by highlighting two primary characteristics. First—and most important—godliness is the result of the combination of goodness, knowledge, self-control, and perseverance and a cause of mutual affection. Second, godliness is to perform the actions appropriate to God.

I wrestled for a month with this chapter, as I did not want to misspeak on anything related to this pivotal virtue that denotes godlikeness. The more I researched, the more overwhelmed I became with the task at hand. Godliness is a deep and rich virtue that is the culmination of its precursor virtues and the tipping point at which the purpose of our very being on this earth aligns itself with that of the Creator of the universe. After much prayer and numerous revisions, I have decided to break this chapter into four components: (1) the path to godliness, (2) the outward effect of godliness, (3) the internal power of godliness, and (4) the privilege of godliness. Although placed early in this chapter, this paragraph is actually the last I'm writing on this subject. I do feel that although godliness is so rich that it is only possible to scratch the surface, I am faithful that this chapter has at least put bookends in place and sufficiently describes the concepts within, such that it will create a foundation for a lifetime of deeper study. With at that in mind, let's dive in.

1.   The path to godliness

I pray that you share my excitement in discovering more complete meanings of God's words, and I expect that doing so is bringing 2 Peter 1:5–8 to life in unexpected but logical ways. You see, it makes perfect sense that someone who is adding to his faith each of the four virtues Peter has thus far listed would now have an identifiable form of godliness to those around him. To further confirm this point, consider that in the original Greek, the words translated in our theme scripture as "and to" are more accurately translated as "and in." It is not that the translation "and to" is incorrect; it simply lacks the more complete meaning. It is therefore likely that what God is really communicating to us is that every virtue that Peter listed is both inter-reliant with the previous and the foundation of the next.

If the original Greek was translated word for word, without a scholarly interpretation, 2 Peter 1:5–7 would actually read, "Bring in supply in the faith of you, goodness; and in goodness, knowledge; and in knowledge, self-control; and in self-control, perseverance; and in perseverance, godliness; and in godliness, mutual affection; and in mutual affection, love." Contrast that with the New International Version translation, which reads,

> Make every effort to add to your faith goodness; and to goodness, knowledge; and to knowledge, self-control; and to self-control, perseverance; and to perseverance, godliness; and to godliness, mutual affection; and to mutual affection, love.

I am not inferring in the slightest that the scholars who worked on the NIV were errant, only that it is sometimes helpful to see the original construction of these sentences because doing so can often highlight something that we might otherwise not see. The NIV translation can appear to infer that we are to add each virtue to the previous, but the original Greek makes clear that each virtue actually emerges from and is rooted in the previous—a small but significant difference in meaning.

Think of it this way: beginning to understand God's goodness drives a desire to more intimately know Him (gnōsis). An ever-increasing knowledge of Him drives us to put God's passions ahead of our own and a willingness to surrender our thoughts to Him because intimacy is foundational for trust. It also motivates us to flee temptation since we do not want to hurt the one with whom we are falling more in love. From that conscious exercise of self-control emerges perseverance, which builds with each passing spiritual success. We also learn to be patient with God as our trust is built through ever-increasing intimacy, and we learn to view suffering as an essential ingredient to fully understanding our heavenly Father. These breed endurance, and endurance combined with goodness, knowledge, self-control, steadfastness, fortitude, and a mustard seed of faith all come together to produce in us a form of godliness. Peter is also confirming for us what was spoken by James, who states that faith alone is insufficient (James 2:14–17). It must be accompanied by a journey in which we strive to be molded to reflect our heavenly Father.

In Western culture, we sometimes associate godliness with aloofness, and sometimes we associate godliness with a position of status in the church. But God says that godliness has nothing to do with talent, natural or spiritual gifts, a position in church leadership, or the mystique of the aloof. Rather, godliness is the culmination of specific virtues built upon each other. People who do not understand which virtues comprise godliness often misconstrue other qualities in people as godliness, but true godliness is never mistaken by God. For God knows those who are His (2 Timothy 2:19).

I have many friends, but there is no lack of clarity in my mind on which friends are my most intimate relationships. Why would it be any different with God? He is fully aware of those who are making every effort to know Him and to embody His character as their own. Many Israelites missed the Messiah when He was standing directly in front of them because they were associating godliness with military might and political leadership. Let us be the ones who accurately wear the name Christian (little Christ) and place righteousness (relationship) with God above any other endeavor (Matthew 6:33).

This journey to godliness is also discussed in Titus 1:1–3, which states:

> Paul, a servant of God and an apostle of Jesus Christ
> to further the faith of God's elect and their knowledge
> of the truth that leads to godliness—in the hope of
> eternal life, which God, who dies not lie, promised
> before the beginning of time, and which now at his

appointed season he has brought to light through the preaching entrusted to me by the command of God our Savior.

Here, Paul affirms for Titus what we are learning in 2 Peter. The furtherance of one's faith includes knowledge of truth that leads to godliness, and our hope lies in eternal life, where we will finally be with the object of our affection. God chose the time for the apostles to reveal the mystery of the path to godliness that the prophets longed to see but which had been kept hidden from them.

> If I am delayed, you will know how people ought to conduct themselves in God's household, which is the church of the living God, the pillar and foundation of the truth. Beyond all question, the mystery from which true godliness springs is great: He appeared in the flesh, was vindicated by the Spirit, was seen by angels, was preached among the nations, was believed on in the world, was taken up in glory. (1 Timothy 3:15–16)

Brothers and sisters, godliness is a mystery because it simply cannot be obtained absent an ever-deepening relationship with God Himself. Over time in a healthy marriage, a husband and wife fall more and more in love, as they discover more about each other, experience the best of life together, witness each other wrestle with character sin, seek forgiveness from each other, work together, endure suffering together, confront life together, raise children together, share financial victories and hardships together, sacrifice together, etc. Many years into these marriages, spouses complete each other's sentences, know each other's thoughts, and communicate volumes to each other with nothing more than a look, and with every passing year, the two become more one. Marriage provides us with a physical example of the path to godliness. With each passing year, God's plan is that you discover more about Him, experience life with Him, seek forgiveness from him, work alongside Him, suffer with Him, confront challenges with Him by your side, manage His money, sacrifice for His desires while He fulfills yours, and, over time, become one with Him (Ephesians 5:31–32).

Peter is pleading with us in 2 Peter 1:5–8 to heed his advice on how to discover the mystery from which true godliness springs. You cannot shortcut the process to godliness. You cannot put godliness on as a mask. It must be built on a relationship that includes understanding God's goodness, which inspires an intimate knowledge, which results in self-control, which produces perseverance. Any other form of godliness denies its very power. We are so blessed to live in a time where the complete Bible is so readily available to each of us. We are able to look at it in its entirety and discover the mysteries that the prophets could only see pieces of. Let's not squander the indescribable privilege we have of embodying a more complete form of godliness so that our Savior may be more accurately seen by the nations and believed in by those seeking and that we may join Him in His glory.

2. The outward effect of godliness

> While the man held on to Peter and John, all the people were astonished and came running to them in the place called Solomon's Colonnade. When Peter saw this, he said to them: "Fellow Israelites, why does this surprise you? Why do you stare at us as if by our own power or godliness we had made this man walk? (Acts 3:11–12)

It is interesting that the Israelites clearly identified godliness in Peter and John. In fact, it was such a powerful trait in Peter and John that the people thought their godliness may have resulted in the healing of the beggar.

To date, we have looked at God's goodness, His knowledge, His self-control, and his perseverance. We have explored what these very traits should look like in one who claims to be a Christian, which literally means "little Christ." We have also discussed how the world admires the virtues listed in 2 Peter, yet it does not recognize that those virtues come from God. But as we approach godliness, we will see a departure from the world's admiration. For once goodness, knowledge, self-control, and perseverance are combined to form godliness, it appears from scripture that this is the tipping point where the world becomes overwhelmed and intimidated, and persecution often begins.

For those of us who struggle with a desire to please people, this can be a challenge. For as we begin to embody the virtue of godliness, we take on an identifiable form of holiness, which means that our thinking and behavior begin to be noticeably separated from the world. This is a challenge that cannot be overstated. It is not easy to simply "behave like God" when you are trying to balance godliness with relatability and without appearing judgmental or condescending.

First, we must understand that our true motivation is key. Those who are still primarily motivated by fear of consequence or punishment will be handicapped in this journey because spiritual insecurity is like kryptonite to embodying godliness. Second, we need not to simply "behave like God." Rather, we need to make every effort to focus our attention on embodying the virtues of goodness, knowledge, self-control, and perseverance.

Those who do will discover two distinct truths: First, having these specific virtues in mind when encountering life situations is easier and more practical than telling yourself to be more "godly," which can be nonspecific and overwhelming. For example, when we find ourselves in a situation where gossip is occurring, consider how much more practical it can be to focus on goodness by finding the best in people—the way that God sees them; to make sure that our words are rooted in true knowledge of the individual; to exercise self-control over our emotions and frustrations; and to remain steadfast in our commitment to bettering the relationships involved—to bring them back to righteousness. One who approaches this situation through the lens of specific virtue will embody godliness without ever having focused on it.

Second, focusing on each of these virtues will cause you to fall more and more in love with the character of God. The desire to please the love of your life will cause you to become emboldened and empowered to reflect God, regardless of the world's reaction. In fact, those who focus on applying specific virtues to challenging situations will sometimes even find encouragement and affirmation in the world's negative response. Read Jesus's words below, paying special attention to the italicized verse.

> Blessed are you when people insult you, persecute you and falsely say all kinds of evil against you because of me. Rejoice and be glad, because great is your reward in heaven, for in the same way they persecuted the prophets who were before you. "You are the salt of the earth. But if the salt loses its saltiness, how can it be made salty again? It is no longer good for anything, except to be thrown out and trampled underfoot. "You are the light of the world. A town built on a hill cannot be hidden. Neither do people light a lamp and put it under a bowl. Instead they put it on its stand, and it gives light to everyone in the house. *In the same way, let your light shine before others, that they may see your good deeds and glorify your Father in heaven.* (Matthew 5:11–16, italics added)

This is godliness.

When my children were young, we worked diligently with them on goodness, which encompassed kindness and the consideration of others. We worked intently with them on their relationship with us and with each other and made sure that we did not allow any unresolved conflict (little foxes) to reside within our family fellowship. We worked consistently with them on self-control, strength of character, not quitting, and enduring hardship. And do you know what? The world was very impressed with our children. Playmates would tell their parents that they couldn't wait to play with the Ryter kids. Parents would go out of their way to compliment our children's behavior and respectfulness.

But as our children got older and they began to incorporate Jesus's instructions in Matthew 18 regarding conflict resolution, they found that some other children didn't know how to process these conversations emotionally or respond biblically. When our children would redirect a conversation among friends that was turning to gossip or an inappropriate topic, these other children began to find times and places that excluded our kids from conversations. The very character traits that the world had admired in our children were suddenly becoming too much for them to handle. These other children did not know how to react to confrontation. A surprising number of them did not know how to react to godliness. The more some of their friends' lives became defined by sinful discussions, thoughts, and pursuits, the more uncomfortable those children became with ones who were exhibiting godliness.

Don't think for a second that this didn't deeply hurt my children's feelings. We have spent hundreds of hours in conversation with our kids, trying to help them process the effects of godliness on relationships. And I will tell you that those hours of helping my children to appropriately process this part of the Christian experience *are the difference* between them becoming callous toward the lost and bitter toward God and their developing a compassion, empathy, and understanding for the lost and a kinship with God.

The primary motivator of godliness must be a passion to honor God by becoming like Him, and the secondary motivator must be such a deep love for the preciousness of others that we will withstand the negative effects of godliness, if only to provide a path to salvation for one (see Matthew 22:37–40). We will soon see that this is why godliness falls in a very specific place among Peter's list of seven virtues.

What I have described here with my children is what happens as one becomes godly, regardless of age. But how magnificent is

God's plan that He does not intend for us to endure the effects of godliness until we first come in contact with His goodness, develop an intimate relationship with Him, learn self-control, and gain strength of character, endurance, and steadfastness. Just as my children were afforded a timeline on which they could become good, develop intimacy with their mom and me, and learn self-control and perseverance before having to deal with the relational separation caused by their conviction, so too does God offer that time of relational development to us. Tragically, too many of us rush to appear godly in a good-hearted effort to display God to the world, but we reflect an errant view of godliness that is not built on goodness, knowledge, self-control, and perseverance. As a result, our version of godliness lacks power and our lives are more reflective of being tied to Ulysses's mast, rather than enjoying Odysseus's more beautiful song.

Regardless of where you are today, let's pause, respond to Peter's plea to learn the more beautiful song, and then continue on our journey with the motivation and passion that God has made available to all of His children.

> I urge, then, first of all, that petitions, prayers, intercession and thanksgiving be made for all people— for kings and all those in authority, that we may live peaceful and quiet lives in all godliness and holiness. This is good, and pleases God our Savior, who wants all people to be saved and to come to a knowledge of the truth. (1 Timothy 2:1–4)

Here again we see godliness and holiness together, and we are reminded that godliness and holiness are similar, in that they both highlight a clear separation from the world. In fact, there is no definition for the word *godliness* in most topical Bibles; rather, you will be redirected to the words *holiness* and *righteousness*, for godliness is the culmination of the two. Allow that to sink in for a moment. The virtues we have looked at thus far in this book are the path to righteousness (uninhibited and purified relationship with God) that culminates in a Christian reflecting the very character of God, which results in a clear separation from the world, which is holiness. Consider Ephesians 4:22–24, which reads,

> You were taught, with regard to your former way of life, to put off your old self, which is being corrupted by its deceitful desires; to be made new in the attitude of your minds; and to put on the new self, created to be like God in true righteousness and holiness.

Read Jesus's prayer in John 17:

> My prayer is not for them alone. I pray also for those who will believe in me through their message, that all of them may be one, Father, just as you are in me and I am in you. May they also be in us so that the world may believe that you have sent me. I have given them the glory that you gave me, that they may be one as we are one—I in them and you in me—so that they may be brought to compete unity. Then the world will know that you sent me and have loved them even as you have loved me. (John 17:20–23)

Do you see it? As you embody God's goodness, knowledge, self-control, and perseverance, you become more like God. And in doing this, you become a modern-day confirmation that Jesus was the Messiah, through which your neighbors can find redemption. Godliness denotes becoming like God, and you cannot become like God if you are not making every effort to add His virtues to your every fiber. Those in the world may possess a form of goodness, knowledge, self-control, or perseverance. But when these virtues (as God defines them) come together in a single person, a godliness emerges that cannot be reproduced by the world.

As a result, there is no need to boast of godliness for godliness speaks for itself. It is clearly noticeable by the world, even if those in the world are blind to the specific virtues coming together to form it. We must also guard against Satan's temptation—or that of our own pride—to think that we must present a certain level of togetherness to the world, lest we put on masks that hide our true selves in an effort to display what we think Christ should look like. Instead, we should make every effort to embody virtue, which includes the vulnerability and openness of knowledge, so that godliness will be perceived as God working through us, rather than our presenting a facade to try to appear more like God than we actually are (2 Corinthians 12:9).

It bears repeating: there are no shortcuts to godliness. If we skip the pursuit of virtue and put on a mask of godliness, we are left with something that might appear to be godliness but lacks any power. And what is that power? It's the power to see people in the way God sees them. It's the power to interpret world events as God does. It's the power to expend our energy in areas important to God and avoid foolish controversies and arguments. It's the power that leads to true biblical peace and pure joy. It's the power of comfort in affliction. It's the power of freedom in surrender. It's the power of confidence at the judgment. It is the power to reflect the characteristics of the God, who formed everything. If we are lacking in any of these areas, then all praise be to our heavenly Father, who has given us the road map to godliness and made it available to all of His children, regardless of natural talent, spiritual gifts, innate IQ, or upbringing.

3.   The internal power of godliness

We have thus far explored the power of godliness on those around us, but we would be remiss if we did not spend some time on the impact of godliness on the person striving to embody it. The first thing we see is that godliness produces a mindset.

> Those who have believing masters should not show
> them disrespect just because they are fellow believers.

Instead, they should serve them even better because their masters are dear to them as fellow believers and are devoted to the welfare of their slaves.

These are the things you are to teach and insist on. If anyone teaches otherwise and does not agree to the sound instruction of our Lord Jesus Christ and to godly teaching, they are conceited and understand nothing. They have an unhealthy interest in controversies and quarrels about words that result in envy, strife, malicious talk, evil suspicions and constant friction between people of corrupt mind, who have been robbed of the truth and who think that godliness is a means to financial gain.

But godliness with contentment is great gain. For we brought nothing into the world, and we can take nothing out of it. But if we have food and clothing, we will be content with that. Those who want to get rich fall into temptation and a trap and into many foolish and harmful desires that plunge people into ruin and destruction. For the love of money is a root of all kinds of evil. Some people, eager for money, have wandered from the faith and pierced themselves with many griefs.

But you, man of God, flee from all this, and pursue righteousness, godliness, faith, love, endurance and gentleness. Fight the good fight of the faith. Take hold of the eternal life to which you were called when you made your good confession in the presence of many witnesses. In the sight of God, who gives life to everything, and of Christ Jesus, who while testifying before Pontius Pilate made the good confession, I charge you to keep this command without spot or blame until the appearing of our Lord Jesus Christ, which God will bring about in his own time---God, the blessed and only Ruler, the King of kings and

Lord of lords, who alone is immortal and who lives in unapproachable light, whom no one has seen or can see. To him be honor and might forever. Amen.

Command those who are rich in this present world not to be arrogant nor to put their hope in wealth, which is so uncertain, but to put their hope in God, who richly provides us with everything for our enjoyment. *Command them to do good, to be rich in good deeds, and to be generous and willing to share. In this way they will lay up treasure for themselves as a firm foundation for the coming age, so that they may take hold of the life that is truly life.*

Timothy, guard what has been entrusted to your care. Turn away from godless chatter and the opposing ideas of what is falsely called knowledge, which some have professed and in so doing have departed from the faith. Grace be with you all. (1 Timothy 6:2–21, emphasis added)

I love this scripture, for it begs us to elevate our thinking above what we believe is fair and just and instead remember the role God has given us. On our own, we had failed abominably and were destined for eternal separation from our heavenly Father. But God became a man, not only to purchase us with His own blood but to provide us an example of what He looks like in the flesh so that we can imitate Him. He wants us to live by virtue, whether we are slaves or free. He wants us to avoid foolish controversies and unhealthy interests.

Not only does this scripture beg us to elevate our thinking, but it informs us that godliness includes a mindset that emanates from the culmination of virtue. There is simply no way that we can avoid getting sucked into the quagmire of political arguments or the temptation to sit in judgment of and legislate morality on a fallen world unless we are growing in virtue that results in a godly perspective. There is no way to avoid unhealthy interests unless our interests are becoming aligned with God's. Absent the right perspective, we can be so fickle in our thinking and easily persuaded. We find ourselves becoming discontented and making comments on how much better it was for previous generations, all the while forgetting that in the not-too-distant past, society forced blacks and whites to use separate bathrooms and drinking fountains. In the not-too-distant past, women were not considered equal with men. In the not-too-distant past, we lost millions, rather than thousands, in world wars. We can pontificate on how good it used to be for the middle class, while completely blind to the fact that an average middle-class home in 1957 was 1,300 square feet, and the average middle-class family owned a single automobile, one home radio, and no televisions. All of these fixations are unhealthy interests.

Instead, we need a godly perspective. God controls the impacts of world leaders, even if those leaders are immoral. God is able to bring good out of natural disasters, famines, recessions, and depressions for those He loves. But we who are becoming goodness by fixating on transparency and surrendering every thought to God *have nothing to fear and everything to give.* We should exhibit calm in our workplace. We should be confident regarding world leaders and fearless in the face of world events because we know that they are all subject to the One who knows us and calls us by His name.

Next, we see that ungodliness is displayed by its focus. Consider 2 Timothy 3:1–5, which states:

> But mark this: There will be terrible times in the last days. People will be lovers of themselves, lovers of money, boastful, proud, abusive, disobedient to their parents, ungrateful, unholy, without love, unforgiving, slanderous, without self-control, brutal, not lovers of the good, treacherous, rash, conceited, lovers of pleasure rather than lovers of God—having a form of godliness but denying its power. Have nothing to do with such people.

Just as godliness includes a mindset that mirrors God's perspective of this world's trials and timelines, ungodliness is revealed by what you focus on. It is easy to look at this passage as a list of sins, but what if we looked at it as describing those who lack virtue? Those who are lovers of themselves are those who lack an ever-growing intimate knowledge of God's goodness. Those who love money are those who fail to exercise the self-control to make their every thought subject to the mind of God. Those who are boastful are those who lack knowledge of their true selves and their rightful places in God's creation. Those who are abusive are those who lack the *mutual affection* that proceeds from godliness—and the list goes on. I cannot imagine how God feels when those who claim publicly to be Christian refuse to be like Christ (Ezekiel 36:20–21).

Those who put on a mask of godliness without first embodying God's virtue are not generating a return in this life or the next. They may be active evangelistically. They may attend every meeting of the church body. They may be known for being reliable contributors and have many friends within the congregation. But if they are not making every effort to understand virtue and then embody it, as to reflect their heavenly Father, then their godliness is without power.

I beg God that as you have been studying these lessons, you have fallen more in love with the true character of your spiritual Father, and that, as a result, you also have felt a motivation to be like Him, which you may not have previously experienced. If so, then you are experiencing the effects of solid food. Those who continue to live on milk, motivated only by the fear of consequence and punishment, cannot experience the power that comes from godliness because that power is rooted in the love of virtue. But to those who make every effort to embody the character of the Creator of the universe by burying themselves in His virtue, there is no end to their spiritual growth and impact.

Peter, who wrote our theme scripture, sums up the necessity for the pursuit of virtue in the passage below with two descriptors: *holiness* and *godliness*. If you have godliness, then you have holiness, and if you have godliness, then you also will have mutual affection and love (our last two virtues).

> Since everything will be destroyed in this way, what kind of people ought you to be? You ought to live holy and godly lives as you look forward to the day of God and speed its coming. That day will bring about the destruction of the heavens by fire, and the elements will melt in the heat. But in keeping with his promise we are looking forward to a new heaven and a new earth, where righteousness dwells. So then, dear friends, since you are looking forward to this, *make every effort to be found spotless, blameless and at peace with him.* Bear in mind that our Lord's patience means salvation, just as our dear brother Paul also wrote you with the wisdom that God gave him. He writes the same way in all his letters, speaking in them of these matters. His letters contain some things that are hard to understand, which ignorant and unstable people distort, as they do the other Scriptures, to their own destruction. Therefore, dear friends, since you have been forewarned, be on your guard so that you may not be carried away by the error of the lawless and fall from your secure position. But grow in the grace and knowledge of our Lord and Savior Jesus Christ. To him be glory both now and forever! Amen. (2 Peter 3:11–18, emphasis added)

4. The privilege of godliness

> Have nothing to do with godless myths and old wives' tales; rather, train yourself to be godly. For physical training is of some value, but godliness has value for all things, holding promise for both the present life and the life to come. This is a trustworthy saying that

> deserves full acceptance. That is why we labor and
> strive, because we have put our hope in the living
> God, who is the Savior of all people, and especially
> of those who believe. (1 Timothy 4:7–10)

I would like to highlight two things in the above passage of scripture. First is a reminder that virtue is not obtained via osmosis. It cannot be attained simply by reading these chapters or listening to sermons. It requires personal training, and that training has a payoff, both in this life and the next. What are those payoffs? In this life, as we have discussed, pursuing virtue results in confidence in our salvation, an ever-deepening conversational relationship with our heavenly Father, true peace, pure joy, godly perspectives, becoming less so that He can become more, spiritual endurance and fortitude, a purpose in suffering, and a hope in Christ.

Paul reminds Timothy that our endurance is inspired by hope; he also reminds him that God is not only the Savior of the saved, but "He is the Savior of all people, especially to those of us who have faith in Him." I simply cannot state this enough. When you are making strides to embody goodness—becoming vulnerable so that others can see God's power at work within you, surrendering yourself and your thoughts to the mind of God, increasing your endurance, strengthening your fortitude, and growing in patience—then you are becoming godly, *and that is noticeable to those around you who are still suffering without hope.* Your godliness can overwhelm them. It can intimidate them. But it also does something that none of us can do on our own: it puts on display for them what the power of God has done in our lives and, therefore, what the power of God can do in their lives. And therein lies the concept of reverence (σέβ) that is contained within the definition of the word itself.

Second, according to Paul, godliness is a spiritual currency, and that currency may be spent both here and in the life to come. In the life to come, that currency will be cashed in when we recognize God and He recognizes us on the day the world is judged. But where should we spend this currency while still here? Jesus states in

John 15:5, "I and the vine and you are the branches. If you remain in me and I in you, you will bear much fruit; apart from me you can do nothing." We often take this verse to mean that if you pray enough, you will convert the lost. While this is certainly an element of what Jesus is describing, it is so much more than that. The only source of nutrients for the branch is the vine. The branch cannot photosynthesize; it cannot gather nutrients from the soil; in fact, it cannot do anything except take the nutrients supplied from the vine and transfer them to the leaves and fruit. In other words, the branch is a perfect conduit for the vine. It doesn't get to select which nutrients it carries; it simply takes whatever the vine gives it and transfers it.

Is that how you view yourself as a Christian? Do you see yourself as someone who is tasked with absorbing every last drop of what Jesus provides you through His spirit and His words and then meticulously transferring that to those around you who are in need? The Bible doesn't use the word *evangelize* or the phrase *invite to church*. Rather, it says to "share your faith," "make disciples," and to be godly. Has your pursuit of goodness compelled you to share your faith to help others find their heavenly Father? Has your intimate knowledge of God compelled you to reveal yourself to those with whom you are sharing your faith, as well as prompting you to self-control? Has your self-control produced a steadfastness and endurance? Has your perseverance rounded out your godliness? That is what it means to remain in the vine, and those who do so are guaranteed to produce much fruit—healthy fruit, a fruit that will last. Only then will the sharing of our faith result in the full understanding of every good thing we have in Christ (Philemon 6). Is there a greater privilege than revealing God to His lost children? Is there a greater place we could spend our spiritual currency than in buying back God's lost sons and daughters?

SUMMARY

Brothers and sisters, if you feel stale in your spiritual walk—unfruitful, unmotivated, or lacking passion, love, compassion, or empathy—then you need to make every effort to add virtue to your life. Too many Christians who are in a spiritual slump fear God's disappointment and ensuing punishment. Fixation on these outcomes leads to spiritual insecurity, feeling like a failure, and doubting God's promises in one's life, including the promise of salvation. While it is helpful from time to time to receive a proverbial kick in the rear, most Christians need to begin—or restart—their transition from milk to solid food in the manner that Peter describes. Let's commit together to the passionate pursuit of goodness, knowledge, self-control, perseverance, and godliness so that we can excel in mutual affection and love in a manner that reflects God in the way He desires to be revealed to a lost world. This is part of the mystery that the prophets could not see because they could neither see nor comprehend God in the flesh. Let us ensure that we who are privileged to see God in the flesh will make every effort to become godly (Godlike) and accurately wear the name we have been given, Christian.

> For in Christ *all the fullness of the Deity lives in bodily form, and in Christ you have been brought to fullness.* He is the head over every power and authority. In him you were also circumcised with a circumcision not performed by human hands. Your whole self ruled by the flesh was put off when you were circumcised by Christ, having been buried with him in baptism, in which you were also raised with him through your faith in the working of God, who raised him from the dead. When you were dead in your sins and in the uncircumcision of your flesh, God made you alive with Christ. He forgave us all our sins, having canceled the charge of our legal indebtedness, which stood against us and condemned us; he has taken it

away, nailing it to the cross. And having disarmed the powers and authorities, he made a public spectacle of them, triumphing over them by the cross. (Colossians 2:9–15)

What magnificent imagery! All the fullness of God lives within the bodily form of Jesus. But it doesn't stop there. You are being brought to fullness in Christ. How? First by a circumcision done by Christ through baptism but then by the indescribable privilege of imitating God in bodily form by wrapping yourself in His virtue and allowing that to drive you to the finish line. My passion is that, by the end of this book, you will be inspired and equipped to become as God already sees you and that in doing so, you may truly enjoy His favor without inhibition in this life and the next.

I'll close with the following anecdote: I recently spoke with a brother who, along with his wife, has spent the last twenty years investing in the moral development of his children. He has done this by modeling godliness for his children, as well as instructing them in the way they should go. Not long before our conversation, he and his teenage son arrived at a store to pick up a medical device and receive some instruction on its use. Because the father had just come out of shoulder surgery and also was confined to a wheelchair as a paraplegic, he had called ahead and let the store employee know that his teenage son would be coming in on his behalf. He asked the employee to telephone him with any questions his son was unable to answer. Approximately fifteen minutes after arriving at the store, the son returned to the car with the medical device—but also with a store employee. When the father rolled the window down to interact with the store clerk, the clerk said, "Sir, I was so impressed with your son that I was compelled to meet you. Whatever you are doing at home, please keep it up."

Brothers and sisters, I cannot think of a more perfect metaphor for godliness, and I am not speaking here of our children. Rather, we are to strive with every fiber of our beings to understand and adopt God's virtues so that we accurately reflect His image. When we do, those whom God brings into our lives will be compelled to meet our heavenly Father after having seen glimpses of Him through us.

Let us close this chapter by recapping where we have traveled thus far. There is a spiritual law at work here that is as valid and inescapable as the law of gravity, which is that those who first understand and then work to embody God's goodness will be compelled to pursue an intimacy with our spiritual Father, which will incentivize them to control themselves in thought and action, which will train perseverance, which will produce godliness and holiness. Each of these virtues has an inward and outward effect. For example, understanding God's goodness drives us to love Him but also to be good to those around us. Knowledge of God creates an ever-increasing intimacy with our heavenly Father but also produces compassion and empathy within us for others. Self-control and perseverance also have both inward and outward results that we have discussed at length in those lessons. But the virtue of godliness in the list that Peter provides is an inflection point. For the virtues that follow are the natural and inescapable result of the previous five.

I so look forward to diving into the virtues of mutual affection and love. God does not want us to live a Christian life absent godly motivation, and God does not want us to live a life absent spiritual intimacy. Instead, God has given us a path to the fruits of the Spirit, which are love, joy, peace, forbearance, kindness, goodness, faithfulness, gentleness, and self-control. As we absorb God's virtues from the vine, we can continuously and reliably transfer them to the fruit of His tree in their pure form.

Chapter 8

MUTUAL AFFECTION

I N THIS CHAPTER, WE WILL EXPLORE THE SECOND TO LAST VIRTUE that Peter lists: *mutual affection*. I am indebted to you for partnering with me on this journey and have complete confidence that you are being transformed if you have invested the time and energy to examine these aspects of God's character *and* are making every effort to add His virtues to your faith. If this is the case, then this transformation is affecting not only your outward behavior but your internal motivation, which is being compelled by an ever-increasing knowledge of your heavenly Father and a passion to honor Him with the life He has breathed into you, who are perfectly crafted for this very purpose.

In the last chapter, we learned that Peter chose to use the words ἐν δὲ (and in) to describe that these virtues not only build upon each other in the order that Peter prescribed but that each virtue is a by-product of the previous and the foundation of the next. In short, our study to date may be simply summarized as follows: in order to transition from milk to solid food, we must bring in supply to our faith God's virtues, beginning with goodness.

I love the imagery the wording "bring in supply to your faith" produces. Imagine that fifteen minutes have passed since the start time of your five-year-old's birthday party, and none of the twenty children you invited has showed up. The party hats still sit on the table, and the game stations are empty, except for the one your still-oblivious child is enjoying with his sibling. Your immaculately decorated yard is vacant, and you have a sickening feeling that your passion to encourage your child is not enough to overcome the sadness of his realizing he has no friends. Just then, to your surprise and relief, a caravan of cars arrives, carrying over a dozen playmates. Within a moment or two, children are scrambling across the front lawn to get to the festivities, with their parents following closely after, carrying birthday presents. Emerging from behind the cars, you see that one father is hauling a wagon full of party favors and another carries a bag full of games that are sure to entertain all of the children well beyond the duration of the party. Tears well up in your eyes as relief floods through your body.

This may seem like a strange analogy, but consider this story for the moment that we become aware of God's goodness being added to our mustard seed of faith. God's goodness emerges from our faith but also transforms our faith. It overwhelms our faith, it inspires more faith—we could argue that it saves our faith—and it motivates us, the recipients of God's goodness, to want to reflect that goodness to others, all while compelling us to want to know the God responsible for bringing all of this goodness to our otherwise anemic "birthday party."

And it doesn't stop with goodness. God brings all of Himself *in supply* to our relationship. The reason we only need a mustard seed of faith is because God supplies everything we need to flourish in our walk with Him. Does it not make perfect sense that the God who created us for the sole purpose of having a relationship with Him would have taken care of every detail to pave the way for that relationship to happen? Unfortunately, a resounding number of disciples are trying to navigate the Christian experience by surviving on a single mustard seed, while completely oblivious to what God has brought to the party. I pray that this study of God's virtues is opening wide your eyes to the majesty of the One who is pouring Himself out to you.

If goodness, knowledge, self-control, and perseverance build upon each other to form godliness, and we have learned that godliness is to perform the actions appropriate to God, then which virtue flows from godliness? Well, I can think of no better person to answer this question than the apostle Peter, who instructs us that mutual affection is the resulting virtue.

The Greek word for *mutual affection* is φιλαδελφίαν (pronounced *philadelphian* in English) and means the type of love one has for one's physical brother or sister; in the scriptures, it also encompasses the love that Christians cherish for each other as "brethren."

You may be aware that the Greek language has different words for specific types of love. To minimize the number of words used in translation, scholars frequently use the English word *love*, rather than inserting additional descriptors into the scriptures to differentiate the meanings. Unfortunately, these simplifications sometimes mask what the scriptures are really trying to convey. *Philadelphian* is one of the words that is often translated into English as *love*. Therefore, in order to understand what the scriptures are really telling us about both this and the next chapter's virtues, we will need to identify which Greek words actually were used. It is no coincidence that the passage we are about to look at records a discussion between Jesus and Peter, who later wrote our theme scripture about making every effort to add virtue to our faith as the means by which we embody the nature of our heavenly Father.

In this chapter, we are going to look at *mutual affection* by breaking it into the following four topics of discussion: (1) what is God's expectation, (2) what does it look like, (3) why is this virtue so important, and (4) what are the practical aspects of implementing God's definition of mutual affection in our lives?

1. What is God's expectation regarding mutual affection?

    When they had finished eating, Jesus said to Simon
    Peter, "Simon son of John, do you love me more than

these?" "Yes, Lord," he said, "you know that I love you." Jesus said, "Feed my lambs."

Again Jesus said, "Simon son of John, do you love me?" He answered, "Yes, Lord, you know that I love you." Jesus said, "Take care of my sheep."

The third time he said to him, "Simon son of John, do you love me?" Peter was hurt because Jesus asked him the third time, "Do you love me?" He said, "Lord, you know all things; you know that I love you."

Jesus said, "Feed my sheep. Very truly I tell you, when you were younger you dressed yourself and went where you wanted; but when you are old you will stretch out your hands, and someone else will dress you and lead you where you do not want to go." Jesus said this to indicate the kind of death by which Peter would glorify God. Then he said to him, "Follow me!" (John 21:15–19)

I believe this is one of the more important passages in the Bible because it provides such clear insight into God's thinking. Please allow me a moment to place this scripture into context. At the time of this interaction, Peter had already betrayed Jesus by publicly denying knowing Him on three separate occasions. Even worse, immediately after Peter's third and most passionate denial, he looked up to see that Jesus had been led out of His trial just in time to witness Peter shouting this denial. That angry betrayal was the last impression that Peter left with Jesus prior to His crucifixion.

Days later, Peter was holed up in an upper room along with the other disciples. He had heard that Jesus had raised from the dead, and Peter had, in fact, gone to see the empty tomb himself. But if the last thing that you, as one of Jesus's closest confidants, had done before His death was to deny knowing Him in front of His face, how excited would you be to see Jesus again? Do you think Peter felt saved at that moment? Likely not. Do you think Peter felt more like Judas or like the other faithful disciples in the room? Suffice it to say that it was a pretty dire time for Peter. He had betrayed the Messiah. He had humiliated himself. He was fully exposed and felt unforgiven, unrestored, unhealed, unworthy, and, likely, unwanted. Satan was having a field day with him.

Have you ever felt this way? I have. It's a bad place to be, but it's a place we will all be at some time in our Christian journey when we have sinned against someone we deeply care for and have not yet restored that relationship.

It is in this upstairs room that Jesus first appears to the eleven and tries to calm their fears by helping them to find peace. But He does not restore His relationship with Peter. In fact, there is no record of the two of them conversing at all.

A full week later, Jesus again appears to the disciples and restores Thomas to Him by addressing his lack of faith and challenging him to stop doubting and, instead, believe. But again, Peter remains unrestored, likely terrified to approach the Messiah, whom he had betrayed to His face. Can you relate? Have you ever sinned against a brother or sister, and although you long to be reconciled, you just cannot bring yourself to address the elephant in the room? Maybe you were waiting for that person to make the first move. Maybe you were still entertaining a justification for your actions and allowing that justification to counter your drive for restoration. Maybe you were waiting for a moment alone because you were too proud to seek forgiveness in a public setting. Whatever the case may be, all of us can relate to Peter. Jesus has brought the women back under His wings. He has restored Thomas. He has embraced, offered peace, and given direction to the other ten disciples, but Peter remains painfully outside of this circle.

Days later, Peter tells Thomas, Nathanael, James, John, and two other disciples that he is going out to fish. To their credit, the other disciples appear to know that this is not a good time to leave Peter by himself, so they tell him that they are coming with him. All night long they fish, indicating that Peter remains a broken man, looking for distraction from guilt. The other brothers likely are trying simply to be there for him. But as morning comes, they have yet to catch a single fish.

Do you ever need time like this to grieve a mistake, a sin rooted in your own character weakness? I do, and if you are like me, as the hours or days pass, one of two things happens: either the passion for restoration builds and the excuses for remaining unrestored become less and less justifiable, or self-pity grows, isolation becomes a viable option, and old ways of life become more attractive. Even if we feel the former, we must be cautious, as the passion for restoration only builds for so long before we begin to settle for our new unrestored reality and to play the victim once again.

Then, to their surprise, a man calls out from the shore, asking if they had caught any fish. Upon hearing they had not, he recommends they try the other side of the boat, a ridiculous and illogical suggestion. I can visualize these professional fishermen, exhausted after hours of failure, looking at each other, shrugging their shoulders, and, with a smirk, saying "Why not?" Immediately, the net becomes so full of fish that seven grown men are unable to haul it into the boat.

If you will, pause for just for a moment and think back to our birthday party metaphor, and consider how much God supplies to our relationship, in contrast to what we bring to Him. Peter knows in his heart that the man on shore must be Jesus, and if you wonder how badly Peter wanted to be reconciled to Jesus, consider that solely on the possibility that this was Jesus, Peter abandoned the net, threw off his outer garment, and began swimming to shore.

But for a reason on which the scriptures don't elaborate, even after reaching the shore, the seven are unable to visually confirm that this is actually Jesus. It says that they knew it in their hearts, but they were afraid to ask. Peter sits and eats the breakfast that Jesus prepared for him, and all the while, his heart burns inside of him. It is in this setting that Jesus initiates the following conversation with Peter. It is a conversation that changes everything about who Peter is and how he behaves. For the reason we discussed earlier, I will replace the English word *love* in this passage with the original Greek words to make sure that we capture Jesus's full intent. Please read this passage with those substitutions.

> When they had finished eating, Jesus said to Simon Peter, "Simon son of John, do you *agapas* me more than these?" "Yes, Lord," he said, "you know that I *philō* you." Jesus said, "Feed my lambs."
>
> Again Jesus said, "Simon son of John, do you *agapas* me?" He answered, "Yes, Lord, you know that I *philō* you." Jesus said, "Take care of my sheep."
>
> The third time he said to him, "Simon son of John, do you *philies* me?" Peter was hurt because Jesus asked him the third time, "Do you *philies* me?" He said, "Lord, you know all things; you know that I *philō* you." Jesus said, "Feed my sheep. (John 21:15–17)

Agapas is the type of love beautifully described in 1 Corinthians 13. In the New Testament, agapas is used to describe a love that reflects marital intimacy but not sexual love. It involves faithfulness, commitment, and an act of the will.[6] This is the word Jesus chose when He asked Peter for the first time whether he had agapas for Him. But Jesus did not only ask if Peter had agapas for Him; He asked Peter whether he had *more* agapas for Jesus than the others who were with him in the boat. Wow! Talk about being put on the spot. To his credit, Peter answers honestly by saying, "You know that I philō you." *Philō* is the appropriate tense for the Greek word *philadelphian* (the virtue that we are studying in this chapter). As we learned earlier in the lesson, it denotes a brotherly love that God's children cherish for each other. And in that moment, Peter wouldn't dare claim anything more than philō for Jesus, in light of his betrayals. Note Jesus's response: He accepts Peter's answer but then commands him to feed Jesus's lambs, a likely reference to other Christ-followers.

---

[6] "What is Agape Love" (n.d.). Retrieved from https://www.gotquestions.org/what-is-agape-love.html

But the interaction doesn't stop there. Jesus again asks whether Peter has agapas for Him, but this time He lowers the standard by leaving out the phrase "more than these." Don't think for a minute that Peter didn't notice that Jesus had left out the comparison between Peter's love for Him and the love that the others displayed for Him. Once again, Peter answers honestly by stating that Jesus already knows he has philō for Him. Jesus again accepts Peter's answer but now orders him to take care of His sheep, likely referring to those of His children who are still lost in the darkness.

But the last question stings Peter because Jesus no longer asks whether Peter has agapas for Him. Instead, He asks whether Peter even has *philies* for Him. I cannot imagine what Peter must have felt. He has now been laid bare before his peers. There is no playing around with Jesus. He is going to use our own shortcomings, our own betrayals, and our own failures to help us identify the absolute truth of the condition of our hearts. Far too often, we try to move quickly from conviction to action because we do not like feeling the pangs of guilt associated with exposing our hearts. But Jesus wants to make sure that Peter has clearly identified the state of his own heart. Having said that, we cannot miss the most vital point; that is, regardless of the condition of Peter's relationship with Jesus, there was one command on which Jesus would not compromise. God expects us to take care of His children, both the lambs who have been found and the sheep who are still lost!

I have one biological brother, and there has never been any question in my mind that I would lay down my life for him, not just literally but in any way needed. If he needed money, no question. If he and his wife lost their lives, I'd be a father to his kids, regardless of what his will said. If he needed shelter, my house would be his. If he needed clothes, all I have would be his (despite my utter lack of fashion). Why do I feel this way? Because he is my brother. We share the same blood. We share a life experience that others have only witnessed from the outside. If I feel this way because we are biological brothers, how much more should we feel this way toward those who share the spilled blood that saves our souls and opens the door to an eternity of fellowship together?

What was God saying to Peter, while in the form of a Jesus? He was stating that regardless of the current condition of their relationship, God has one uncompromising expectation of His children; that is, to take care of each other. What do goodness, knowledge, self-control, and perseverance have in common? They are all character traits of God that profit you. But we learned in a previous chapter that with godliness comes the expectation to take what we have been given and supply it to others for *their* profit.

> For everyone who has been given much, much will be demanded; and from the one who has been entrusted with much, much more will be asked. (Luke 12:48b)

If you wonder how seriously Peter took Jesus's challenge to feed and take care of His children, all you need to do is read Acts 2:44–47 to see the character of the new church founded under Peter's leadership:

> All the believers were together and had everything in common. They sold property and possessions to give to anyone who had need. Every day they continued to meet together in the temple courts. They broke bread in their homes and ate together with glad and sincere hearts, praising God and enjoying the favor of all the people. And the Lord added to their number daily those who were being saved.

What do you think? Does it look like Peter took Jesus's charge in John 21 seriously? It certainly does to me. Does the fledgling Jerusalem church behave more like physical brothers and sisters or like acquaintances who happen across each other only at Sunday services? Does your congregation resemble the description of the Jerusalem church? If not, do you resemble the description of the

Jerusalem disciples? Is there any question that Peter's conviction to take care of God's children was indelibly stamped on the believers in Jerusalem?

Let's look at another passage of scripture to see if we can confirm how specifically God exhibited mutual affection for His children.

2. What does mutual affection look like?

> A new command I give you: Love one another. As I have loved you, so you must love one another. By this everyone will know that you are my disciples, if you love one another. (John 13:34–35)

As you are likely aware, *love one another* was not a new command. It is found throughout the law of the prophets, most notably in Leviticus 19:18. So what is the new part of this command? It is the manner in which we are to love one another. Jesus says, "You *must* love one another *as I have loved you*." This is so very rich! God so loved His lost children that He became a man, was born to a woman, submitted to His earthly parents, learned obedience through what He suffered, and became a voluntary living sacrifice. Not only did He become a living sacrifice, but He was put to death on the cross for us in a public display of what we might think was the ultimate sacrifice. But it was not. The ultimate sacrifice took place when Jesus became sin for us and took on the spiritual separation from His Father that only we deserved (2 Corinthians 5:21, Matthew 27:46). He sacrificed in life, in death, and, through spiritual separation from God, in death. This is beyond a high bar; this is the highest bar. And after Jesus set that bar, He turned to Peter and said, now it is time for you to do as I have done, up to and including the manner by which you will die. But Jesus didn't say this only to Peter; He says it to anyone who would come after Him. He commands it in John 13:34–35 and again in John 13:12–17 after washing the feet of His disciples, including the one who was to betray him.

When he had finished washing their feet, he put on his clothes and returned to his place. "Do you understand what I have done for you?" he asked them. "You call me 'Teacher' and 'Lord,' and rightly so, for that is what I am. Now that I, your Lord and Teacher, have washed your feet, you also should wash one another's feet. I have set you an example that you should do as I have done for you. Very truly I tell you, no servant is greater than his master, nor is a messenger greater than the one who sent him. Now that you know these things, you will be blessed if you do them. (John 13:12–17)

Brothers and sisters, do we really "understand what [He has] done" for us? In the depths of our hearts, how do we really view Jesus? Is He nothing more than the sacrifice for our sins and a good example for us to strive for, or do we believe that when we look at the way Jesus lived, loved, spoke, and sacrificed that we are actually witnessing God in the form of a man—living, loving, speaking, and sacrificing? He set us an example of what it means to sacrifice in life and in death, and He defined mercy and grace. But He set this example so that we should do as He has done for us. This isn't an option. If we are to embody godliness, we must absorb goodness, knowledge, self-control, and perseverance from the vine, and then we must transfer those virtues to our spiritual brothers and sisters, having made every effort not to tarnish God's virtues with our own impurities. Those who do so will be blessed and will bear much fruit, the Spirit's fruit.

But this command is not simply an option for those who want to bear much fruit and receive blessings; it is a requirement that our Father has for all of His children—that we will take care of each other in the same manner that He exemplified for us while embodying the form of our brother. Doing so is the purest form of godliness, as it allows us to reflect the Father to His other children, both saved and lost.

Since we are commanded and expected to love as Jesus loved, let us look at how Jesus exemplified mutual affection.

a. He committed Himself first to God.

This might sound like a strange point when discussing mutual affection, but if you are going to genuinely love your spiritual brothers and sisters, rather than just act the part, then you must remain in the vine. We learned earlier that sin is anything that damages relationships. As a result, there is simply no way we can enter God's family without bringing our own past hurts and poor relational habits. When first joining God's family, the vast majority of us enjoy a honeymoon phase, during which we see God's people through rose-colored glasses. It is inevitable, however, that at some point, someone will sin against us, and we will sin against someone, and it's going to happen again and again. The realization that God's family is composed of sinners on their own journeys toward maturity can sometimes dredge up many negative feelings of old hurts and result in a lack of trust and a desire to pull back relationally. Therefore, we must first commit to remaining in the vine.

If we do not rely on faith that our heavenly Father knows best, then we can become driven by fear. If we fail to see God's goodness poured out in our lives, even while we were still unreconciled with Him, then we will be tempted to become critical of others. If we fail to deepen our knowledge of God, who is saving us, then we will be handicapped in our ability to see the true value of each of God's children. If we don't practice self-control, then we will not have the mental discipline to capture our worldly thoughts and make them a slave to God's expectation of reconciliation. If we fail to learn to persevere in relationships, with the knowledge that others are working through their own past issues, we can inadvertently stifle their spiritual journey if we try to impose on them our own timetable for their character development. And, of course, if we fail to embody godliness, we will never be able to perform the actions appropriate to God.

Said simply, how can we claim to love each other as Jesus loved if we are not doing our best to imitate God? The first step in embodying mutual affection and loving *as Jesus loved* is for us to make every effort to pursue God's character. To do that, we must remain in the vine.

b. He became all things to all men.

> Who, being in very nature God, did not consider equality with God something to be used to his own advantage; rather, he made himself nothing, by taking the very nature of a servant, being made in human likeness. (Philippians 2:6–7)

> For we do not have a high priest who is unable to empathize with our weaknesses, but we have one who has been tempted in every way, just as we are— yet he did not sin. (Hebrews 4:15)

> Though I am free and belong to no one, I have made myself a slave to everyone, to win as many as possible. To the Jews I became like a Jew, to win the Jews. To those under the law I became like one under the law (though I myself am not under the law), so as to win those under the law. To those not having the law I became like one not having the law (though I am not free from God's law but am under Christ's law), so as to win those not having the law. To the weak I became weak, to win the weak. *I have become all things to all people so that by all possible means I might save some.* (1 Corinthians 9:19–22, emphasis added)

In this last verse, we see Paul's conviction beautifully laid before us. He so loved Jesus and so appreciated the gift of his own salvation that he considered his own rights and freedoms to be worthless in comparison to the salvation of others. In your life, what is difficult to surrender? Is it your dream for a big home or the perfect location in which to reside? Is it your "me time" that you cherish? Is it your right to afford a nice car at the expense of being more benevolent? Is it your right to free speech and to vocalize your opinions? Is it your right to fairness? Jesus left His throne to become the son of an uneducated carpenter and his young bride. Acknowledging that He was the Messiah made Him a man without a country. He submitted Himself to a pagan government and to the judgments of people who were consumed with self, driven by power, and morally bankrupt. He was often without a home, income, or a meal. He allowed Himself to be tempted in every way that we are tempted, only so that He could relate to temptations that we brought upon ourselves by rejecting Him. With that firsthand knowledge, He has devoted Himself to interceding on our behalf before the Father. If this is how the Creator of the universe behaves, then certainly we can sacrifice ourselves to connect with people from different racial and socioeconomic backgrounds, those with different interests, and those with different temperaments. Although we could come up with dozens of ways to be all things to all people, allow me to share three specific examples.

First, we must take a vested interest in others. Kevin Robbins was a campus minister of mine, and one of Kevin's strengths was in taking a genuine interest in people by endeavoring to learn things about them so that he could become an encouragement to them. Kevin wouldn't just ask questions; he would listen intently to the answers. Once he discovered your strengths, what made you special, and what you had to offer the world, he would engage you from that perspective. When Kevin would introduce people, he would always add encouraging information about them that might connect them. I cannot think of a sermon that Kevin delivered that was not rife with examples of Christian virtue lived out by those in the congregation. This simple life skill had the effect of making everyone around Kevin feel important, noticed, and loved. He became all things to all people by taking a genuine interest in who they were and building a vision for himself of how God viewed them.

Second, we must be willing to step beyond our comfort zones. Sometimes, in order to connect with others, we simply need to be willing to do something that interests them. How about endeavoring to learn someone else's culture, trying their cultural foods, or learning the different ways that those in that culture perceive the world around them? What about participating in hobbies that someone else enjoys, even if you don't? What about making time in our schedules to truly draw people out and find out how they are doing in their walk with God, their understanding of who God is, their life goals and spiritual ambitions, and their pursuit of purity?

In my experience, most of us have a tendency to avoid topics of conversation that could be uncomfortable. As a result, our relationships can either remain relatively superficial, or we deceive ourselves by thinking that our relationships are deep because we share about our personal goals and challenges, but we don't sacrifice the time and emotional energy to learn the personal goals of others and partner with them in overcoming their challenges. But we are not loving in the way that Jesus loved if we don't ask our brothers and sisters the uncomfortable questions and provide a safe place for them to share. These are not the easiest conversations to enter, but they are exactly what differentiate loving others from loving others *as Jesus loved*.

Third, we need to pray specifically for others. If you want to draw near to others, then go to God regularly with someone else's needs and the desires of his or her heart. Often, our prayers for others are generic. We pray for them to have peace, to be close to God, etc. Those are good prayers, but what about praying for the things on that person's prayer list. If you don't know what those are, why not ask? What about praying that God will give you a vision of what a brother or sister will look like, once they overcome a weakness that is plaguing them. Regularly doing so will allow you to see others for what they can become, rather than a sum of their current struggles. You may end up being the only person in their lives who sees them the way God sees them.

There are so many other ways to become all things to all people.

I have listed these three to spur your own thoughts and ideas on this subject. I encourage you to write down the names of those brothers and sisters with whom you have relationships, and next to each name, write down your vision for that person, as well as one or two things on that person's prayer list. This simple step will begin to transform the way you pray for others, as well as the way you see them.

c. He met people's physical needs.

> What good is it, my brothers and sisters, if someone claims to have faith but has no deeds? Can such faith save them? Suppose a brother or sister is without clothes and daily food. if one of you says to them, "Go in peace; keep warm and well fed," but does nothing about their physical needs, what good it is? In the same way, faith by itself, it if is not accompanied by action, is dead. (James 2:14–17)

The above passage is not about taking care of each other; rather, James is making the case that faith is an action. To drive this point home, James gives what he believes is such an obvious and indisputable example that no one will be able to argue otherwise. In James's opinion, meeting the physical needs of others is an irrefutable obligation of a rational society. Contrast that with our culture in the United States, where it is the norm to delegate the responsibility to handle the needs of others. We give money to the church and expect that its benevolence fund will be used to help those in need. We pay taxes to fund programs that care for the poor. As individuals, however, we do virtually nothing to routinely meet the needs of others. In fact, national statistics reveal that United States citizens who classify themselves as religious contribute an average of 2.5 percent of their annual income to charity (this includes their church tithe). What makes this more notable is the fact that the average annual donation for all Americans who give to charitable causes is

4.3 percent of their annual income.[7] The difference between our cultural norm and God's expectation could not be more disparate.

In this context, Jesus's words, recorded in John 13:35, make so much sense: "By this everyone will know that you are my disciples, if you love one another [as I have loved you]." There are so many physical needs among our brothers and sisters in the church, not to mention those outside of the church. And if I may be blunt, far too many of us step over these physical needs to invest in "spiritual activities" that are more pleasant, less expensive, or less time-consuming. This is not reflective of our heavenly Father. Approximately 70 percent of the gospel accounts of Jesus record Him as meeting a physical need. We simply cannot claim to be Christian (little Christ) if we are not characterized by personally meeting the physical needs of those around us.

Here are some ideas for consideration: If you feel that you don't have the time to bring a dinner to someone who is ill because you are studying the Bible with an individual, why not delay the Bible study by an hour so that you can both serve someone in need? What about downsizing your Christmas so that you can adopt a family who cannot afford presents for their own children? How about making a commitment to call one brother or sister every day while driving home from work to encourage them. What if each of us kept notes of people's needs and then ventured to meet them as God opens doors for us to do so? How about asking people what needs they have so that you can keep them at the front of your mind and pray for them? Are you in a position in life where you can "adopt" a college student or organize meals for new parents? How often do you ask people whether you can meet with them one morning to pray together? If we are going to love *as Jesus loved*, then we have no option but to commit to meeting the needs of others.

When my father was undergoing painful recovery from open-heart surgery, a member of his church, Jay Leach, who was a studio

[7] Taylor Schulte, "Charitable Giving Statistics for 2022," Define Financial, January 3, 2022, https://www.definefinancial.com/blog/charitable-giving-statistics/.

musician by profession, showed up on our front porch one night with his guitar in hand. He played acoustical guitar music to my father for thirty to forty-five minutes and then prayed with my dad before excusing himself to attend his own family dinner. Jay didn't have food to bring, money to give, or a minister's training on meeting spiritual needs, but he had a gift. I will never forget how beautiful that moment was and how much it calmed my family—in particular, my father—during a very challenging recovery period.

Matthew 9:35 states, "Jesus went through all the towns and villages, teaching in their synagogue, proclaiming the good news of the kingdom and healing every disease and sickness." We cannot miss Jesus's example here. Yes, he attended synagogue, and yes, he taught the good news, but he did so while healing every disease and sickness that he encountered. Let's make sure that we introduce people to the character of God in the scriptures, while also displaying the character of God through our own actions and behavior.

d. He told the truth.

Jesus loved people, but He did not flatter them. He encouraged people, but He did not avoid the difficult conversations about the condition of their hearts. His commitment to His own purity of heart was deeper than His desire to please others. Look at how Jesus engaged the rich young man in Matthew 19. He told him the truth about the idol that was standing in the way of his relationship with God, but He simultaneously laid out the following vision: "If you want to be perfect … [then] you will have treasure in heaven." Jesus is the master at telling the whole truth—the truth about the current condition of our hearts (as He does with Peter in this chapter's theme scripture)—while also telling us the truth about our future, should we surrender our wills and follow Him.

How often do you have conversations with brothers or sisters in which you respectfully bring up something you see in their lives that is not formed in Christ? If individuals are posting divisive political speech on social media, do you reach out to them privately to gain understanding of their motivations and help to gently restore them to a more righteous path of communication? If a brother is failing to lead family devotionals or to routinely pray with his wife, do you speak up and offer to work alongside him to help develop biblical habits? If a sister is struggling with seeing herself as a victim of circumstance, are you helping to bring her back to a godly perspective? If a brother is not characterized by opening up about personal struggles, are you actively drawing him out? If you feel that someone was condescending toward you, did you bring it to that person's attention in an effort to seek understanding before passing judgment on his or her intentions?

For some of us, these conversations are one of the most difficult callings of the Christian walk, but we will see, later in this chapter, that our commitment to overcome this weakness will factor in to whether we are categorized with the sheep or the goats on the day of our judgment. Others have little to no insecurity over having these conversations, but they can sometimes come across as superior, judgmental, and condescending. Suffice it to say that regardless of your God-given temperament, you can work to be better at telling the truth with patience, grace, steadfastness, and vision.

e. He interceded on our behalf.

How much do you truly intercede with God on behalf of others? When you pray for someone who is struggling with a sin, does your prayer sound something like, "Father, Frank has such magnificent character strengths and is going to be such an asset to your family. Please don't hold his current struggle against him. Please help me or someone else to connect with Frank so that he can see your more beautiful way and become untangled from Satan's lies and the baggage from his past."

I have often been guilty of praying for individuals to change because their sin annoys me, or I have lost patience with their lack of progress. But that is not reflective of Jesus. He saw men for what they could become while not turning a blind eye to who they were.

And it is that vision that Jesus brings before the Father when He intercedes on our behalf.

> Who then is the one who condemns? No one. Christ Jesus who died—more than that, who was raised to life—is at the right hand of God and is also interceding for us. (Romans 8:34)

Look also in Luke 23 at Jesus's prayer for those who stood at the foot of His cross: "Father, forgive them, for they do not know what they are doing."

One of my favorite verses, Galatians 3:26–27 reads, "So in Christ Jesus you are all children of God through faith, for all of you who were baptized into Christ have clothed yourself with Christ." Consider what God is telling us here; that when baptized, we put on Christ as our clothing, so when God looks down upon us, He no longer sees us for what we are but for what we are becoming.

Jesus knows the condition of our hearts. He tells us the truth. He maintains His vision for us, He intercedes for us, and He never gives up on us. Oh, how we need to imitate this part of God's character!

f. He sacrificed His own expectation of fairness.

I do not want to spend a lot of time on this point, but we simply cannot look at how Jesus loved without pointing out His sacrifice of fairness. Brothers and sisters, it is a cultural fallacy that any of us is promised fairness in this life, and hallelujah! For if we truly received what was fair, we would all face eternal separation from our Creator with no chance at salvation. Consider how illogical it is that those of us who receive the gift of salvation (grace)—which we could never earn, let alone deserve—can then be so bothered by life's lack of fairness. Was it fair that Jesus was raised by sinners? Was it fair that the King of the universe had to surrender to an earthly and pagan government? Was it fair that Jesus often had to be the one to initiate conversations in order to restore relationships that he wasn't responsible for damaging? Was it fair that the wicked enjoyed health and wealth, while the Messiah lived as a nomad with no place to lay his head? If we are going to embody mutual affection, we must relinquish the expectation that life will be fair to us, while simultaneously expecting that our eternity will be determined by what is not fair to God. On the contrary, it is in our reaction to life's unfairness that the character of God can be most clearly seen through us, for life's unfairness provides the perfect moment for us to behave like Jesus.

There are so many other practical ways that Jesus loved. I have only scratched the surface with these six examples. Nonetheless, we are commanded to love as Jesus loved, and we will be judged on whether we do so. We can choose to obey reluctantly and out of obligation, or we can choose to plug into the vine for proper perspective, sustainable food, and abundant motivation. For this reason, Peter implores us to make every effort to add mutual affection to the virtues he has thus far listed. The beauty of mutual affection is that there is no right place to start; just let God's Spirit lead you. There is no lack of physical and spiritual needs, and there is no shortage of people who need encouragement. If we will only open our eyes and commit to loving as Jesus loved, we will have no trouble finding ways to do so.

3. Why is mutual affection so important?

Gary Ezzo tells a story about his young daughter, who asked him if he would take care of her doll while she accomplished a chore. Gary looked at the doll and was internally repulsed. It was dirty, torn, and had saliva stains on it; quite frankly, he didn't want to touch it, let alone cuddle with it. But Gary knew how important this doll was to his daughter, and he knew that in order to honor his daughter, he needed to treat the doll based on the value his daughter placed on it, rather than the value he placed on it. So he did just that. He took the tattered and filthy doll and cuddled with it, treating it as his daughter would want it treated.[8]

What a perfect analogy for how we should view this great command *and* this great honor. We are not to treat our brothers and sisters based on the value they have to us. Instead, we are to treat them based on the value they have to God. Many years later, Gary's daughter shared with him that when she saw the manner with which he took care of her doll, that was the moment she knew that she could trust her dad with anything. And that is how God will feel about you when He sees you taking care of His other children in the same manner and with the same passion that He exhibited while in the form of a man.

Consider the following two passages in the context of the story above:

> Dear friends, let us love one another, for love comes from God. Everyone who loves has been born of God and knows God. *Whoever does not love does not know God, because God is love.* This is how God showed his love among us: He sent his one and only Son into the world that we might live through him. This is love: not that we loved God, but that he loved us and sent his Son as an atoning sacrifice for our sins. Dear friends, since God so loved us, we also ought to love one another. *No one has ever seen God; but if we love one another, God lives in us and his love is made complete in us.*
>
> This is how we know that we live in him and he in us: He has given us of his Spirit. And we have seen and testify that the Father has sent his Son to be the Savior of the world. If anyone acknowledges that Jesus is the Son of God, God lives in them and they in God. And so we know and rely on the love God has for us.

---

[8] Gary and Anne Marie Ezzo, *Growing Kids God's Way*. Growing Families International, 1994.

God is love. Whoever lives in love lives in God, and God in them. This is how love is made complete among us so that we will have confidence on the day of judgment: In this world we are like Jesus. There is no fear in love. But perfect love drives out fear, because fear has to do with punishment. The one who fears is not made perfect in love.

We love because he first loved us. [20] Whoever claims to love God yet hates a brother or sister is a liar. For whoever does not love their brother and sister, whom they have seen, cannot love God, whom they have not seen. And he has given us this command: Anyone who loves God must also love their brother and sister. (1 John 4:7–21, emphasis added)

We cannot miss what John is telling us here. The scriptures say that if you do not love in action, then you do not know God. But Peter tells us that if you *know* God, then *mutual affection* is an inescapable by-product. We cannot be deceived. We are either practicing mutual affection, or we are deceiving ourselves to think that we are loving God, when we are not actively loving His children. This could not be more clearly stated than by the Lord Himself.

When the Son of Man comes in his glory, and all the angels with him, he will sit on his glorious throne. All the nations will be gathered before him, and he will separate the people one from another as a shepherd separates the sheep from the goats. He will put the sheep on his right and the goats on his left.

Then the King will say to those on his right, will share those in a moment, "Come, you who are blessed by my Father; take your inheritance, the kingdom prepared for you since the creation of the world. For I was hungry and you gave me something to eat, I was thirsty and you gave me something to drink, I was a stranger and you invited me in, I needed clothes and you clothed me, I was sick and you looked after me, I was in prison and you came to visit me."

Then the righteous will answer him, "Lord, when did we see you hungry and feed you, or thirsty and give you something to drink? When did we see you a stranger and invite you in, or needing clothes and clothe you? When did we see you sick or in prison and go to visit you?"

The King will reply, "Truly I tell you, whatever you did for one of the least of these brothers and sisters of mine, you did for me."

Then he will say to those on his left, "Depart from me, you who are cursed, into the eternal fire prepared for the devil and his angels. For I was hungry and you gave me nothing to eat, I was thirsty and you gave me nothing to drink, I was a stranger and you did not invite me in, I needed clothes and you did not clothe me, I was sick and in prison and you did not look after me."

They also will answer, "Lord, when did we see you hungry or thirsty or a stranger or needing clothes or sick or in prison, and did not help you?"

He will reply, "Truly I tell you, whatever you did not do for one of the least of these, you did not do for me." Then they will go away to eternal punishment, but the righteous to eternal life. (Matthew 25:31–46)

Did you notice the deciding factor when God renders His judgment? Very simply, it is whether or not we adhered to His instruction to take care of His sheep, regardless of the momentary condition of our hearts. Verse 40 states, "whatever you did for one of the least of *these brothers and sisters of mine*, you did for me" (my emphasis). We cannot miss that choice of words. While God views us as His children, Jesus views people as His actual brothers and sisters.

He laid down His life for them and expects us to do the same. Peter was present for this sermon, but it was not until he was restored to Jesus after his betrayal and Jesus's crucifixion that the conviction took a lasting root in his heart.

Before we get into our fourth and final topic, I want to acknowledge that I am aware that this chapter is long, and for that reason, I hope you are breaking it into digestible amounts and using it in your personal prayer times over a number of days. Nonetheless, mutual affection is too important a virtue to cut it short for convenience. Quite frankly, brothers and sisters, since many of us have backed away from a consistent expectation on structured discipling in our churches, far too many of us have yet to find and commit to a biblical expectation of being discipled and discipling others. I fear that if we endeavor to get back into traditional discipling roles but fail to understand the biblical principles behind these structured relationships, we will fall back into legalism, judgment, and criticalness and will shortcut the individual journey on which God has each of us, due to our own impatience or insecurity with others.

I beg you to take the time to digest what the scriptures teach us about the role God expects us to take in the lives of our spiritual brothers and sisters. God's plan is always better than our implementation, and the more aggressive we are about aligning our implementation with His example, the more effective we will be as spiritual brothers and sisters to each other. Absent this, we will be in danger of our relational expectations falling into what Isaiah prophesied against when he said, "They worship me in vain; their teachings are merely human rules."

If that is unclear, let me be even more blunt. The word *discipling* is not found in the scriptures. On the other hand, the virtue of mutual affection is not only found but commanded. It is a product of godliness and will, in part, influence our very salvation. The concept of discipling others is certainly biblical, but it will remain true to God's intent only if it is modeled after biblical virtue, rather than man-made constructs, worldly wisdom, or varying methods for motivating obedience that have little or no basis in scripture. Let's make every effort to ensure that our discipling is modeled after the magnificent virtue of mutual affection.

4. Implementation made practical

Over the course of this study, we have looked specifically at how Jesus loved. The purpose of this is so that we may be able to walk away from this chapter with a clear mind on how we must embody the virtue of mutual affection. We cannot conclude this study, however, without addressing the elephant in the room, which is the requirement to capture and deal with the foxes that ruin His vineyard, which are unrestored relationships among God's children.

> You have heard that it was said to the people long ago, 'You shall not murder, and anyone who murders will be subject to judgment.' But I tell you that anyone who is angry with a brother or sister will be subject to judgment. Again, anyone who says to a brother or sister, 'Raca,' is answerable to the court. And anyone who says, 'You fool!' will be in danger of the fire of hell. *Therefore, if you are offering your gift at the altar and there remember that your brother or sister has something against you, leave your gift there in front of the altar. First go and be reconciled to them; then come and offer your gift.* (Matthew 5:21–24, emphasis added)

We know from scripture that all sin is of equal significance in God's eyes; it is the earthly consequences that vary. But Jesus is not focused on earthly consequence. He is focused on righteousness, of which a primary component is the relationships between His children as His eternal family. As such, Jesus sometimes makes comparisons to help us understand the gravity of behaviors we otherwise might deem less important. He does this when He equates the lust of the eye to adultery, and He does it again in Matthew 5, when discussing the feelings we hold toward each other.

For context, *Raca* is a term of verbal abuse, believed to be derived from an Aramaic word meaning empty-headed, numbskull, and fool. You can see how very serious God is here. He makes it clear that exhibiting outward niceties toward each other is insufficient. Quite the contrary, those of us who hold anything against our brothers and sisters in Christ are in danger of losing our place in God's family, possibly through expulsion but more likely through the slow deterioration of unrestored relationships that leads to bitterness toward God and His church, while opening wide the door to the temptation that the world offers something better.

Upon reading this, you might think of those brothers and sisters in the church with whom you have unresolved issues. We are given two options in addressing relational hurts. We can either forgive and overlook an offense, or we must engage to reconcile the relationship. There is no third option. Are you struggling with a minister or small-group leader because of something he or she said in a lesson? Are you struggling with a sister who hurt you when she made a statement that came across as judgmental? Have you lost patience with a brother who struggles repeatedly with a weakness that seems trivial to you? Are you wounded by someone's harsh joking? Have you been hurt by someone's expectation that you follow her advice when you can find no biblical justification for it? Are your children resolved in their relationships with each other? Are there any unresolved areas in your marriage that you have decided to settle for, rather than address? Whatever the case may be, God tells us exactly what to do about it.

Proverbs 19:11 addresses forgiveness: "A person's wisdom yields patience; it is to one's glory to overlook an offense." This is a biblical and righteous option, whereby you decide to overlook the intentions of another and forgive them from your heart without bringing your hurt to their attention. *God gives us this option so that we may exhibit grace, not so that we can avoid conflict.* There is only one acid test to determine whether or not this option was successful, and that is time. After choosing to overlook and forgive, if you still have hurt feelings or any kind of anger or resentment toward that individual, then you must move on to the second option, reconciliation.

Reconciliation is addressed in Matthew 5:21–24 (above) and 18:15–17. This option requires you stop whatever you are doing and be reconciled to whomever you have hurt or to whoever has hurt you. I am going to offer some specifics on reconciliation below, but before I do, it will help to remember that God's goodness encompasses God's decision to sacrifice Himself, first in becoming a man, then in His daily life on earth, and finally on the cross, all while you were still His enemy. It encompasses His decision to offer to abolish your sins from His memory (Hebrews 8:12), an offer He made before you had even begun the process of repentance. Herein lies another reason why Peter states that these virtues build upon each other.

In order to successfully reconcile, we must be rooted and growing in goodness. This does not mean that you become a pacifist and continue to endure abuse as a good soldier. For that is neither what this verse says nor what Jesus teaches in Matthew 18:15–17. However, we are called to remove the little foxes from our vineyard (Song of Songs 2:15). We are called to reconciliation (Matthew 5:23–24). We are called to love as Jesus loved (John 13:34–35). We are called to forgive as God forgives (Ephesians 4:32). We are called to keep no record of wrongs (1 Corinthians 13:5). And if we are going to rise to this challenge, then we will need to continually ingest the solid food that comes from virtue, lest we not have the spiritual strength to complete the task.

How do we engage someone who has hurt us or whose weaknesses we find off-putting?

a. First and foremost, we must train ourselves to withhold judgment.

If anyone hears my words but does not keep them, I do not judge that person. For I did not come to judge the world, but to save the world. (John 12:47)

There is a difference between observing facts and making judgments. That difference is in attaching intent to what you observe without first gaining understanding.[9] Years ago, when I would return from work, my young children would run to the door and attack me with hugs and stories from their day. I felt compelled to sit with them and speak with them as a means to show them my love. One day, Tami and I got into an argument, and after a while, what came to the surface was that she wasn't feeling loved. She was unaware that she had been attaching intent to my spending time with the kids upon returning home, rather than seeking her out first. That judgment left her feeling that she was less important to me than our children. Over time, that little fox began to define every area of our relationship. It was good for Tami to hear my reasoning, and it was good for me to hear how she felt about my actions. The understanding I received from our discussion motivated me to prioritize her when returning home from work so that I could close that door on Satan. What Tami took from that conversation was the conviction that she needed to seek understanding on things she was feeling before assuming that she knew the intent behind my actions.

Proverbs 20:5 states, "The purposes of a person's heart are deep waters, but a man of understanding draws them out." If we are going to be effective as a brother's keeper, then we need to learn to ask nonjudgmental questions so that we can gain understanding before making judgments. Those who do this effectively attest that they often finish conversations without needing to give any advice at all because the people they were drawing out got in touch with their own hearts and came to their own convictions, simply by answering questions that helped to reveal the true condition of their hearts.

> Do not judge, or you too will be judged. For in the same way you judge others, you will be judged, and with the measure you use, it will be measured to you. (Matthew 7:1–2)

---

[9] Dr. James Richards, *How to Stop the Pain* (Whitaker House, 2001).

What an amazing promise God makes us. If you choose to withhold judgment and, instead, practice mutual affection, God will do the same for you. But if you choose to sit in the judge's seat and attach intent to observable behavior without first seeking understanding from the offender, then you inevitably will mete out your love based on your judgment. Let's commit ourselves to imitating God, whose only desire in drawing us out is to restore us to Him.

b. Commit to reconciliation.

> For Christ's love compels us, because we are convinced that one died for all, and therefore all died. And he died for all, that those who live should no longer live for themselves but for him who died for them and was raised again. So from now on we regard no one from a worldly point of view. Though we once regarded Christ in this way, we do so no longer. Therefore, if anyone is in Christ, the new creation has come: The old has gone, the new is here! All this is from God, who reconciled us to himself through Christ and gave us the ministry of reconciliation: that God was reconciling the world to himself in Christ, not counting people's sins against them. And he has committed to us the message of reconciliation. We are therefore Christ's ambassadors, as though God were making his appeal through us. We implore you on Christ's behalf: Be reconciled to God. God made him who had no sin to be sin for us, so that in him we might become the righteousness of God. (2 Corinthians 5:14–21)

How can we hope to embody godliness if we refuse to embrace the ministry of reconciliation? And how can we successfully reconcile unless we imitate God by choosing to withhold judgment while on this earth?

One of the most challenging aspects about treating the disease of cancer is that if surgeons happen to overlook a single cancer cluster or a therapy leaves behind a single cancer cell, the disease will return and try to snuff out the life of the survivor. As a result, people will subject themselves to postsurgical rounds of chemotherapy, with the havoc that treatment wreaks on the body and the crushing blow it brings to their lifestyles, just to kill any cancer that might possibly have been missed.

Yet when it comes to the cancer of unrestored relationships, we willingly and knowingly let them fester. We have already reviewed scriptures, in which God commands us to suspend our worship of Him in order to first restore a broken relationship, and another where God warns us that those who fail to do so place themselves in danger of entering eternity with an unresolved relationship with our heavenly Father. Yet unrestored relationships permeate the church like an unchecked cancer, and we continue to pretend it is without consequence.

Brothers and sisters, if you hold anything against someone, you need to commit this very moment to resolving it. First, I would encourage you to journal on how you actually feel toward this person and the specific actions or events that led to this feeling. Second, ask God to help you trust that He has your best interests in mind and that obedience to His words will not return to you empty (Isaiah 55:11). Third, take a few steps back and remove any judgment you may have placed on the other party's intent. Then make the time to speak with that person with a commitment to reach reconciliation. I do have some thoughts on how to have an effective conversation and will share those in a moment, but I am much more concerned that we commit to having these conversations than I am about how masterfully they are carried out, for a house divided against itself cannot stand (Mark 3:25).

As for technique, I offer the following suggestions:

1. Clearly differentiate between observable facts and resultant feelings. For example: "Brother, the other day I came across a Facebook post you forwarded that contained prejudicial statements and generalizations toward a particular race of people. I was already aware those sentiments were out there, but I felt hurt when I saw that you had posted it on your own page."

   Here, you have stated a fact about the post and explained how you felt about it. You have not mixed the two by saying something like, "You really hurt me by posting that," which is much more likely to put the person on the defense.

2. Ask questions aimed at gaining understanding, rather than using questions to make a point. For example, you could follow up on the statements above by asking, "Do you agree with this post? Does it support your views regarding this group of people?"

   By asking questions that are genuinely aimed at finding truth, you accomplish two things. First, you exhibit humility by not assuming that you already know the person's intent, and second, you give the person an opportunity to tell his or her own truth on the matter.

3. Allow the person to respond and endeavor to genuinely hear his answer. For example, let's assume the brother answered, "Oh man. I'm so sorry that hurt you. That wasn't my intent. I didn't necessarily agree with those sentiments, but the post brought up something from my own past, and I thought that reposting it might generate a legitimate conversation on the subject."

   If that was the answer, you might be able to offer some suggestions on how he could have initiated the same conversation with a short explanation, rather than just reposting something that could be construed by others as promoting or supporting the original post. On the other hand, if the brother was struggling with some racial issues, you would now be in a position to help him process those things by coming up alongside him, rather than down on him. His simply seeing the hurt his unresolved issues caused you is a motivator that God can use to begin healing his heart and forming his racial opinions to mirror those of Christ.

Here is one more example: "Brother, the other day when I was giving John some advice, you interrupted my comments and gave your own advice, which was contradictory to mine. I don't know your intentions, but I do know that I felt undermined and disrespected." In this example, you stated observable facts without judgment, and then you connected how those observations impacted you. The recipient of this information now has the option to choose humility, seek your forgiveness, maybe offer an explanation for understanding or clarification, and be restored to you. He or she also has the option to react defensively or pridefully, which may prompt you to continue obeying Matthew 18:16 by seeking assistance from another. Regardless, the end result remains the same—we must be absolutely committed to ridding God's family of any unresolved conflict.

4. When someone apologizes or seeks forgiveness, do not minimize it. I cannot tell you how many times I have sought forgiveness from someone, only to hear, "Ah, don't worry about it," or "Thanks, but it wasn't a big deal." We make these statements because we don't like people to be uncomfortable, and we want to get back to "normal" as quickly as possible. But trivializing or minimizing a hurt robs the offender of the opportunity to receive forgiveness and—equally, if not more importantly—it also robs the person of the opportunity for God to "form" Himself in him or her.

When individuals ask you to forgive them, say, "I forgive you," and leave it at that. If you're not ready to forgive someone because the wound is too deep for you to process what you're feeling on the spot, then be honest and say something similar to, "Brother, I will forgive you, but I need some time to process this. I am really hurt, and I don't just want to forgive;

I want to be restored with you as well. So please give me some time, and we can continue this conversation in a day or two."

Mastering these techniques takes time, but not to worry; it is inevitable that we will give each other much opportunity for practice. Nonetheless, achieving proficiency in these interactions is *not* a prerequisite for having them. We have seen that God is uncompromising in His expectation that we make every effort to become godly and that godliness is not without effect. Godliness that does not produce mutual affection is a form of godliness that denies its power. One of Satan's most effective tools is to infuse God's family with seemingly small unresolved hurts and attitudes. We often justify them by convincing ourselves that we are simply overlooking and forgiving, but we carry around these attitudes in our hearts, and they stifle our love. Furthermore, they block us from an uninhibited relationship with our heavenly Father because we fail to imitate His goodness, His revelation of the most intimate parts of His heart to us, and His affection for His children (1 John 4:20). It is time to eviscerate this cancer from our fellowship. We need to identify these foxes, ready ourselves for these conversations, and then be reconciled to each other so that we can be brought to complete unity and become one, just as Jesus and God are one (John 17).

c. Become an encourager.

For everything that was written in the past was written to teach us, so that through the endurance taught in the Scriptures and the encouragement they provide we might have hope. May the God who gives endurance and encouragement give you the same attitude of mind toward each other that Christ Jesus had, so that with one mind and one voice you may glorify the God and Father of our Lord Jesus Christ.

Accept one another, then, just as Christ accepted you,
in order to bring praise to God. (Romans 15:4–7)

The above is another rich scripture that bears breaking down. Did you catch the importance that endurance and encouragement have on our spiritual journey? We have already studied how endurance is a component of perseverance (our fourth virtue), which, combined with encouragement, form an essential part of the foundation for finding hope. It is God who gives endurance and encouragement, but He also gives another blessing: the ability to have the same attitude of mind toward each other that Jesus possessed. Why? So that with one mind and one voice we can make God bigger to a lost world. Accepting each other and exhibiting mutual affection toward each other brings praise to God and reveals His true nature to a world of people longing for acceptance and importance.

Brothers and sisters, we all need encouragement. The number-one place to find that encouragement is to remain in the vine by making every effort to understand and then embody God's virtues. The second place we find encouragement is from our spiritual brothers and sisters who are working hard to withhold judgment and, instead, to love without condition and with vision.

Let us hold unswervingly to the hope we profess, for he who promised is faithful. And let us consider how we may spur one another on toward love and good deeds, not giving up meeting together, as some are in the habit of doing, but encouraging one another— and all the more as you see the Day approaching. (Hebrews 10:23–25)

How are we to hold to that hope? Unswervingly. And what is the best way to avoid swerving? First, pray to God and depend on Him. As we have now spoken about numerous times, we will not be able to practice genuine mutual affection if we are not being fed through our intentional connection to the vine and then choosing to love God's children because of the value He places on them. Second, surround yourself with *reliable* brothers and sisters who are all headed in the same direction. Isn't that what this scripture says? We need to put conscious thought into spurring one another on, and then we must meet together often enough to provide that constant and targeted encouragement.

Nowhere in the scriptures does it say that we are to receive our encouragement from a weekly sermon. Similar to a sermon, this discussion can help to spur you on toward change and equip you with the tools to be successful. But neither a sermon nor this chapter are a biblical prescription that rivals the need to receive encouragement through philadelphian relationships. In fact, if you choose to absorb knowledge but fail to act on it, then you, unfortunately, will be defined by the first description in 1 Corinthians 8:1b–3, which states,

> But knowledge puffs up while love builds up. Those who think they know something do not yet know as they ought to know. But whoever loves God is known by God.

Instead, let's commit to living up to the name we are honored to wear—Christian. Let's commit to loving as Jesus loved in all areas, especially in our commitment to encourage each other, "and all the more as we see the day approaching."

CONCLUSION

Brothers and sisters, thank you for taking the time to read this entire chapter. We have seen that if we are going to be like Christ, then we must embody mutual affection. If we are going to embody mutual affection, we need to first remain in the vine to continually absorb goodness, knowledge, self-control, and perseverance so that we can exhibit godliness.

Then we need to commit to and train our minds to place value on people, not as their actions deserve but based solely on the value they have to their heavenly Father.

Then we need to commit to dying to ourselves so that we free up our personal ambitions in order to be others-focused.

We need to practice withholding judgment and become competent in seeking understanding so that we can be completely restored to—as well as adequately counsel—our spiritual brothers and sisters.

We will need to encourage one another more and more as we mature in Christ.

Let's close by listening to the heart of Jesus, poured out to His heavenly Father as His time on earth was coming to an end.

> My prayer is not for them alone. I pray also for those who will believe in me through their message, that all of them may be one, Father, just as you are in me and I am in you. May they also be in us so that the world may believe that you have sent me. I have given them the glory that you gave me, that they may be one as we are one—I in them and you in me—so that they may be brought to complete unity. Then the world will know that you sent me and have loved them even as you have loved me. Father, I want those you have given me to be with me where I am, and to see my glory, the glory you have given me because you loved me before the creation of the world. Righteous Father, though the world does not know you, I know you, and they know that you have sent me. I have made you known to them, and will continue to make you known in order that the love you have for me may be in them and that I myself may be in them. (John 17:20–26)

The seventeenth chapter of John contains the only complete prayer we have of Jesus. I would encourage you to read the entire prayer, as I highlighted only verses 20–26. Jesus, who was God in the flesh, prays that we will be one with God's other children in the same manner that He is one with God. Why? For the same reason you want your children to love each other. You realize the incredible role they play in helping each other through this life and that they will be each other's greatest earthly support, once you are no longer around to guide them.

Jesus then states that He has given to us the glory that God gave Him (you may recall that this glory is the ability to make God bigger as we become smaller). And why this undeserved privilege? So that the world may believe that we are genuine representatives of the only true God. Jesus wants us to be "brought to complete unity" so that we become one as He and God are one. Then, we will reflect God to a lost world, and God will be comforted, knowing that His lost children, who are being drawn back to Him through the glory He is displaying in us, will be surrounded by His other children, who will love them just as He did when He was in bodily form. This is the conviction that Jesus impressed upon Peter in John 21 and that became part of Peter's legacy.

Reflecting God to His lost children is the ultimate glory. Loving God's saved children as He wants them loved is one of our greatest privileges. How unbelievable that we have each gone from being lost and condemned with no hope of salvation to all of us having an essential role in presenting the bride of Christ as holy and blameless to the God who formed us for this very purpose—that is a perfect, righteousness, untarnished relationship and complete oneness.

Chapter 9

LOVE

M Y FRIENDS, WE HAVE REACHED THE LAST OF OUR CHAPTERS ON the virtues that Peter highlights regarding our Father. I am so very grateful that you have sacrificed your time to stick with it. This has been a labor of love for me because pursuing a virtue-based Christianity has transformed my spiritual life. I am therefore compelled to share these thoughts in the hope of cracking open the door to a transformative relationship with God for all who connect with this material.

My own journey began when I found myself surprisingly unequipped to teach my children why obedience to God's commands was always more beautiful than anything the world had to offer. Because I didn't know how to paint this more beautiful picture for my own children, I found myself relying on demands of obedience "because I said so," with threats of punishment hanging over their little heads, should they choose to disobey. The older my children became, the more incomplete this type of parenting felt. Not only was it incomplete, but it was damaging, as it left my children frustrated with my decisions and wondering if my commands were meant only to make Dad's life easier, rather than founded in their best interest.

Certainly, it could not be God's perfect plan that we trudge through this life desiring so much of what is off limits, with no more motivation to choose righteousness than the fear of eternal damnation for disobedience and the hope that our inconsistent application of self-denial over the things we really want to do will be sufficient to prove to God that He should let us into heaven, where we finally will find happiness and contentment.

Little by little, and with the help of many advisers, I began to build my own library of moral reasoning, and in doing so, I found an entirely new side to Christianity that lifted my spirit and opened my eyes to the truth that, in this life, God is singing a song to us that is so beautiful that Satan's temptations and the lusts of the flesh pale in comparison. My prayer is that, through these chapters, you also are empowered to grab onto that hope and start the journey that Jesus envisioned when He said, "I have come so that you may have life and have life to the full" (John 10:10).

I pray that you are now convinced beyond any doubt that God is committed to revealing Himself to those who want to know Him. I pray also that you now see a living and breathing image of God's perfection, for we have learned that He is so good that He is the embodiment of moral excellence and virtue. This goodness compels Him to pave for us a road to salvation that included becoming a man and sacrificing Himself, in life and in death, as the only acceptable offering for our forgiveness.

He wants so intently to be known by us that He has revealed Himself not only in scripture but by coming and living among us so that we could witness Him in human form. His incomprehensible self-control allows Him to treat us not as our sins deserve but as He envisions us to be, once we are fully formed in Him. Every action He takes in our lives is on our behalf. He exudes perseverance, as seen in His indescribable patience, not wanting any of His children to be lost. These virtues culminate in the image of perfect godliness that draws all nations to Him, while simultaneously separating the sheep from the goats. As a man, He lived and breathed mutual affection for His spiritual brothers and sisters, while showing us how to love each other as our Father desires. All virtue, placed together in perfect form in the same being, can be expressed in three words—God is love—which is the topic of our study in this chapter.

The Greek word Peter uses in 2 Peter 1:7 for love is ἀγάπην (*agapēn* in English). Rather than use a Greek Bible lexicon to define this word, let's allow God to define it for us.

> Love [agapēn] is patient, love [agapēn] is kind. It does not envy, it does not boast, it is not proud. It does not dishonor others, it is not self-seeking, it is not easily angered, it keeps no record of wrongs. Love [agapēn] does not delight in evil but rejoices with the truth. It always protects, always trusts, always hopes, always perseveres. Love [agapēn] never fails. (1 Corinthians 13:4–8a)

I am going to take a different approach in this chapter. We have spent the previous six chapters learning that "making every effort" to add to our faith each of the virtues Peter lists is the path to sustainable spiritual maturity (solid food) and a functional relationship with our heavenly Father. We have also seen that being motivated by the majesty of God's virtue is incalculably more powerful than living in fear of consequence and that God's way is much more beautiful than anything that the world offers us. Therefore, I see no reason to try to convince you further. Instead, let's take our new convictions and conclude this series of lessons by looking at what these fifteen elements of agapēn look like when applied to everyday life.

Love is …

1. **Patient** and **not self-seeking**

   Patient:

   The Lord is not slow in keeping his promise, as some understand slowness. Instead he is patient with you,

not wanting anyone to perish, but everyone to come
to repentance. (2 Peter 3:9)

Is not self-seeking:

Do nothing out of selfish ambition or vain conceit.
Rather, in humility value others above yourselves,
not looking to your own interests but each of you to
the interests of the others. (Philippians 2:3–4)

In December 1967, outside of Knoxville, Tennessee, a young
man named Lynn Weaver had just finished his first semester at
Howard University and was home in Sevierville for the holidays.
The following words are his recounting of that evening:

I was walking up the street Christmas Eve and I see
this kid riding down the street on this bicycle and I
said [to myself] 'boy that looks like my brother's bike.'
I get to the house and I say, "Wayne, where is your
bike?" and he said, "It's down on the steps" and I said,
"No it's not. It's gone." It's a small neighborhood, so
we find out where the kid lives who has the bike.
And it's a shack in the alley. Now my brother and I,
we're gonna beat this boy but my father was there
and he said, "Just shut up and let me talk." So we
knock on the door, and this old black guy comes on
a cane. The house was cold. The only light he had
was a candle. It was his grandson who has stolen the
bike. He was the same age as my brother, about ten
years old. The little boy starts crying and he says, "I
just wanted something for Christmas." So we get the
bike and we leave.

We go back to my house. My father tells my
mother and she doesn't say anything. She just starts
cutting the turkey in half and all the fixings—she

started packing it up. My father went to the coal yard and got a big bag of coal. And then he told my brother, "You've got another bike, don't you." My brother said, "Yeah." So we went back with the food, coal—so they could have some heat—and the bike. The little boy was just crying but the thing that moved me the most was the old man. My father gave him twenty dollars, which was a huge deal back then and said, "Merry Christmas." He said, "Thank you" and then just broke down in tears. My father was a chauffeur. My mother was a domestic. So, we didn't have a lot of stuff and that Christmas, I don't even remember what gift I got but I do know that made me feel better than any Christmas I ever had.[10]

William "Lynn" Weaver went on to become the chief of surgery at Morehouse School of Medicine in Atlanta, Georgia. He passed away on May 25, 2019.

2. **Kind**

Those who are kind benefit themselves, but the cruel bring ruin on themselves. (Proverbs 11:17)

Therefore, as God's chosen people, hold and dearly loved, clothe yourselves with compassion, kindness, humility, gentleness and patience. (Colossians 3:12)

"What do you see today?" asked Jim of his ailing roommate.
"It's another beautiful day, Jim," answered Bill, who went on to describe the brilliantly colored sunny day, with puffy cumulus clouds floating by in the gentle breeze and the various activities of the people in the impeccably kept park across the street from

---

[10] William Weaver. "In the Spirit." Produced by Jud Esty-Kendall, StoryCorps, December 15, 2017, https://storycorps.org/stories/william-lynn-weaver-171215/.

the hospital. This daily ritual seemed to be the only thing that kept Jim from succumbing to deep depression over the loss of his vision. What a godsend to be placed in a room with Bill, whose remaining days on earth were short but who seemed to see the beauty in everything outside of his window, regardless of the kind of day he was having.

Multiple times each day, Jim would ask Bill for an update, and Bill would provide his friend with every detail he could make out. In between these daily recaps, these men began to have deeper talks about Jim's fears regarding his new blindness. Those conversations led to more intimate discussions over personal failures, wayward children, and loneliness. But it was Bill's positivity, his understanding, and his contentment that Jim could not put out of his mind.

During their few weeks together, Bill shared the gospel with Jim by revealing the aspects of his personal faith and how they had played out in his life. As the days passed, Jim became more and more convinced that the only way he was going to survive his new reality was with God by his side.

It was a Thursday morning when Bill's vital signs took a turn for the worse, setting off numerous alarms. Nurses ran in and whisked Bill from the room. Sadly, that morning's update from the window was the last Jim would ever receive from Bill.

Later that afternoon, while an orderly was preparing Bill's bed for a new patient, Jim asked him if he would do him a favor. He asked the orderly to look out the window and describe what he saw.

The orderly answered, "Sir, there is no window in this room. That is why we only use these rooms for our visually impaired patients."

3. **Always protects**

No temptation has overtaken you except what is common to mankind. And God is faithful; he will not let you be tempted beyond what you can bear. But

when you are tempted, he will also provide a way out
so that you can endure it. (1 Corinthians 10:13)

Kob Sinn arrived early at his food stand in the center of the outdoor market, as he did every day. He began by washing the fruits and vegetables, and then he readied a variety of soups in time for the morning rush. As the crowd filled the streets, and his regular customers funneled into the market, Mr. Sinn's customer line was interspersed with the homeless, and, as was his custom, he generously provided them with a to-go cup of warm soup—and a smile. One afternoon, he heard a commotion, and upon turning his attention toward the sound, he saw a woman gripping a young boy's arm while rebuking him for stealing medicine from her store. The boy was crying, clearly scared, and trying to explain that he wasn't a bad boy but that his mom was ill and needed the medicine.

Mr. Sinn asked his daughter to tend to the counter while he stepped into the street. With a smile, he kindly engaged the fuming store owner and asked her the price of the medicine. Upon obtaining the amount, he paid the woman and walked the boy back to his food stand, where he gave the boy some warm soup, handed him the bottle of medicine, and said, "Go on home, and take care of you mother."

Fifteen years later, Kob Sinn again arrived early to prepare for the outdoor market. As always, he began to prepare enough soup for his paying customers, plus enough extra for those who were homeless. Little did he know that within a few moments, he would suffer a massive heart attack. Three days later, his now-adult daughter sat weeping by his hospital bedside, not only for her father who had yet to wake from his coma but also over the hospital bill, which she could not pay, even if she and her father were to commit all profits for the remainder of their working lives.

But it was the last page of the bill that confused her. The complete amount of the itemized services totaled over 200 million Thai baht, but the amount-due line simply read *zero*. Under the zeroed-out amount due was a handwritten note:

In return for an act of kindness showed to my mother and me fifteen years ago. God bless.—Dr. Prajak Arunthong[11]

4. **Does not envy**

But godliness with contentment is great gain.
(1 Timothy 6:6)

Emily walked into her college Spanish course and saw the same group of kids assembled in the corner of the room that she saw before every class. She had come to perceive them as a clique that avoided interaction with the rest of their classmates and insulated their study group from any outsiders.

On this particular morning, Emily was carrying the stress of that day's examination, which was to consist of the professor placing students into pairs and then expecting them to hold a five-minute, uninterrupted conversation in Spanish. Feeling the temptation to judge this group of kids and the anger welling up inside of her, Emily decided to set down her books and excuse herself to the restroom to pray. While praying, Emily asked God to help her to withhold judgment of these classmates, who seemed so exclusionary. She asked God to forgive her for projecting her own stress onto her perception of others' actions. She prayed to be kind, controlled, and to reflect God's character rather than her own emotions. She then returned to her class.

As soon as Emily opened the classroom door, one of the girls in the perceived clique asked, "Emily, do you want to join us?"

Emily felt a pang of guilt over her perception of these students and a simultaneous affirmation from the Spirit, having not given in to judgment on that particular day. To her great surprise, the group asked if she wanted to prep with them for the examination, and she

---

[11] Reprinted by permission of True Corporation, Ogilvy Bangkok Advertising Agency, and Phenomena Film Production.

happily agreed. For the next fifteen minutes, Emily prepared for the exam with one of these girls.

Soon after, the professor entered the room, and the examination began. When the time came for Emily to receive her pairing, the professor unknowingly paired Emily and the girl with whom she had been studying. To no surprise, the two of them aced their exams, receiving the highest possible score.

As Emily walked back to her dormitory that afternoon, she could not stop herself from expressing gratitude to God for His Spirit of self-control and for the powerful example He had provided that the success He had already prepared for her that day had been dependent on her obedience.

5. **Does not dishonor others**

> Be devoted to one another in love. Honor one another
> above yourselves. (Romans 12:10)

Abel Mutai was only thirty feet from winning the Burlada cross-country race when he stopped running, believing he had just crossed the finish line. Spanish runner Ivan Fernandez was closing in from behind, hoping to beat the Olympic bronze medalist, when he realized that Abel had become confused. Without a second thought, Ivan began yelling to the Kenyan runner, trying to explain that he hadn't yet finished the race.

When it became clear that Abel didn't understand the Spaniard's encouragement, Ivan fell in behind him and began pushing Abel until the two crossed the finish line in tandem.

When a reporter asked Ivan why he had given away the victory, he replied, "My dream is that one day we can have some sort of community life where we push ourselves and others to win." Unsatisfied with the answer, the reporter pushed the Spanish runner further on the subject, to which Ivan replied, "I didn't deserve to win it. I did what I had to do. He was the rightful winner. He created a gap that I couldn't have closed if he hadn't made a mistake. As soon as I saw he was stopping, I knew I wasn't going to pass him."

Again, the reporter urged, "But you could have won!"

Ivan looked at the reporter and said, "But what would be the merit of my victory? What would be the honor of this medal? What would my mother think of it?"[12] [13]

6. **Is not easily angered** and **does not boast**

Is not easily angered:

> My dear brothers and sisters, take note of this: Everyone should be quick to listen, slow to speak and slow to become angry, because human anger does not produce the righteousness that God desires. (James 1:19–20)

Does not boast:

> Do nothing out of selfish ambition or vain conceit. Rather, in humility value others above yourselves, not looking to your own interests but each of you to the interests of the others. (Philippians 2:3–4)

Having reached his dinner stop, social worker Julio Diaz had exited the subway and was heading for the staircase when he was stopped by a knife-wielding teenager who demanded his money. Realizing no one was available to help on this otherwise empty platform, Julio complied and handed over his wallet. As the thief turned to leave, Julio said, "Hey, wait a minute. You forgot something.

---

[12] "Honesty of the Long-Distance Runner," Fair Play International, December 19, 2012, www.fairplayinternational.org/honesty-of-the-long-distance-runner.
[13] Keith Stevens, "It's How You Finish that Matters," KTIS, August 3, 2021, https://myktis.com/2021/09/its-how-you-finish-that-matters-most/.

If you're going to be robbing people for the rest of the night, you might as well take my coat to keep you warm."

The young man looked back, expecting to encounter more sarcasm, but instead, he saw Julio holding out his jacket for the young man to take. The young thief reached out for the jacket and asked, "Why are you doing this?"

Julio answered, "If you're willing to risk your freedom for a few dollars, then I guess you must really need the money. All I wanted to do was get dinner, and if you want to join me—hey, you're more than welcome."

To Julio's surprise, the teenager accepted his invitation. While the two of them sat across the table from each other having dinner, deli customers and employees alike came over to say hello to Julio.

After a number of such interactions, the teenager said, "You know everybody here. Do you own this place or something?"

"No, but I do eat here a lot," Julio answered.

"Yeah, but you're even nice to the dishwasher," the teen remarked.

"Haven't you been taught you should be nice to everybody?"

"Yeah," the teen replied, "but I didn't think people actually behaved that way."

As the conversation progressed, Julio asked the teen what he wanted out of life. The boy looked sad and elected not to answer. When the bill arrived, Julio said to the teen, "Look, I guess you're going to have to pay for this 'cause you have my money and I can't pay for this. If you give me my wallet back, I'll gladly treat you."

Without hesitation, the teen pushed Julio's wallet back across the table. Julio paid for the dinner and then handed the teen a twenty-dollar bill—but Julio asked the teen for something in return. "I need your knife," he said.

The teen placed the knife on the table and walked away.[14]

---

[14] Julio Diaz. "A Victim Treats His Mugger Right." Produced by Michael Garofalo, StoryCorps, NPR, March 28, 2008, https://www.npr.org/2008/03/28/89164759/a-victim-treats-his-mugger-right.

7. **Keeps no record of wrongs** and **always trusts**

Keeps no record of wrongs:

For I will forgive their wickedness and will remember their sins no more. (Hebrews 8:12)

Always trusts:

Trust in the Lord with all your heart and lean not on your own understanding; in all your ways submit to him, and he will make your paths straight. (Proverbs 3:5–6)

Elizabeth Howard met her husband, Jim, at Wheaton College, where she was studying in pursuit of her dream to translate the Bible into a language that did not yet have its own translation. Little did she know that this relationship would eventually lead her and her new husband to Quito, Ecuador, where they would serve as missionaries. Quito also became a home base for Jim while he and a small group of missionaries began building a relationship with the Auca Indian tribe. Prior to Jim's making contact, the Auca tribe had not had any interaction with the outside world. Because of their lack of familiarity with the Aucas and the Aucas' reputation for cannibalism, it took many months of engaging the tribe and building trust by dropping gifts from a small airplane while slowly circling at low altitudes before Jim felt that he would be able to conduct an in-person meeting. It was also in Quito that Elizabeth gave birth to a daughter, Valerie; she was the primary caretaker for their new daughter while Jim and his team were venturing into Auca territory, trying to foster a relationship with this violent tribe.

Eleven months later, convinced that a sufficient relationship had been built with the Aucas, Jim and four other missionary friends hiked into Auca territory for their first face-to-face meeting. There, the five missionaries were slaughtered by the Aucas. When their bodies were later discovered, it was clear that all of the missionaries had chosen to leave their guns holstered and surrender their lives to the Auca spears without putting up a fight.

Now widowed and a single mother, Elizabeth elected to continue her work as a missionary to the Quechua Indians, a much less violent tribe that was integrated into the more modern society in Quito. But by the work of the Holy Spirit, two Auca refugee women also lived among the Quechua Indians, and over time, they taught Elizabeth the Auca language.

One year after Jim's death at the hands of the Auca Indians, one of the Auca refugee women, Dayuma, returned to her tribe and found them suffering under the guilt associated with slaughtering the missionaries, who had willingly surrendered their lives. When Dayuma reported to Elizabeth that the Aucas wanted to make amends, Elizabeth, her daughter, and fellow missionary, Rachel Saint, went to live among the Auca tribe, sharing the gospel with them and converting many. Elizabeth remained with this tribe for five years, ministering to their spiritual and physical needs.

Although Jim Elliot will forever be remembered for his passion, his courage, his martyrdom, and his famous quote—"He is no fool who gives what he cannot keep to gain what he cannot lose"—it was Elizabeth's unqualified forgiveness that ultimately allowed the one true God to be revealed to a lost people.

8. **Always hopes** and **always perseveres**

Always hopes:

> Therefore we do not lose heart. Though outwardly we are wasting away, yet inwardly we are being renewed day by day. For our light and momentary troubles are achieving for us an eternal glory that far outweighs them all. So we fix our eyes not on what is seen, but on what is unseen, since what is seen is temporary, but what is unseen is eternal. (2 Corinthians 4:16–18)

Always perseveres:

Be strong and courageous. Do not be afraid or terrified because of them, for the Lord your God goes with you; he will never leave you nor forsake you. (Deuteronomy 31:6)

Keep your lives free from the love of money and be content with what you have, because God has said, "Never will I leave you; never will I forsake you. (Hebrews 13:5)

Near the entrance to Australia's Sydney Harbor is a rocky cliff known as the Gap. A short distance away lived Don and Mora Richie. After serving in the Royal Australian Navy during World Way II, Don and his wife decided to settle there to raise their three children. To do so, Don took up a job as a life insurance salesman. Not long after moving in, Don noticed that it was common to see someone walk to the cliffside alone, never to return.

Don came to learn that since the 1880s, an average of one person per week had used cliffs at the Gap to take their life. Although not entirely understood, the Gap apparently provided enough solitude and peace that for over one hundred years, it had been the most common place that distraught Australians chose to end their lives.

Rather than fret over the impact of this reality on his real estate value, Don decided that his proximity to these tragedies was a blessing. Every morning after waking, Don scanned the cliff from his bedroom window, watching for anyone walking alone who appeared to be out of place or whose body language appeared distraught. Whenever Don saw such a person, he hurried over and, with the largest smile he could muster, said, "May I help you in some way?" To those who were willing to speak with him, he invited them back to his home for tea.

Don once told his daughter that an offer of help "was all that was needed to turn people around" and "not to underestimate the power of a kind word and a smile." And Don's words proved accurate many times over.

Years ago, a man jumped to his death from the Golden Gate Bridge in San Francisco. On his suicide note, he wrote the following words: "If one person smiles at me on the way to the bridge, I will not jump." Tragically that morning, not a single smile came his way.

Since moving into his Australian home in 1964, Don has been credited for saving more than 160 lives. "My ambition has always been to just get them away from the edge, to buy them time, to give them the opportunity to reflect, and give them the chance to realize that things might look better the next morning," Don once told a reporter. "You just can't sit there and watch them. You've got to try and save them."

He would later tell friends "I was a salesman for most of my life, and I sold [these people] life," referring to those he helped away from the cliff. In 2006, Don Richie was awarded the Medal of Order of Australia, the highest civilian honor. It hung in Don's home, directly above a painting that had been left anonymously in his mailbox. The inscription on the painting read, "An angel walks among us." Don Richie died in 2012 at the age of eighty-six.[15][16]

9. **Does not delight in evil** and **always rejoices with the truth**

Does not delight in evil:

Love must be sincere. Hate what is evil; cling to what is good. (Romans 12:9)

---

[15] Kristen Genineau, "Australian "Angel" Saves Lives at Suicide Spot," *CBS News,* June 14, 2010.

[16] Max Reed, "Meet the Australian Who's Saved 160 People from Suicide," *Gawker,* June 15, 2010.

Rejoices with the truth:

> Yet now I am happy, not because you were made sorry, but because your sorrow led you to repentance. For you became sorrowful as God intended and so were not harmed in any way by us. (2 Corinthians 7:9)

In the times of kings and kingdoms, there was a young prince who grew up under the guidance of a watchful king. The prince's closest friend was the son of a castle servant who was of very little means. The two were inseparable and because of the innocence of youth, the disparities of status and wealth were inconsequential and mostly unnoticed.

But over time, as the prince's grooming for kingship began, the two friends spent less and less time together. Eventually, the requirements of life forced the relationship to drift apart, until ultimately it became necessary for the servant's son to leave the castle grounds to find work.

A number of years later, the king died, and the prince assumed the throne. In an effort to assert his leadership among a citizenry whose behavior had waned during the failing health of the king's latter years, the newly anointed king established a number of laws, not the least of which was a proclamation that whoever was caught stealing would lose his hand and whoever was caught cheating would be sentenced to hard labor until the thief could provide full restitution for his behavior.

The kingdom responded in kind, and a year of peace passed. Then, on one spring day, the king was alerted that a thief had been apprehended. The king's stomach sank as the reality of his proclamation and the responsibility that he now shouldered sank in. Nonetheless, the new king had prepared himself for this moment. He demanded that the criminal be brought into the throne room so that he could personally impose the first application of his law. *After all,* he thought, *one should not require obedience to a law that he is not willing to personally enforce.*

The king took to his throne, and while the guards stood at attention, his childhood friend was dragged into view. The king's heart felt as if it had skipped a beat, and his face grew pale. The crime was the theft of food, and the criminal clearly was in need of it. The king's forehead began to sweat, and he had to focus his mind just to keep his trembling hand from being seen by his subordinates. After a few seconds of stunned silence, which felt like minutes, the king authoritatively excused himself, stating that he would return shortly.

The king could barely make it out of the room before sickness began to swell in his throat, causing him to sit on the floor before it overtook him. His mind raced, and it was hard to focus on what was happening. *How could this be?* he thought. Had his law been irresponsible? Was he cut out for this? Who allowed this to happen? What would his father have done? How could he reconcile the competing perceptions that if he forgave his friend, then the entire kingdom would know that this new king showed favoritism. If he imposed the consequence, then the entire kingdom would believe him harsh, distant, and without compassion. Grasping focus seemed impossible, but as he searched his soul and his racing heart slowed, the answer became clear, and the young king's vision blurred as his eyes swelled with tears.

The chief guard called the others to attention as the king reentered the chamber. The king was pale but convicted; the pain in his face was obvious, but his countenance was unwavering. The king walked to the throne; he rested his hand on the armrest but stood beside it, rather than sitting.

The room was deathly silent, as those who had not earlier understood the connection between the king and the criminal had been so informed during the king's brief absence. As a result, every eye was riveted on the king, and not one man could bring himself to guess what the king might do.

The king's words hit each man in attendance like a punch to the gut, and an audible gasp filled the room when he announced that on this day, his law would stand. The punishment would be imposed. And every eye was glued to the king as he descended the stairs and walked toward his friend, who was already being shoved against the wooden block on which his hand would be removed. Words could not describe the flood of thoughts that raced through each head and heart when the king gently took his friend by the wrist, removed his arm from the wooden block, and replaced his friend's hand with his own.

You see that on this day, the king's law was upheld, and the punishment was applied but not to the guilty. Instead, it was borne by the one who, through love and compassion, imposed the punishment upon himself so that the guilty could reenter life with another opportunity to choose right.

We will never know the thoughts and emotions of the king's childhood friend as he watched the king's hand removed. It might be safe to assume that from that day forward, that man's behavior was not dictated by fear of consequence but instead out of deep love, knowing that his life choices were the only currency through which he could show gratitude to the king.

10. **Never fails**

> Everyone who believes that Jesus is the Christ is born of God, and everyone who loves the father loves his child as well. This is how we know that we love the children of God: by loving God and carrying out his commands. In fact, this is love for God: to keep his commands. And his commands are not burdensome, for everyone born of God overcomes the world. This is the victory that has overcome the world, even our faith. Who is it that overcomes the world? Only the one who believes that Jesus is the Son of God. (1 John 5:1–5)

The Race
—Dr. D. H. "Dee" Groberg

Whenever I start to hang my head in front of failure's face,
my downward fall is broken by the memory of a race.
A children's race, young boys, young men; how I remember well,
excitement sure, but also fear, it wasn't hard to tell.
They all lined up so full of hope, each thought to win that race
or tie for first, or if not that, at least take second place.
Their parents watched from off the side, each cheering for their son,
and each boy hoped to show his folks that he would be the one.

The whistle blew and off they flew, like chariots of fire,
to win, to be the hero there, was each young boy's desire.
One boy in particular, whose dad was in the crowd,
was running in the lead and thought "My dad will be so proud."
But as he speeded down the field and crossed a shallow dip,
the little boy who thought he'd win, lost his step and slipped.
Trying hard to catch himself, his arms flew everyplace,
amidst the laughter of the crowd he fell flat on his face.
As he fell, his hope fell too; he couldn't win it now.
Humiliated, he just wished to disappear somehow.

But as he fell his dad stood up and showed his anxious face,
which to the boy so clearly said, "Get up and win that race!"
He quickly rose, no damage done, behind a bit that's all,
and ran with all his mind and might to make up for his fall.
So anxious to restore himself, to catch up and to win,
his mind went faster than his legs. He slipped and fell again.
He wished that he had quit before with only one disgrace.
"I'm hopeless as a runner now, I shouldn't try to race."

But through the laughing crowd he searched and found his father's face
with a steady look that said again, "Get up and win that race!"
So he jumped up to try again, ten yards behind the last.
"If I'm to gain those yards," he thought, "I've got to run real fast!"
Exceeding everything he had, he regained eight, then ten …
but trying hard to catch the lead, he slipped and fell again.
Defeat! He lay there silently. A tear dropped from his eye.
"There's no sense running anymore! Three strikes I'm out! Why try?
I've lost, so what's the use?" he thought. "I'll live with my disgrace."
But then he thought about his dad, who soon he'd have to face.

"Get up," an echo sounded low, "you haven't lost at all,
for all you have to do to win is rise each time you fall.
Get up!" the echo urged him on, "Get up and take your place!
You were not meant for failure here! Get up and win that race!"
So, up he rose to run once more, refusing to forfeit,
and he resolved that win or lose, at least he wouldn't quit.
So far behind the others now, the most he'd ever been,
still he gave it all he had and ran like he could win.
Three times he'd fallen stumbling, three times he rose again.
Too far behind to hope to win, he still ran to the end.

They cheered another boy who crossed the line and won first place,
head high and proud and happy—no falling, no disgrace.
But, when the fallen youngster crossed the line, in last place,
the crowd gave him a greater cheer for finishing the race.
And even though he came in last with head bowed low, unproud,
you would have thought he'd won the race, to listen to the crowd.
And to his dad he sadly said, "I didn't do so well."
"To me, you won," his father said. "You rose each time you fell."

And now when things seem dark and bleak and difficult to face,
the memory of that little boy helps me in my own race.
For all of life is like that race, with ups and downs and all.
And all you have to do to win is rise each time you fall.
And when depression and despair shout loudly in my face,
another voice within me says, "Get up and win that race!"[17]

SUMMARY

We have learned that part of maturing in Christ (moving from milk
to solid food) is discovering the magnificence behind the virtues
that make up God's character and therefore moving away from any
prohibitive lens we may have looked through. For example, when
we think of placing our desires second to God's, we can feel an
anxiety move into our hearts because we may have a propensity to
view Christianity more from the perspective of what we give up,
rather than what we gain. But let's place this into a different context
for a moment.

When you first fell in love with your spouse, how hard was it
for you to adopt his or her passions and dreams? In fact, it is more
common for someone who is newly in love to delay or put on
hold their own dreams to become the greatest fan, supporter, and
promoter of their love interest. Doing so isn't a burden because
there is a return on this investment—requited love. Why, then,
when we think of denying ourselves for an ever-increasing intimate
relationship with the one who created us to know Him, do we view
self-denial as prohibitive and restrictive? True, it is because Satan is
constantly lying to us, and yes, we are in a spiritual war for our souls.
But I put before you that the difference between winning that war
and surviving that war is how inspired you are by the outcome.

Young men dream about fighting to protect a woman's honor;
why don't we dream about protecting the honor of our Father, the
King? Young women dream about finding their life partners and

---

[17] Reprinted by permission of Dr. D. H. "Dee" Groberg.

will often make deep personal sacrifices to support their husbands and children; why is that hard to do for the groom of the church?

Ironically, the world loves God's virtues when it sees them lived out in people. That's why CNN has its annual Hero Awards for those who excel in service and compassion, and the Olympic Games are filled with journalistic in-depth looks into the discipline, hard work, perseverance, and excellence of the competing athletes. The great tragedy is that the world does not recognize those attributes as originating from and existing in their heavenly Father. What is even worse is that the primary reason the world does not recognize God's virtues as coming from God is because those of us who proclaim the name of Christ are often not the ones exhibiting them. And therein lies a challenge—to become like Christ by literally becoming like Him. As Peter says, "Make every effort" for goodness to seep from your every pore. "Make every effort" to intimately know God and to make yourself known to those Christians *and* non-Christians around you. "Take captive every thought" so that you may subject it to the mind of Christ, while you put yourself second to God's passions, and so on.

In light of the stories above, take a minute to visualize the following: What if Christians made up the most empathetic and philanthropic doctors? What if Christians presided over courts with godly justice and mercy? What if Christians became the most astute politicians with unshakable integrity? What if Christians were the hardest-working athletes with a Barnabas-level encouragement and sportsmanship? What if Christians were the kindest and most helpful retail workers? What if Christians were the most professional and respectful police officers? What if Christians lit up their offices with kindness and generosity? What if Christians were the most patient and understanding schoolteachers? What if Christian managers consistently exhibited servant leadership? What if every person who claimed to be Christian was becoming more and more reflective of God's attributes with every passing day? Can you visualize this?

Imagine the fellowship at church among people who are ambitious to reflect God, every minute of every day without excuse. Imagine the contrast that would be drawn between the world and its Creator. Now consider that this is not just some fantasy for the afterlife; this is how we are to glorify God in this life (Colossians 3:23–24). This is how we honor Him. This is how we fulfill the role of ambassadors of Christ; it is part of God's plan to reveal Himself to His lost children, and this plan is not new.

In Israel, there are numerous hills (*tels*) that are not natural. Instead, they are ancient cities that, over centuries, have been covered in dust and soil and now simply appear as hills. During excavation, archaeologists will sometimes find cities built upon other cities. One such discovery was Tel Gezer. This great city stood along the road that led from ancient Mesopotamia to Egypt. It is located halfway between Jerusalem and the Mediterranean Sea and was first settled in the early Bronze Age, thousands of years before Jesus. This city existed when Solomon was king, when Abraham transited the area, and when Jesus walked the earth.

Gezer stands on the edge of the coastal plain, a very fertile area with the Mediterranean Sea to the west and the foothills to the east. If you traveled southwest from Gezer, you would come to Egypt, the most technologically advanced country of its day. If you traveled to the north, you would come to the Oriental civilizations, including Mesopotamia, Persia, and Assyria. The Oriental and Egyptian empires needed each other for economic and cultural reasons, and the life artery between those two empires was a road called Via Maris, which ran right through Gezer. If you went east from Gezer, you would pass by Jericho and the Dead Sea before intersecting another north–south thoroughfare called King's Highway. Because of its location, Gezer was able to control *all trade* between these dominant empires, making it one of the most strategically significant cities on earth at that time. As such, people from all nations would routinely transit Gezer and be exposed to the culture of its citizens as they rested and replenished their supplies.

With this in mind, consider that Gezer is one of the cities that God gave to the Israelites, as recorded in Joshua 21:20–26. It was God's intention for His people to reside in the crossroads of the world, through which everyone who moved commerce traveled, rested, and replenished. In placing them there, God was showing that He didn't want His people to live in seclusion or communes. Rather, it was part of God's plan that His people would affect the world by defining morality, justice, and salvation, while displaying His system of living. He wanted His people located where all nations would be exposed to the love, integrity, hospitality, and beauty of His virtue, lived out in His people.

Instead of remaining in the town God had given the Israelites, however, archaeologist tell us that the Israelites chose to retreat to the foothills and allow the Canaanite people to populate the most influential city of its day. Because God's people were content to live in the shadows of the foothills, the people of that day did not come in contact with God. Instead, it saw a very worldly Canaanite people, and with nothing more beautiful to contrast it, the Canaanite way appeared the acceptable norm.

Brothers and sisters, I put before you that God, who is the same yesterday, today, and tomorrow (Malachi 3:6; Hebrews 13:8), has no different expectation from us. He has put us dead center in the middle of the world. Many of us live in one of the world's richest nations and work among some of the world's most influential people. The question is whether we are inspired to embody godly virtue so that the world can see how beautiful our heavenly Father is, or we are content to live in the shadows.

If I'm being honest, sometimes I live in the shadows because I give in to laziness and don't want the responsibility of being a good example. Sometimes I live in the shadows because I am struggling with a sin that I do not want to deal with. But most of the time, I live in the shadows because I have allowed Satan to convince me (or I have convinced myself) that I don't have anything to offer. And that is one of the worst types of self-deceit. We alone have the Spirit of the Creator of the universe that empowers us to both understand and embody His traits and His virtues. When people see God's traits, they are stirred spiritually, even if they don't recognize it as coming from God.

Consider the people's response to Jesus:

> People were overwhelmed with amazement. "He has done everything well," they said. "He even makes the deaf hear and the mute speak." (Mark 7:37)

Let that verse sink in for a minute. Jesus had just healed a deaf and nearly mute person. I don't know about you, but over the course of my fifty-one years on this earth, I have yet to see that repeated. The Bible, which we know tends toward understatement, says that people were not just amazed but *overwhelmed* with amazement. Did you notice why? Was it just the miracle that amazed them? On the contrary, the Bible says that the people were overwhelmed with amazement at the fact that Jesus did everything well; the miracle was just an example of His doing so. That is one of God's traits—He does everything well. In Mark 7:37, we see an example of the world's reaction to a human who embodies God's attributes.

How about you? Do you do everything well, even if it means you need to commit to less? Do you love thoroughly, completely, and sacrificially? Do you honestly strive for excellence at your job? Do you give your absolute best to your schoolwork? Do you listen intently, withhold judgment, and strive for empathy with others? When people pass through your "Gezer," are they overwhelmed with amazement, even if they do not yet know that your every virtue flows from the God who is pursuing them? If not, then let's commit together to making every effort to add each of God's virtues to our faith so that the world can meet God through us.

Biblical historian Ray Vander Laan put it this way:

> We need to live in the crossroads of life. People need to be able to see me so that they can see God. We tend to isolate ourselves, sit in judgement of others, and settle for mediocrity rather than seeing that we are to live so publicly, so front and center, that we become a flavoring influence, so that people can see

God. Wouldn't it be awesome if every time someone saw my life, they would say, "Wow. Your God must truly be awesome."[18]

In ancient Israel, it was common practice to set up a stone memorial on a site of great historical significance. We see this occur many times in the Old Testament. The stones chosen were usually about the height of an adult and were placed vertically so that they would stand out as having been placed there intentionally, rather than by natural events. When someone would travel by these historical markers, they would be compelled to ask what had happened there, and stories of God's glory would then be shared.

Throughout this book, we have studied the words of Peter, who authored our theme scripture regarding which of God's virtues we should make every effort to embody and in what order we should go after them. It is appropriate to see what Peter said regarding the way we are to live our lives.

> You also, like living stones, are being built into a spiritual house to be a holy priesthood, offering spiritual sacrifices acceptable to God through Jesus Christ. For in Scripture it says: "See, I lay a stone in Zion, a chosen and precious cornerstone, and the one who trusts in him will never be put to shame." Now to you who believe, this stone is precious. But to those who do not believe, "The stone the builders rejected has become the cornerstone," and, "A stone that causes people to stumble and a rock that makes them fall." They stumble because they disobey the message—which is also what they were destined for. But you are a chosen people, a royal priesthood, a holy nation, God's special possession, that you may declare the praises of him who called you out of darkness into

---

[18] Ray Vander Laan, "Promised Land," *That the World may Know*, Focus on the Family, 1998.

his wonderful light. Once you were not a people, but now you are the people of God; once you had not received mercy, but now you have received mercy. Dear friends, I urge you, as foreigners and exiles, to abstain from sinful desires, which wage war against your soul. Live such good lives among the pagans that, though they accuse you of doing wrong, they may see your good deeds and glorify God on the day he visits us. (1 Peter 2:5-12)

Wow! What a scripture. We are becoming living stones, a living and visible monument to God that brings attention to Him. Each day that I live as a Christian, I am becoming more and more of a living monument to what God is doing. When people pass by me, they are to say, "What happened here?" or "How is this person (family or home) so peaceful and loving?" and there is then an opportunity to introduce them to God. We are a chosen people. We are not just a priesthood (priests intercede between God and man), but we are a *royal* priesthood because we are also children of the King. We are a holy nation—holy because we reflect God and are therefore *set apart* by His attributes, His virtues. We are God's special possession because our very lives declare the praises of God, who called us out of darkness into His wonderful light. Ask yourself honestly whether you are characterized by feeling that His light is wonderful or burdensome. Once, we were nomads—not a people—because we had not received mercy, and we were therefore condemned. But now we have received mercy from the only one who has the authority to condemn and forgive.

And what are we to do with all of this? According to Peter, the answer marries up perfectly with what we have been studying the previous eight chapters. We are to live such good lives among those still lost that, despite accusations, they may see our good deeds and glorify God on the day He visits us.

Brothers and sisters, the lost have absolutely no idea what God looks like or who He is. They have many preconceptions—the big punisher in the sky, out of touch with human realities, oppressive, repressive, judgmental, hateful of people who are born different than what is morally acceptable, and the list goes on and on. But when they see you embodying goodness, knowledge, self-control, perseverance, godliness, mutual affection, and love, they are overwhelmed with amazement and say, "He (or she) does everything well," and that is the first time they begin to see God for who He really is. This is what Jesus envisioned when He spoke of the shining light on a hill. He put you in Gezer and has given you His Spirit to empower you, a family of disciples to encourage you, a hope and a future, complete forgiveness, and an inheritance that can never fade or spoil.

Join with me in committing to make every effort to more accurately represent God with every passing day. Only then will those who surround us, flailing about in the sea, recognize God on the day He visits us because they will have already seen Him in us. We need to be the ones who use everything that God has given us to serve Him. It starts by passionately striving to make every effort to embody every one of God's virtues. But it does not end there. We must then foster every talent He has bestowed upon us so that we can reach those lost, who God ordained for us to encounter.

CONCLUSION

> For this very reason, make every effort to add to your faith goodness; and to goodness, knowledge; and to knowledge, self-control; and to self-control, perseverance; and to perseverance, godliness; and to godliness, mutual affection; and to mutual affection, love. For if you possess these qualities in increasing measure, they will keep you from being ineffective and unproductive in your knowledge of our Lord Jesus Christ. But whoever does not have them is nearsighted and blind, forgetting that they have been cleansed from their past sins. (2 Peter 1:5–9)

In light of our discussions regarding the limited motivation that fear is capable of producing and, therefore, the need to come in contact with God's more beautiful way, it might seem strange to you that Peter seems to end this thought with a statement in verses 8 and 9 that highlight words of vice and warnings of consequence. Just so there is no misunderstanding, let me reiterate one final time that fear is not bad. On the contrary, fear is the beginning of wisdom, and just like physical pain, it is intended by God to grab our attention and prompt a change in direction.

But we have learned together that fear can only motivate so far. Young children are not motivated by the impact of their decisions on their relationship with their parents. Instead, they are motivated by fear of pain, either resulting from the natural consequences of disobedience or inflicted by a parent as the result of disobedience. At some point during childhood, however, every child should transition from a motivation of fear and consequence to being motivated by a deep love and respect for his or her parents, an obedience driven by the passion to honor them, which is rooted in an ever-increasing intimate relationship with them.

This, however, doesn't define most of our upbringings because most of us never completely made that transition. Rather than being driven by our relationship with our parents, most of us felt that our parents had become more oppressive and punitive as we entered our teen years. This failure to transition resulted in fear running its course. Absent the motivation of God's more beautiful way, many of us began to sin in secret in order to avoid punishment. We hid behind our outward appearances or productivity and worked diligently to display our independence so that our parents would be impressed enough with our capabilities to grant us the freedoms we desired. Others of us sinned publicly and without hindrance, knowing that doing so would distance us from our parents and gain us the freedom we desired.

The world's mental health experts and educators have categorized these behaviors as a natural part of being a teenager, but that is worldly wisdom and not of God. Rather, these behaviors are not part of being a teenager; they are biblical dysfunction, for nowhere in the Bible does it authorize or condone hidden sin, unresolved conflict with parents, pride, and independence, regardless of age. In fact, if the Bible says anything about the teenage years, it speaks loudly that this is the exact time (before marriage) during which we should experience a rapid development in our relationship with our heavenly Father and actively transition from milk to solid food.

After everything we have learned about the unsustainability of fear of consequence and punishment as a lifelong motivator, it would be improper for us to end our lesson in verses 8 and 9. Remember that Peter did not write his letters in chapters and verses. Instead, let's conclude by placing our theme passage into its rightful context and see what reason Peter gives for making every effort to add these seven virtues to our faith. To do so, we need to look no further than the four verses that precede our theme scripture.

> Simon Peter, a servant and apostle of Jesus Christ, To those who through the righteousness of our God and Savior Jesus Christ have received a faith as precious as ours: Grace and peace be yours in abundance through the knowledge of God and of Jesus our Lord. His divine power has given us everything we need for a godly life through our knowledge of him who called us by his own glory and goodness. Through these he has given us his very great and precious promises, so that through them you may participate in the divine nature, having escaped the corruption in the world caused by evil desires. (2 Peter 1:1–4)

Do you see it? After all that we have looked at, can you hear Peter's passionate plea, quite possibly written to us from his subterranean jail cell adjacent the magnificent Roman Forum. He writes to us, who, through righteousness (relationship), have received a faith so very precious, but it is not through our righteousness that we received this faith. It comes through the relationship that God and Jesus freely extend to us. Grace and peace are ours in abundance. How? Through the knowledge (gnōsis) of God and Jesus, our Lord. For we could never have known God if not for Him becoming a man. God's divine power has given us everything we need for a godly life. How? Through our knowledge of Him, who called us by His glory and goodness.

We have learned that His goodness compelled His grace and mercy. It is through these great and precious promises that we may participate in the divine nature (godliness) and escape the corruption of the world caused by evil desires. How is it that we escape the corruption of the world and our own evil desires? How do we hear Odysseus's song? By making every effort first to comprehend goodness, knowledge, self-control, perseverance, godliness, mutual affection, and love and then to embody these virtues, as God displayed for us while in the flesh.

Now let me ask you: which is more motivating—2 Peter 1:9 or 2 Peter 1:1–4? If you answered 2 Peter 1:1–4, then you understand why Peter could walk confidently to his death, passing the earthly magnificence of the Roman Forum—the house of power to which the whole world submitted—and not bat an eye. He knew that God was the groom of the church, and therefore, God would see His will accomplished in His time and with His power. Peter knew that his job was neither to judge nor to fix the world. He knew that his number-one job was to know God with an ever-increasing intimacy, and his second job was to become like God so that God could be revealed to a lost world.

Let's conclude in Hebrews 12:1–3:

> Therefore, since we are surrounded by such a great
> cloud of witnesses, let us throw off everything that
> hinders and the sin that so easily entangles. And let
> us run with perseverance the race marked out for us,
> fixing our eyes on Jesus, the pioneer and perfecter of
> faith. For the joy set before him he endured the cross,
> scorning its shame, and sat down at the right hand of

the throne of God. Consider him who endured such opposition from sinners, so that you will not grow weary and lose heart.

I cannot think of a better passage on which to end this study of spiritual solid food. If we are going to run the race marked out for us with perseverance, it will benefit us to understand that we are surrounded by a great cloud of witnesses, both living on earth and cheering us on from heaven. More important than our cloud of witnesses, we must throw off everything that hinders us from running, which includes the sin that impedes our relationship with God. We have spent seven chapters learning that the most sustainable way to throw off sin is to fix our eyes on the beauty of God's more beautiful way, demonstrated by Him while He inhabited the flesh, so I trust that this needs no further clarification.

We need not miss the second clause of this sentence, which is to run, with perseverance, *the race marked out for us.* Jesus used the phrase, "carry your cross," because that described the race marked out for Him.

His race was meant to last thirty-three years. It did not include marriage or children but did include the early and voluntary forfeiture of His earthly life for people who still were His enemies. Whatever the race that has been marked out for you, trust God that He has created the course for you and is leveling the paths before you (Isaiah 26:7). Once you have accepted that fact, then fix your eyes on Jesus (God in the flesh), for He was the pioneer of our faith. He left the comforts of the law, religious tradition, family, and culture in order to forge a path for us to get from wherever life has landed us to the promised land. All we have to do is place Jesus in our sights and keep running. Behave how He behaved. Speak like He spoke. Love as He loved. Live as He lived. And do not quit.

Not only did He pioneer our faith, but He perfected it. Jesus did it for the joy set before Him. We should do it not only for the joy set before us but also out of honor and gratitude to our big brother, who pioneered our path, perfected it, and now stands at the finish line with outstretched hands, longing to welcome us home.

I beg God that through this study of Peter's words, you have either begun or furthered your transition to spiritual maturity. God's plan for your life is the only option for true peace, joy, and fulfillment. God's ways are always more beautiful than anything the world has to offer. The more we fix our eyes on Jesus, the pioneer and perfecter of our faith, and make every effort to add God's virtues to our own lives, the more in love with God we will fall, the more faithful we will become, the more peace we will experience, and the more our confidence will grow as our fear is driven out by perfect love. Thank you, brothers and sisters, for joining me on this journey.

Chapter 10

GOD'S SOVEREIGNTY

NOW THAT WE HAVE TAKEN CONSIDERABLE TIME TO EXPLORE Peter's charge to make every effort to add God's goodness, knowledge, perseverance, self-control, godliness, mutual affection, and love to our faith, I am compelled to include one final chapter. It seems incomplete to have looked intently into the virtues and character of God without a discussion on His sovereignty. It also may be unfair to expect anyone to comprehend God's sovereignty without first getting a basic grip on His character. Therefore, if you have skipped ahead to this chapter, I would encourage you to go back and start this book from the beginning. Embracing God's sovereignty is a big ask if you are not already growing in your faith through an ever-increasing knowledge of your Father.

Let's begin this final lesson by diving into one of the most important biblical truths—God's sovereignty, which in its simplest form means His supreme power and authority. Before we begin our discussion, please meditate on and consider the following verses, including both of the complete chapters listed last.

> The Lord does whatever pleases him, in the heavens
> and on the earth, in the seas and all their depths.
> (Psalm 135:6)

Our God is in heaven; he does whatever pleases him.
(Psalm 115:3)

I make known the end from the beginning, from
ancient times, what is still to come. I say, 'My purpose
will stand, and I will do all that I please.' (Isaiah 46:10)

All the peoples of the earth are regarded as nothing. He
does as he pleases with the powers of heaven and the
peoples of the earth. No one can hold back his hand
or say to him: "What have you done?" (Daniel 4:35)

"For no word from God will ever fail." (Luke 1:37)

"I know that you can do all things; no purpose of
yours can be thwarted." (Job 42:2)

See Job 38 and 39.

These verses can strike each of us very differently, depending
on our personal background, our relationships with our parents and
other authorities, and our current understanding of who God is.
For some of us, the above verses can come across harsh, controlling,
and unbending. Others are on the opposite end of the spectrum,
finding great peace in these promises. Therefore, in order to have
a constructive discussion, I would like to focus our thoughts in a
couple of specific directions.

First, in these verses we clearly see the theme that God's sovereignty
is more specific than just His supreme power and authority. They
also encompass the truth that nothing in all creation occurs without
His conscious knowledge and permission. He is in complete control,
even when it appears that creation is in opposition to Him. His plan
is bigger and more comprehensive than we are capable of imagining,
and He does what pleases Him, regardless of opposition. All things
are under God's power and control.

> And we know that in all things God works for the
> good of those who love him, who have been called
> according to his purpose. (Romans 8:28)

We may feel, from time to time, that things in the world and things in our lives are out of control, and we would be partially right. Things are out of *our* control, but they are completely and absolutely under God's control, in every way, at all times, and in all places. He is King of everything. He is Creator of all. He is not flustered. He is never caught off guard, and nothing happens outside of His perfect plan, not even the death of a single bird, according to Jesus in Matthew 10:29.

Second, we only matter because we matter to Him. Absent our Creator and His perfect eternal plan, we are a useless flash in the timeline of all creation. The earth we live on was here before us, and absent Christ's return, it will survive long after us. We worry about human impact on nature, including the climate, and rightly so. But in truth, whatever damage we do to the climate likely will kill off only us. The earth and the cosmos will bounce back, just without humans to enjoy it. In fact, the earth and the cosmos are God's playground, His invention, His pallet, and we are placed here by His design for a very specific purpose. Quite frankly, most of our purpose may not be for this world. Think of the infant who does not make it out of his mother's womb or the one whose life on earth lasts only a few minutes. No doubt, God orchestrated that life to impact his parents and immediate family, but only after this life will we have a clear view of God's eternal plan for that child.

Consider the following verses in Romans:

> What then shall we say? Is God unjust? Not at all!
> For he says to Moses, "I will have mercy on whom
> I have mercy, and I will have compassion on whom
> I have compassion." It does not, therefore, depend
> on human desire or effort, but on God's mercy. For
> Scripture says to Pharaoh: "I raised you up for this

very purpose, that I might display my power in you and that my name might be proclaimed in all the earth." Therefore God has mercy on whom he wants to have mercy, and he hardens whom he wants to harden. One of you will say to me: "Then why does God still blame us? For who is able to resist his will?" But who are you, a human being, to talk back to God? "Shall what is formed say to the one who formed it, 'Why did you make me like this?' "Does not the potter have the right to make out of the same lump of clay some pottery for special purposes and some for common use? What if God, although choosing to show his wrath and make his power known, bore with great patience the objects of his wrath—prepared for destruction? What if he did this to make the riches of his glory known to the objects of his mercy, whom he prepared in advance for glory. (Romans 9:14–23)

Allow this passage to sink in for a minute. God, with foreknowledge of who would accept Him and who would reject Him, wove into His eternal and perfect plan a plan for even those who would reject Him. Paul doesn't beat around the bush on this issue. We cannot read the above verse without wondering why God would make a person whom He foreknew would reject Him and suffer eternal damnation. With that realization in mind, we are compelled to ask how God can hold those accountable who were created with foreknowledge of their damnation. But look at how Paul handles this question: "But who are you, a human being, to talk back to God?" Paul grasped God's sovereignty.

We are created by God, for God, and to fulfill God's purpose. Those of us in the United States have been taught since childhood that all people are equal, with equal rights and an expectation of fairness. I am thankful to live in a country where that is the accepted belief, even if not fully practiced. But we cannot overlay that cultural expectation on our understanding of God's sovereignty.

The scriptures never promise fairness. We are but clay, molded by a Creator in order to fulfill a specific purpose, a purpose of His choosing. Brothers and sisters, if you are not in awe of God, in love with God, and passionate about your relationship with your heavenly Father, then these concepts are offensive and can seem harsh. How does God respond to our offense? "But who are you, a human being, to talk back to God."

Step back with me for a moment to God's perfect world, before sin entered into the heart of man. The Genesis story records that God created Adam, and the two of them walked the earth together, conversing with each other. In fact, the Bible states that God brought to Adam each animal that He had created, and Adam named each one. Although the Bible describes this process in a single verse, imagine, for a moment, how long it took for God to allow Adam to come in contact with each creature that He had created and for Adam to then name those creatures, based on his observations of them in their natural habitat.

But something else occurs, something that will not be confirmed for us for a few more verses. While naming each of God's animals, Adam realizes that every animal has a counterpart of its own kind—every animal, that is, except for Adam. Once that realization takes place, God—who previously had noted that it was not good for man to be alone—creates Eve, and only then are we witnesses to the longing that Adam had developed for one of his own kind. When he first sees Eve, he exclaims, "You have my skeleton! You have my flesh!" In other words, "I have found one that is like me!"

These verses are so often brushed over as just a piece of the creation story, but let's take a moment to ponder what occurred here. Adam walked with God in a sinless environment. This was perfection, a literal heaven on earth. Yet even in perfection—before the fall of man—we see the scriptures describe a part of creation as "not good." How can that be? How can something "not good" exist in a place without sin? The answer is simple yet profound: loneliness is not a sin; it is a state. It is a reality. God allows Adam to live long enough to experience loneliness and to feel it deeply. Only after

God determines that Adam sufficiently understands what it feels like to long for another of his own kind does He give Adam a human counterpart, and Adam's excitement is unabashed. We cannot miss the fact, however, that following the union of Adam and Eve, there is still one being left without a counterpart. Did you catch that? God made man in His very image so that He can have a relationship with one like Him, but man was lonely without one of his own kind. So God made Adam a counterpart, which began the process of God, once again, being left alone.

God is sovereign, so this is not a mistake. In fact, this is one of the most essential elements of God's plan for us that we should understand. God made man so that man could choose to love God back. The only way man could choose whether or not to love God back was to be given the full freedom to choose otherwise. God knows that there will be a remnant of His creation that *does* choose Him, and for that remnant, He will work to restore them to Him. He will work to refine them to remove their errant ways of thinking, of behaving, and of believing. He will heal them and, ultimately, the bride of Christ—composed of those who choose a relationship with God above all else—will be presented to Him, just as Eve was presented by God to Adam. Only then will God have one like Him, with whom to fellowship for eternity.

What can we gather from these truths? You may recall from chapter 4 that the first aspect of the virtue of self-control is capturing our thoughts and continually reminding ourselves that this is all about God. We exist for God. We will only find joy, comfort, assurance, peace, and healing in God. With these thoughts in mind, consider how much you mean to God. The entire, vast, seemingly eternal universe exists to woo you to Him. He adores you and wants fellowship with you. He has an eternal paradise for you that will make the years of this earthly life appear like a mist that vanishes as quickly as it appeared.

If it's all about God, then everything that happens in our lives— even if those happenings are the results of decisions by sinful men— are fully within God's control. He will use those very happenings to draw you to Him, to reveal Himself to you, and to refine you into what He created you to become. Although those children who endure physical abuse from their earthly fathers do so as the result of their fathers' sinful decisions, God, in His sovereignty, will weave that child's experience into His perfect plan for that child to find Him and perhaps reach out to Him. If that child does so, then God will use that child's experiences, brought about by sinful men, to mold that child into a tool that God can use to reach other lost children, while simultaneously refining that child into a perfect part of the bride of Christ. Those born to abject poverty, with little to no hope of escape, may be there because of the greed of others, but God, in His sovereignty, will use that very condition to accomplish His will. God knew which parents will lose their teenage daughter in an automobile accident with a drunk driver. With that foreknowledge, God acts to build that tragedy into His perfect plan.

You see, nothing surprises God, and nothing happens that He doesn't foresee. He cannot be beaten by Satan or by the sinful will of man. God also determines your earthly citizenship—whether first world or developing nation—whether, you lived as a slave or in freedom, whether you will be taken home early or at the end of a long life, whether you will succumb to cancer as a young father, or whether you will endure a physical or mental disability.

It is this same God who determines whether you are an object of mercy or an object of wrath. If we try to explain away this passage or alter its meaning, then we fail to grasp the wholeness of God's sovereignty. In all of my years, I have come up with only two ways to feel about this passage. Either we allow ourselves to feel bitter, which is rooted in entitlement and pride, or we allow ourselves to be open to the truth that God's plan is so big, so awesome, so indescribable, and so incomprehensible that all earthly trials, regardless of how insurmountable they may feel, pale in comparison to the majesty of what He has in store for those who choose a relationship with Him.

Some might find that last sentence contradictory. How can I use the phrase "choose a relationship with Him" when Romans 9 states that God has chosen who He made to be an object of wrath or mercy. Herein lies the burden of being God.

> This is good, and pleases God our Savior, who wants all people to be saved and to come to a knowledge of the truth ... the man Christ Jesus, who gave himself as a ransom for all people. (1 Timothy 2:3–6a)

To have any chance at understanding that which we cannot fully understand, we need to take the Bible in entirety. Consider this: God can passionately desire for all people to be saved, but He cannot impose His will on them without subverting His ultimate purpose—to create for Himself a people who will choose Him *of their own free will*. Just because His omniscience allows Him to see the entirety of your life before it begins doesn't impede your full freedom, in any way, to choose Him or reject Him.

> But now, this is what the Lord says—he who created you, Jacob, he who formed you, Israel: "Do not fear, for I have redeemed you; I have summoned you by name; you are mine. When you pass through the waters, I will be with you; and when you pass through the rivers, they will not sweep over you. When you walk through the fire, you will not be burned; the flames will not set you ablaze. For I am the Lord your God, the Holy One of Israel, your Savior; I give Egypt for your ransom, Cush and Seba in your stead. Since you are precious and honored in my sight, and because I love you, I will give people in exchange for you, nations in exchange for your life. (Isaiah 43:1–4)

This is one of the most beautiful and poetic love letters in the scriptures. The Israelites are reminded that God made them and summoned them by their name and that He takes ownership of them, as a father does his children. He promises that He will be with them when they encounter life's trials but that He will not allow them to be overtaken by those trials. They may be uncomfortable, but they will not perish. You see, God is omniscient. He knows everything that will happen to each one of us, for He gave free will to all humanity. In the exercise of that free will, some humans will hurt other humans. God can foresee it all, but He will let it play out.

But He doesn't let it play out in the way we let things play out with our children. For example, parents might foresee that their teens' lack of discipline likely will cause them to have a very late night of completing homework that will impact how they feel the next day. Parents can intervene with instruction or reminders or sit by and let children suffer the natural consequences of their lack of discipline. Either way, the parents can foresee something coming but do not know exactly how it will play out. God knows exactly how things will play out. With His foreknowledge, He intervenes, not by stopping the trial but by weaving the trial into His perfect plan to refine us, to help us find Him, and to perfect us. Remember that Jesus was made perfect through suffering. Do you really want God to intervene and stop hardship, or would you rather He help you to find Him, see your need for Him, perfect you, and heal you?

This love letter doesn't end there. Rather, we see God's sovereignty in action. He gave over Cush and Seba to the sinful choices He foresaw they would make, but wove that into His plan to reach and teach Israel. Why? Because Israel was precious and honored in His sight. This is unbelievable! You are not just precious to God but honored, meaning that God has chosen to value you higher than He values Himself. How much does He value us? Well, for starters, He will give people in exchange for you and give nations in exchange for your life. Those people and those nations made their own decisions, but God foresaw those decisions and "worked all things to the good of those who love Him, and are called according to *His* purpose." Brothers and sisters, I believe with all my heart that with this understanding, we are supposed to feel the overwhelming love of God, while simultaneously feeling a harsh sobriety that we could easily be one of those who chooses not to love God and, therefore, become part of God's plan to be exchanged for someone who does love God.

One might then ask, how does this sync with the theme of this book—that fear is the beginning of wisdom but not the entirety of wisdom and that we are not to remain in fear because perfect love drives out all fear? Well, brothers and sisters, it all comes down to whether or not you accept that God wants a relationship with you.

When I was first dating my wife, I was much more fearful then of losing the relationship than I was after she committed herself to me in marriage. That's not to say that it is beyond me to make decisions that could destroy my marriage, but it is a different level of commitment. This commitment is one that is not to be undone just because you no longer think he or she is the one for you. Those considerations were allowable while you were courting, but once committed to each other in marriage, the bar is raised significantly (e.g., death and marital unfaithfulness). Remember that marriage exists as part of God's plan as a visible representation of our invisible relationship with Him. The primary difference between a marriage relationship with God and your marriage to your spouse is that your spouse is also a sinner who can damage your marriage. With God, you are the only one who can damage your relationship with Him, and in that knowledge is great peace and tremendous comfort. As a disciple, remaining in Him resides entirely within your control, for He will never leave you or forsake you. Only you have the power to choose to leave and forsake Him.

> For the Lord watches over the way of the righteous, but
> the way of the wicked leads to destruction. (Psalm 1:6)

Do we need further convincing that being in a functional relationship with God is the only place where we can find true joy, inner peace, and a security that will not wither and cannot be taken?

With these truths in mind, let's look at Ephesians 2 as we move into the final part of this lesson and a summation of this book.

> As for you, you were dead in your transgressions and sins, in which you used to live when you followed the ways of this world and of the ruler of the kingdom of the air, the spirit who is now at work in those who are disobedient. All of us also lived among them at one time, gratifying the cravings of our flesh and following its desires and thoughts. Like the rest, we were by nature deserving of wrath. But because of his great love for us, God, who is rich in mercy, made us alive with Christ even when we were dead in transgressions—it is by grace you have been saved. And God raised us up with Christ and seated us with him in the heavenly realms in Christ Jesus, in order that in the coming ages he might show the incomparable riches of his grace, expressed in his kindness to us in Christ Jesus. For it is by grace you have been saved, through faith—and this is not from yourselves, it is the gift of God—not by works, so that no one can boast. For we are God's handiwork, created in Christ Jesus to do good works, which God prepared in advance for us to do. (Ephesians 2:1–10)

In this verse, we see an example of God's sovereignty as it applies to our lives. Consider the truth that we were dead in our sins and transgressions. We were not misguided. We were not off course. We were not simply misled. We were dead. It was irrevocable, irreversible, and unalterable. We were destined to be separated from God and from all that is good for eternity. That is the way of man. God had created perfection, but man, in his pride, chose to forgo God's perfect timing and decided that he was going to know what God knew by eating from the tree of the knowledge of good and bad. That impatience, rooted in pride, led to man's death. This same cycle has occurred in every person ever born—but one. Said simply, God creates what was perfect. Man interferes and choses to jump ahead of God's perfect timing. With that choice, man exchanges his relationship with God and brings about his own spiritual death.

Now contrast that with what we see in Ephesians. Here, we find that man is dead, but God interferes and introduces redemption, which opens the only door for man to return to an eternal relationship with his Creator.

Allow me, if you will, to paint this picture with an analogy. Imagine for a moment that you are standing on the deck of a cruise ship, looking over the railing at the aqua-colored Caribbean Sea, five stories below. The sky is blue, and the gentle breeze caused by the ship's propulsion cools your skin from the sun's more intense rays. In the moment, you decide that you want a better and unobstructed view, a godlike perspective of the Caribbean as you tower over it from fifty feet above. You disregard the "Stay Off the Railing" sign and place your feet on the rung that is second from the top. One leg goes behind the top rung and the other in front of it, pinching the rail between your legs for stability. But you don't account for the moisture on the railing, which causes that railing to be as slippery as ice against the soft rubber soles of your shoes. Before you know what is happening, your feet shoot out from under you, and you are plummeting to the ocean below.

Fortunately, you land feet first and are stunned but uninjured. And once you scramble to the surface in this warm and shallow sea, it seems that all will be OK. Then your clothes and shoes begin to weigh you down, so you shed them—a small price to pay for your ability to easily tread water. But as the moments pass and the ship has no appearance of changing course, the truth of your situation begins to dawn on you. Although the seas are shallow, you cannot reach the bottom. Although the water is warm, it is cooler than your body temperature, which will eventually lead to hypothermia. Although you are a strong swimmer, you will ultimately succumb to exhaustion. If the ship does not turn around, you are capable of delaying death for only a short time.

Everything you have built for yourself and everything you have achieved is about to become meaningless. The family members you love are on that boat, and although they will ultimately realize that you are missing and look for you on the ship, it likely will take too long for them to conclude that you are missing from the boat altogether. The pleasures of life that you enjoyed a moment ago are now cruising away from you, and you are powerless to fix your situation. There is no island within swimming distance and no floatation device to give your muscles a break. Death is inevitable, absent someone's intervention.

"Can it really end this way?" you ask yourself. "What about my spouse? My kids? My job?" But the truth about life is that it will move on without you, as surely as the cruise ship continues to sail. Sure, your loved ones will mourn your loss, but time heals all wounds. Absent someone's intervention, nothing can save you, not even additional time driven by a burst of energy; it will only prolong the inevitable. You are totally incapable of saving yourself. The short-term gift to live your life is coming to an end. It is becoming clear to you that the power you thought you had was on loan to you. In a short time, you will succumb to death, the ultimate surrender, and you are utterly powerless over everything that happens, beginning at the moment your earthly life ends.

This is what Paul is trying to explain to the Ephesians. As we age in our Christian walks, we tend to adjust our history into fond memories. We remember the fun of high school but not the pain, immaturity, and insecurity. We remember the best of previous relationships and not the turmoil and unresolved hurts. As we mature in Christ, we accidentally apply our newfound maturity and self-control to the memories of what we were like before Christ. Our lives before Christ become romanticized, and our opinions of ourselves become skewed. Paul reminds us of the truth that we were treading water as the result of our own disobedience, death was inevitable, and we were powerless to save ourselves. God alone knew that we were treading water, never taking His eye off us. It was our heavenly Father who rescued us. Yes, we agreed to study the Bible and confess our sins, but claiming power over that is as ridiculous as taking credit for grabbing the hand of the boatsman who rescued us from the water. God forgave all of our disobedience. He set aside the hurt we had caused Him in our pride. He restored us to undeserved sonship and gave us an inheritance in what can never fade, spoil, or perish. He placed His Spirit within us and empowered us to change the things we were powerless to change prior to His intervention. And all of this was according to His plan.

If we find ourselves rejecting His plan, resisting His reasoning, disappointed in His choices, or unhappy with His provisions, then we are forgetting or romanticizing our past. Only those who truly connect with the truth of their own deaths—caused by their own life choices—and accept the reality of God's mercy and grace in their lives are capable of surrendering their will and enjoying God's lordship.

If you have not surrendered your life to God, then this is where your earthly story ends. You will stand before the Creator of all, but having rejected a relationship with Him, you will not continue your eternal journey with Him. For those who have surrendered their lives to God, the ship analogy continues, and it plays out as follows: God appears and offers you a lifeline. Despite the appearance of your Savior and the lifeline He is offering you, you still must grab hold of it and hang on. No one in their right mind would claim that he had saved himself by grabbing the lifeline. It was God who appeared and offered a lifeline through the sacrifice of a blameless lamb, His only perfect Son. Yes, you had to grab on and hold tight to the lifeline, but the effort you had to exert was not only minuscule, but it would not have been possible if there was no lifeline to grab. In truth, death was imminent, and you were without any power to stop it, but God …

And that is what Ephesians 2 says. There was God, who made man in perfection. Man desired God's knowledge of good and bad before he was morally ready to handle it, and so he tossed aside God's instruction and God's perfect timeline. In doing so, man brought death upon himself. But "because of His great love for us, God, who is rich in mercy, *made us alive* in Christ, even *while we were dead* in our transgressions. It is by grace [we] have been saved" and "we have been seated by Him in the heavenly realms *in* Christ Jesus."

There is so much here to unpack. We have studied God's goodness, which is described here in Ephesians as "God, who is rich in mercy." What is mercy? It means that *someone else volunteered to take on the punishment due you.* Do you remember the story about the king and his childhood friend in chapter 9 on love? That is a story of mercy. The punishment was carried out, but by mercy alone, it was not given to you. Just as with the king's childhood friend, the acceptance of grace and mercy produces in us a change in behavior and perspective, driven by gratitude. The more in touch we are with what we have done to deserve the punishment due us, the more gratitude we feel and exhibit—hence, the reason we are instructed to regularly commune with Him in remembrance of Him.

But God is not just rich in mercy. He did not just take on our punishment and then kick us back into the world to try again. The scriptures say that God then made us alive in Christ, even while we were dead in our transgressions. That is the definition of grace. Whereas mercy is exhibited when someone else takes on the punishment due you, *grace is a present you are given but do not deserve.* That grace is the undeserved gift of being made alive in Christ.

Galatians 3:27 says it best when it states, "For all of you who were baptized into Christ have clothed yourself with Christ." While dead in our transgressions, God's mercy placed our punishment upon Jesus. Then God clothed us in Christ, just as He clothed Adam and Eve in the skin of a blameless animal. From that moment forward, when God looks down on the earth, He no longer sees us; He sees Jesus. He sees a vision of what we are becoming. The paths are made level for our feet so that He may lead us to fulfill His purpose for us. He seats us in glory, adjacent Jesus. Everything we were powerless to do on our own, He has done for us.

But Ephesians 2 does not end there:

> For it is by grace you have been saved, through faith—and this is not from yourselves, it is the gift of God—not by works, so that no one can boast. For we are God's handiwork, created in Christ Jesus to

do good works, which God prepared in advance for us to do. (Ephesians 2:8–10)

Here, we see God's plan to overcome man's actions. Man's pride leads to his destruction—chaos in an otherwise perfect creation—but God's sovereignty is so great, so all-powerful, that even man's fallen world succumbs to its gravitational pull. Hudson Taylor once said it this way: "God has made no mistake in what He has permitted." Do you see the sovereignty in that statement? Nothing occurs that God has not permitted, and nothing falls outside of His perfect and all-encompassing plan. We look at the chaos caused by man's downfall, and we fret, stress, and worry. But this reaction is due to our myopic perspective and our disconnection with the spiritual truth of God's sovereignty.

I would like to pause, though, and focus specifically on verse 10, which states, "For we are God's handiwork, created in Christ Jesus to do good works, which God prepared in advance for us to do."

The Greek word used here for handiwork is ποίημα (pronounced *poiēma* in English) and means a work of divine creation. This word is only used one other time in the New Testament and is found in Romans 1:20, which reads,

> For since the creation of the world, God's invisible qualities—his eternal power and divine nature—have been clearly seen, being understood from what has been made, so that men are without excuse.

Poiēma is translated "made" here in Romans 1, and in this context, we see the divine nature of the word. Poiēma is not just handiwork; it is divine handiwork (or craftsmanship) that displays—and therefore reveals—God's invisible qualities, His eternal power, and His divine nature, such that men are without excuse. In that light, you see why I could not conclude our lessons on the virtues of God, listed in 2 Peter, without addressing God's sovereignty. It is God's perfect plan that we would exercise the free will He granted us to choose a relationship with Him, and that in doing so, the elect would embody God's character by adopting His virtue and become the revelation of Him to the remainder of His lost children.

Let's hone in on a few concepts in verse 10 that will help to set our minds.

We are God's handiwork, His craftsmanship, his poiēma. Proverbs 8:30 reads,

> Then I was beside Him as a master craftsman; and I
> was daily His delight, rejoicing always before Him.
> (NKJV)

Unfathomably, the Master Craftsman created everything you see and even that which you can't see out of only approximately 118 known basic molecular elements. This Master Craftsman "knit you together in your mother's womb," and you are "fearfully and wonderfully made" to be perfectly suited to completely fulfill God's plan for you, both on this earth and after. He placed you onto the earth at the exact time and place of His choosing, with the parents, upbringing, challenges, gender, gifts, talents, intellectual ability, attractiveness, temperament, height, and surroundings that are part of His perfect plan. And He made it such that the only way you can find true fulfillment while on this earth is when you align and surrender yourself to God's choices.

The world has decided to categorize humanity into divisions based on levels of oppression, and there is reason to do so in the eyes of the world. In the United States, minorities have a steeper road to climb than those in the majority. Women face challenges in the workplace that escape men. Money purchases privilege, and the absence of money makes some privilege unobtainable. But in God's plan, this thinking loses relevance because you were perfectly made in the color, shape, athleticism, gender, attractiveness, aptitude, etc., to perfectly accomplish God's plan and because the only time you will find true peace and joy is when you are aligned with God's plan.

The more you fixate on life's lack of fairness, the more you diverge from God's truth.

I am not minimizing the challenges we face in this world due to our ethnicity, gender, socioeconomic standing, or natural talents. In fact, we should use our energy, God-given talents, and government-granted rights—including our right to vote—to make this world a better and fairer place while we reside in it. But what good is it to fixate on the negative effect life's challenges have on us? God wants us to focus on the opportunities He has created in advance for us to grab, in order to achieve His perfect plan, rather than our own. In this, we need to be transformed by the renewing of our minds, as it says in Romans 12. Let's read that together.

> Therefore, I urge you, brothers and sisters, in view of God's mercy, to offer your bodies as a living sacrifice, holy and pleasing to God—this is your true and proper worship. Do not conform to the pattern of this world, but be transformed by the renewing of your mind. Then you will be able to test and approve what God's will is—his good, pleasing and perfect will. (Romans 12:1–2)

Does this not address exactly what we are discussing?

- "In view of God's mercy"—is the motivation.
- "Offer your bodies as a living sacrifice"—to do the good works He prepared in advance for us.
- "Holy and pleasing to God"—God's sovereign plan is pleasing to Him, and we please Him by displaying trust through surrender.
- "This is your true and proper worship"—which cannot be supplanted by emotional, spiritual highs created through music or sermons that tug at the heartstrings.

- "Do not conform to the pattern of this world"—by succumbing to and defining yourself by the world's categorization of your challenges.
- "But be transformed by the renewing of your mind"—by submitting to God's plan, aligning your thoughts with His, and trusting in His sovereignty.
- "Then you will be able to test and approve what God's will is."

How will you ever know God's will if you refuse to elevate your thinking above the world's categorization of your oppression?

If you need further confirmation of the intent of Romans 12, read verses 3–8, and you will see the continuation of this theme. In fact, the scriptures specifically state that God created you exactly as He wanted and needed you to be so that you would fulfill His role in His family.

Let me expand on this, as I know that we have a propensity to define ourselves by worldly categories. One could say, "I have less opportunity because my socioeconomic status required me to attend a poverty-laden high school with reduced educational opportunities." God would say, "I built my plan for you around that socioeconomic status so that you could perfectly fulfill My role for you, with which I am pleased."

Another might say, "I was denied a college opportunity that I earned because someone else's eligibility was artificially elevated due to Affirmative Action." God would say, "I allowed you to be in that exact place so that you could fulfill My role for you, with which I am pleased."

Another might say, "I have been denied fair and equal pay due only to my gender." God would say, "I chose your gender before you were born, with the foreknowledge of the man-made limits that would be imposed on you and wrote the script of your life around these hindrances to perfect you so that you could fulfill My role for you, with which I am pleased."

I am *not* saying that, as citizens, we should not move to remedy inequalities with our votes, political action, and voices. What I *am* saying is that we need not define ourselves by the categories in which we find ourselves. If we are to elevate our thinking to align it with God, then we must accept that He has everything completely under control. We are where He wants us, with the exact talent, looks, ethnicity, income, number of friends, freedoms, etc., that He deems perfect to accomplish His plan for our lives.

To elevate our thinking, let's insert some truth to our discussion of the world's categorizations. Because the world is flailing around, absent a relationship with God that is based on the truth of who He is and the authority He wields, those of the world spend an inordinate amount of time categorizing each other into those who are oppressed and those who oppress. As a society, we have decided that those categories are race, gender, wealth, and geography. But this is an oversimplification of the truth. There are many more "categories" than these three. For example, studies show that physical attractiveness is an asset both in earnings potential and career advancement. Socioeconomic standing has a roll in education and opportunity. Speech impediments affect career opportunities. Single-parent households add challenge in child-rearing. Physical disabilities clearly affect life opportunities. Physical, sexual, and mental abuse affect self-esteem and future relationships, including one's view of authority. And this is just a small sampling of "categories." What is my point? Well, let's take an example of a woman in the workplace. Studies show that, as a woman, she will have to work harder to obtain pay equal to her male counterparts. But what if she is also unattractive, as defined by the society in which she lives? Research shows that she will have to work harder to achieve promotion opportunities that may be offered to attractive coworkers. What if that woman has abuse in her past that affects her view of authority? What if she is also a minority for whom English is a second language? And what if she is a single mother, raising children?

Here is my point: The world wants to place this person into oversimplified categories so that it can deem her oppressed or an oppressor. But the truth is that this person is an individual with a story written by God so that she would perhaps reach out to Him and find Him (Acts 17:27)—a story crafted by God so that she would learn to surrender to Him and to His will (Matthew 16:24–27), a plan for her to develop a conviction that this world is not her home (Hebrews 13:14), and a path on which she would learn to fully trust God to meet her every need, as He deems fit (Matthew 6:25–32). In doing these things, this woman will begin to reflect the character and virtue of God to those around her and become a pathway to a restoring those whose view of God is skewed. In this, she will find true joy and peace and be able to test God's good, pleasing, and perfect will. Maybe changes will occur in the world that create a fairer life for her, but it is also possible that this might not occur. This is why it is so very essential to possess the self-control to deeply believe that it is not about us; it is all about God.

Brothers and sisters, we will not be able to mature in our relationships with God until we understand our condition without Him and until we learn to surrender completely to His sovereignty. Who do you want planning your course? How absurd is it that we planned our courses, and they led to irreparable and irreversible death? God then interceded and rescued us, entirely on His own and without any foresight by or assistance from us. Yet somehow, after our rescue, we want to reassume control.

Trust the Creator of your soul, your heavenly Father, who has leveled the path before you and charted your course exactly as He sees fit in order to perfect you, to reunite you with Him for eternity, and to prepare you for whatever eternity has planned for you. We must elevate our thinking to see that God uses us to reflect His character and virtue to His lost children, while simultaneously working to perfect us and remake us in His image. Remember our premise that God placed us into perfection, but man's choices led to death (Romans 3:23). But Ephesians 2 provides an opposite path. Man brought about death, but God provided salvation through mercy and grace. And that mercy and grace is not without effect.

The world relies on these oppressor/oppressed categories to explain, excuse, and justify their conditions. The disciple of Christ looks at his condition as the road crafted by God to perfect him and bring him to eternity with God in a place no eye has seen and no mind can fathom.

> For I am the least of the apostles and do not even deserve
> to be called an apostle, because I persecuted the church
> of God. But by the grace of God I am what I am, and
> his grace to me was not without effect. No, I worked
> harder than all of them—yet not I, but the grace of God
> that was with me. (1 Corinthians 15:9–10)

Would you gamble with the life of another? Most people answer this question with a resounding no. Yet most adults choose to have children. Why? Because we want to have someone on whom to lavish our love, another of our kind, someone to make better than ourselves, and someone to carry on our personal legacy and to put meaning to our existence. Yet by choosing to have children, we gamble with their lives. What if they are born with severe challenges? What if they develop cancer? What if they have spouses who are unfaithful to them? What if they reject a relationship with God? Despite all of these potential outcomes, we choose to reproduce and create an individual, at great risk to that individual. Yet we so often look at God in consternation for making us. We are so fickle. We appreciate the life God gave us when we are flourishing, and we blame God for the life He gave us when we are struggling. We appreciate His guidance and direction when we benefit from it being lived out by others, yet we often loathe it when those same behavioral expectations are placed on us. We choose to create children in our own images and impress our paradigms on them, all while wagging our fingers in the face of God for His parenting of us. Oh, what wretched people we are. Who will rescue us from these bodies of death? Thanks be to Christ Jesus, our Lord!

I earlier told a story of a king who paid the price for the sin of his childhood friend. Although the story is an obvious analogy to our Heavenly Father, the analogy is errant in an important way. Unlike the king who was surprised by the sin of his friend and was thrust into a real-time internal debate over how to balance enforcement of his law with his desire to show mercy and grace, God—in His sovereignty—had foreknowledge of the fall of man while man was still nothing more than an idea. With all foreknowledge, God was also fully aware that He would have to send a part of Himself to live as a man among men, be raised by human parents, subject Himself to the authority of corrupt government, be mistreated by those He had created, and surrender Himself to unjust punishment in order for man to have any chance at restoring his relationship with his Creator. Despite this foreknowledge and a limitless period with which to contemplate the cost of the creation of man, God chose to make you because He was so deeply in love with the idea of you. As God slowly knit you together in your mother's womb, He did so with full knowledge and complete understanding of what would be required of Him to restore you to Him. He loved both the idea of you and the reality of you with such indescribable and incalculable depth that not one of us may ever fully grasp the love of our Father. This is the actual story of our King.

Thank you brothers and sisters for taking this journey with me. I pray that you are beginning to hear His more beautiful song. I pray also that you are beginning to see your heavenly Father as the embodiment of goodness, poured out through knowledge, wrapped in self control, with the perseverance of a perfect parent whose godliness results in the mutual affection of a big brother with a love so deep that words fail any adequate description. I pray that your understanding of His sovereignty is wrapping you in His warm embrace and providing you with a freedom from any emotional and mental discouragement that is rooted in a misunderstanding of who God is and what He desires from you. And I pray that these understandings are filling you with a peace that passes human understanding and a joy that is rooted in accepting how deeply you are loved. Lastly, I pray that you too are compelled to make every effort to imitate the virtues that make up your heavenly Father so that you might love Him as He desires to be loved while appropriately representing Him to those of His children who are still lost.

Let's close by meditating on Paul's words to our Roman brothers and sisters.

> Therefore, there is now no condemnation for those who are in Christ Jesus, because through Christ Jesus the law of the Spirit who gives life has set you free from the law of sin and death. For what the law was powerless to do because it was weakened by the flesh, God did by sending his own Son in the likeness of sinful flesh to be a sin offering. And so he condemned sin in the flesh, in order that the righteous requirement of the law might be fully met in us, who do not live according to the flesh but according to the Spirit.
>
> Those who live according to the flesh have their minds set on what the flesh desires; but those who live in accordance with the Spirit have their minds set on what the Spirit desires. The mind governed by the flesh is death, but the mind governed by the Spirit is life and peace. The mind governed by the flesh is hostile to God; it does not submit to God's law, nor can it do so. Those who are in the realm of the flesh cannot please God.
>
> You, however, are not in the realm of the flesh but are in the realm of the Spirit, if indeed the Spirit of God lives in you. And if anyone does not have the Spirit of Christ, they do not belong to Christ. But if Christ is in you, then even though your body is subject to death because of sin, the Spirit gives life because of righteousness. And if the Spirit of him who raised Jesus from the dead is living in you, he who raised Christ from the dead will also give life to your mortal bodies because of his Spirit who lives in you.
>
> Therefore, brothers and sisters, we have an obligation—but it is not to the flesh, to live according

to it. For if you live according to the flesh, you will die; but if by the Spirit you put to death the misdeeds of the body, you will live.

For those who are led by the Spirit of God are the children of God. The Spirit you received does not make you slaves, so that you live in fear again; rather, the Spirit you received brought about your adoption to sonship. And by him we cry, "Abba, Father." The Spirit himself testifies with our spirit that we are God's children. Now if we are children, then we are heirs—heirs of God and co-heirs with Christ, if indeed we share in his sufferings in order that we may also share in his glory.

I consider that our present sufferings are not worth comparing with the glory that will be revealed in us. For the creation waits in eager expectation for the children of God to be revealed. For the creation was subjected to frustration, not by its own choice, but by the will of the one who subjected it, in hope that the creation itself will be liberated from its bondage to decay and brought into the freedom and glory of the children of God.

We know that the whole creation has been groaning as in the pains of childbirth right up to the present time. Not only so, but we ourselves, who have the firstfruits of the Spirit, groan inwardly as we wait eagerly for our adoption to sonship, the redemption of our bodies. For in this hope we were saved. But hope that is seen is no hope at all. Who hopes for what they already have? But if we hope for what we do not yet have, we wait for it patiently.

In the same way, the Spirit helps us in our weakness. We do not know what we ought to pray for, but the Spirit himself intercedes for us through wordless groans. And he who searches our hearts knows the mind of the

Spirit, because the Spirit intercedes for God's people in accordance with the will of God.

And we know that in all things God works for the good of those who love him, who have been called according to his purpose. For those God foreknew he also predestined to be conformed to the image of his Son, that he might be the firstborn among many brothers and sisters. And those he predestined, he also called; those he called, he also justified; those he justified, he also glorified.

What, then, shall we say in response to these things? If God is for us, who can be against us? He who did not spare his own Son, but gave him up for us all—how will he not also, along with him, graciously give us all things? Who will bring any charge against those whom God has chosen? It is God who justifies. Who then is the one who condemns? No one. Christ Jesus who died—more than that, who was raised to life—is at the right hand of God and is also interceding for us. Who shall separate us from the love of Christ? Shall trouble or hardship or persecution or famine or nakedness or danger or sword? As it is written: "For your sake we face death all day long; we are considered as sheep to be slaughtered."

No, in all these things we are more than conquerors through him who loved us. For I am convinced that neither death nor life, neither angels nor demons, neither the present nor the future, nor any powers, neither height nor depth, nor anything else in all creation, will be able to separate us from the love of God that is in Christ Jesus our Lord.

—Romans 8:1–39

Amen.

For Further Study

Matthew 19:26	1 Chronicles 29:11
Ephesians 3:20	Nehemiah 9:6
1 Samuel 2:10	Psalm 121:2
2 Chronicles 20:6	Psalm 134:3
Job 9:12	Luke 10:21
Isaiah 43:13	Acts 17:24
Isaiah 45:9–10	Exodus 17:16
Acts 5:39	Psalm 45:6
Psalm 29:10	Psalm 93:2
1 Chronicles 16:31	Psalm 123:1
Psalm 47:2	Isaiah 6:1
Isaiah 6:5	Isaiah 66:1
Isaiah 43:15	Jeremiah 49:38
Jeremiah 10:7	Lamentations 5:19
Jeremiah 14:9	Ezekiel 1:26
1 Timothy 1:17	Daniel 7:9
1 Timothy 6:15	Matthew 5:34
Revelation 15:3	Psalm 93:1
Revelation 19:6	Isaiah 40:22
Deuteronomy 4:39	James 4:15
Genesis 24:3	Matthew 10:29–30
Deuteronomy 10:14	Luke 12:6–7
Joshua 2:11	Ephesians 1:11

Bibliography

Bauer, Walter. A Green-English Lexicon of the New Testament and Other Early Christian Literature, fourth edition by Arndt, William F. and Gingrich, F. Wilbur. University of Chicago Press, 1979.

Goodrick, Edward W. and Kohlenberger III, John, R. *The NIV Exhaustive Concordance.* Zondervan Publishing House, 1990.

Imes, Carmen Joy. Bearing God's Name, Why Sinai Still Matters. InterVarsity Press, 2019.

Marshall, Alfred. *The new International Version Interlinear Greek-English New Testament.* Zondervan Publishing House, 1976.

Nave, Orville J. *Nave's Topical Bible.* Hendrickson Publishers, 2002.

Vine, W.E. *Vine's Expository Dictionary of New Testament Words.* MacDonald Publishing Company, 1989.